GUNS OF THE ELITE

GUNS OF THE ELITE

SPECIAL FORCES FIREARMS, 1940 TO THE PRESENT

GEORGE MARKHAM

ARMS AND
ARMOUR

Published in Great Britain by
ARMS & ARMOUR PRESS
An Imprint of the Cassell Group
Wellington House, 125 Strand, London
WC2R 0BB

Originally published in 1987
Reprinted 1987, 1989, 1991 1992 1993 1994
Second revised edition first published in 1995
Reprinted 1995

Distributed in the USA by
Sterling Publishing Co., Inc.
387 Park Avenue South,
New York, NY 10016.

Distributed in Australia by
Capricorn Link (Australia) Pty Ltd.
2/13 Carrington Road, Castle Hill, NSW 2154.

British Library Cataloguing in Publication Data
Markham George
Guns of the elite: special forces firearms 1940 to
the present.
1. Special forces (military science)
–Equipment and supplies
2. Firearms–History–20th Century
I. Title
355.8'24 UD380

ISBN 1-85409-198-0

HALF-TITLE PAGE ILLUSTRATION:

1. What the best-dressed CTW man is wearing these
days . . . Note the Heckler & Koch MP5 with an aiming
projector—a highly sophisticated battery-powered
torch—and body armour, including an abdominal
protector. A gas-mask with built-in communications
equipment completes the package. Author's collection.

TITLE PAGE ILLUSTRATION:

2. The 5.56mm CETME Model L, seen here in the hands
of a member of the Spanish police CTW unit, is typical of
the current generation of ultra-lightweight rifles.
Courtesy of Empresa Nacional Santa Barbara, Madrid.

Acknowledgements

The first edition of *Guns of the Elite*, published in
1987, was an instantaneous success—indeed, it
became the best-selling firearms book of the 1980s
and a translation even appeared in Japanese!
However, as comparatively few errors were reported
during the life of the first edition, most of the reprints
(though bound differently) were identical with the
original book.

Owing to wide-ranging political changes
throughout the world, and their effects on the
availability of small-calibre firearms, this new
edition has been substantially revised. The
handguns section has been entirely rewritten, and
the opportunity has been taken to integrate the
appendices formerly devoted to the Kalashnikov
and the AR-15/M16 series into the rifles chapter. The
glossary has been enlarged, and some additional
information has been added in the ammunition
appendix in an effort to broaden the general
appeal of the project.

I am particularly grateful for the assistance
offered by governmental and military departments
throughout the world, and to many of the world's
leading firearms manufacturers—

Pietro Beretta SpA, Gardone Val Trompia, Italy.
Colt's Inc., Hartford, Connecticut, USA.
Department of the Army, Washington DC, USA.
FN Herstal SA, Belgium.
Luigi Franchi SpA, Fornaci/Brescia, Italy.
Glock GmbH, Deutsch-Wagram, Austria.
Heckler & Koch GmbH, Oberndorf/Neckar,
    West Germany.
Imperial War Museum, London.
Ministry of Defence, London.
Royal Ordnance plc, Nottingham, England.
SIG, Neuhausen/Rheinfalls, Switzerland.
Smith & Wesson, Inc., Springfield, Massachusetts, USA.
Steyr-Daimler-Puch AG, Vienna, Austria.
Sturm, Ruger & Co., Inc., Southport, Connecticut, USA.
Tanarmi SpA, Gardone Val Trompia, Italy.
The Pattern Room, The Enfield Building, Royal
    Ordnance plc, Nottingham, England.
Carl Walther GmbH, Ulm/Donau, West Germany.

George Markham. Swanage, 1995.

Contents

Information

GLOSSARY

The most popular abbreviations and acronyms encountered in relation to terrorism, the armed forces, Special Forces, international support organisations and light firearms.

AA. Anti-aircraft
Abu Sayaf. Philippine Muslim fundamentalist group
AF. Airborne forces
AFL. Armed Forces of Liberia
AFV. Armoured Fighting Vehicle
AIT. Army Individual Training (USA)
AK. Avtomat Kalashnikova (Kalashnikov assault rifle. USSR)
AKM. Avtomat Kalashnikova Modernizirovanii (modernized Kalashnikov assault rifle. USSR)
ALF. Afar Liberation Front (Ethiopia)
ANC. (i) Congolese National Army, (ii) African National Congress
ANP. Armée Nationale Populaire (Algeria)
ANZAC. Australia and New Zealand Army Corps
APC. Armoured Personnel Carrier
APN. Armée Populaire Nationale (Congo)
ARGK. People's Liberation Army of Kurdistan
ARVN. Army of the Republic of Vietnam (South Vietnamese)
AUG. Armee-Universal-Gewehr (made by Steyr-Daimler-Puch)
AVS. Avtomaticheskaia Vintovka Simonova (Simonov automatic rifle, USSR, 1936)
AVT. Avtomaticheskaia Vintokva Tokareva (Tokarev automatic rifle, USSR, 1940)

BAR. Browning Automatic Rifle
BGEK. Bundesgendarmerie-Einsatz-Kommando (Austrian state police CTW unit)
BGS. Bundesgenzchutz (West German border guards)
BKH. State security police (Hungary)
BLM. Bolivarian Liberation Movement, Venezuela
Blue Berets. Metropolitan Police marksmen (UK); sometimes also applied to the French Alpine troops, Les Diables Bleus ('Blue Devils')
Blue Devils. See previous entry
BRA. Bougainville Revolutionary Army (Papua New Guinea)
Bren. An acronym of Brno and Enfield
BSO. Palestinian Black September Organization
BSU. Boat Support Unit (USA)
BUD. Basic Underwater Demolition (USA)

CAL. Carabine Automatique Légère (light automatic carbine, made by FN)
CAWS. Close Assault Weapon System (USA)
CCO. Clandestine Communist Organisation (Sarawak, c.1963–6)
CETME. Centro de Estudios Tecnicos y Materiales Especialises (arms manufacturer, Spain)
CIA. Central Intelligence Agency (USA)
CIDG. Civilian Irregular Defense Group (formed by the

US special Forces in Vietnam from local tribesmen, 1960 onwards)
CIS. Commonwealth of Independent States (part of the former USSR, Russia being the principal constitutent)
CMG. Company machine-gun (USA)
CNGSB. Simon Bolivar National Guerrilla Co-ordinating Board (Colombia)
COIN. Counter-Insurgency operations ('COIN-OPS')
Comsubin. Comando subaquei e incursori (Italian naval submarine commando unit)
COPP. Combined Operations Pilotage Parties (UK, Second World War)
CPLA. Cordillera People's Liberation Army (Philippines)
CQB. Close-quarters battle (UK)
CRWW. Counter-Revolutionary Warfare Wing, SAS (UK)
CSLA. Československá Lidová Armadá (Czechoslovakian People's Army)
CTW. Counter-terrorist warfare

Devsol. Revolutionary Left Organisation (Turkey)
DLF. Dhofar Liberation Front (c.1962, succeeded by PFLOAG, q.v.)
DRB. Division Ready Brigade (USA)
DZ. Dropping zone

ECM. Electronic Countermeasures
EDES. National Republican Greek Army (1943–50)
EDRE. Emergency Deployment Readiness Exercise (USA)
EDU. Ethiopian Democratic Union
ELAS. National Popular Liberation Army (Greece, 1943–50)
ELF. Eritrean Liberation Front
ELN. Army of National Liberation (Colombia)
EPDM. Ethiopian People's Democratic Movement
EPL. Popular Liberation Army (Colombia)
EPLF. Ethiopian People's Liberation Front
EPRLF. Eelam People's Revolutionary Liberation Front (Sri Lanka)
EPRP. Ethiopian People's Revolutionary Party
ERNK. National Liberation Front of Kurdistan
ERP. Ejercito Revolucionaria de Pueblo (people's Revolutionary Army, Argentina)
ESI. Escadron Spéciale d'Intervention 'Diane' (Belgian police CTW unit)
ETA. Basque Fatherland and Liberty separatist movement (Spain)
EZLN. Zapatista National Liberation Army (Mexico)

FAA. Federal Army of Angola
FAL. Fusil Automatique Léger (the standard FN semi-automatic rifle)
FALN. Venezuelan guerrilla group
FALO. Fusil Automatique Lourd (heavy-barrel FAL)
FAL Para. Folding-butt 'paratroop' version of the FAL
FAMAE. Fabricaciones Militares do Arsenal de Ejercito, Santiago (Chilean arms manufacturer)
FAN. Forces Armées du Nord (Chad)
FANT. Forces Armées Nationales Tchadiennes (Chad armed forces)
FAP. (i) Fusil Automatico Pesado—the Spanish-language equivalent of FALO (q.v.); (ii) Forces Armée Populaire (Chad)
FAPLA. People's Armed Forces for the Liberation of Angola

FAR. Force d'Action Rapide (France)
FARC. Revolutionary Armed Forces of Colombia
FARP. People's Revolutionary Armed Forces (Cabo Verde)
FAT. Forces Armées du Tchad (Chad)
Fatah Hawks. Splinter group formed from PLO militants
FBI. Federal Bureau of Investigation (USA)
FEG. Fegyver é Gázkészülégyár, Budapest (Hungarian arms manufacturer)
FG. Fallschirmjägergewehr (paratroops' rifle, Germany)
FLCS. Front de Libération de la Côte des Somalis
FLECR. Front de Liberation de l'Erythrée, Conseil de la Révolution (Eritrea)
FLN. Front de Libération Nationale (Algeria, 1954–62)
FLOSY. Front for the Liberation of South Yemen
FLQ. Front de Libération de Québec (Canada)
FMLN. Frente 'Farabundo Marti' para la Liberacion Nacional (El Salvador)
FMS. Foreign Military Sales Programs (USA governmental sales)
FN. FN Herstal SA (Belgian arms manufacturer, formerly Fabrique Nationale d'Armes de Guerre)
FNC. Fabrique Nationale Carabine (successor to the CAL)
FNLA. Frente Nacional de Libertaçao de Angola (Angolan Liberation Front)
FOM. Foreign Material. A prefix used by the US authorities to classify foreign weaponry
FPLE. Front Populaire de Liberation de l'Erythrée (Eritrea)
FRELIMO. Frente de Liberataçao de Moçambique (Front for the Liberation of Mozambique)
FSZS. Federalni Sprava Zpravodajskych, 'Federal Information Service Department' (Czechoslovakian secret police). See also STB

GEO, GEOS. Grupo Especial de Operaciónes (Spanish CTW unit)
GIAT. Groupement Industriel d'Armaments Terrestres (French government arms-sales agency)
GIGN. Groupement d'Intervention de la Gendarmerie Nationale (French CTW group), colloquially known as 'Gigéné'
GIS. Gruppo Intervenzione Speciale (Italian Carabinieri unit)
Green Berets. US Special Forces
GPLM. Gambela People's Liberation Movement (Ethiopia)
GPMG. General-purpose machine-gun
GSG-9. Grenzschutzgruppe-9 (West German CTW unit)

HALO. High altitude, low opening (parachute)
HEAT. High explosive, anti-tank
HEHO. High extraction, high opening (parachute)
HELO. High extraction, low opening (see also HALO)
HESH. High explosive, squash head
Hezb-i-Islam. Islamic Party (Afghanistan)
Hezb-i-Wahdat. Unity Party (Afghanistan)
HK, H&K. Heckler & Koch GmbH, Oberndorf/Neckar (German arms manufacturer)
HMG. Heavy machine-gun
HOS. Party of Rights, Croatian paramilitary organisation
HRT. Hostage Rescue Team (USA, FBI groups)

ICEX. Intelligence, Countermeasures and Exploitation

IDF. Israeli Defense Force
IMI. (i) Imperial Metal Industries Ltd (Britain); (ii) Israeli Military Industries, Ramat ha-Sharon
INLA. Irish National Liberation Army
IPF. Inkatha Freedom Party (Zulu organisation, South Africa)
IRA. Irish Republican Army
IZL. Irgun Zvai Leumi ('National Military Organization', Israel, formed c.1944)

Jamiat-i-Islami. Islamic Society (Afghanistan)
JCG. Joint Command Group (US/ARVN)
JNA. Yugoslavian Federal Army
JSSAP. Joint Services Small Arms Program (USA)

KDP. Kurdish Democratic Party (Turkey)
KDS. Komitet Durzhavna Sigurnost, 'State Security Committee' (Bulgaria)
KGB. Komitet Gosudarstvennoy Bezopastony (secret police, USSR)
Khmer Rouge or KR. Cambodia
KPNLF. Khmer People's National Liberation Front
KTEK. Kirbis Turk Emniyet Kuvvetleri, 'Turkish-Cypriot Security Force' (Cyprus)

LAR. Light Automatic Rifle (English version of FAL, q.v.)
LAW. Light Automatic Weapon (light machine-gun)
LEHI. Lochamei Herut Israel ('Israeli Freedom Fighters', c.1944 onwards)
LMG. Light machine-gun
LRA. Lord Resistance Army (Uganda)
LRDG. Long Range Desert Group (UK, Second World War)
LRPU. Long Range Photographic Unit (predecessor of the LRDG, q.v.)
LSN. Local Stock Number. See 'NSN' below
LSW. Light support weapon
LTTE. Liberation Tigers of Tamil Eelam (Sri Lanka)
LZ. Landing zone

MAB. (i) Marine Amphibious Brigade (USA); (ii) Manufacture d'Armes de Bayonne, Hendaye (French arms manufacturer)
MAC. Manufacture Nationale d'Armes, Châtellerault (French arms manufacturer)
MACV. Military Assistance Command, Vietnam (US)
MAG. Mitrailleuse à Gaz ('gas-operated machine-gun', FN's original name for the GPMG, q.v.); now known as "Mitrailleuse d'Appui Général"
MAP. Military Assistance Program (USA)
MAU. Marine Amphibious Unit (USA)
MCP. Malayan Communist Party guerrillas
MG. (i) Machine-gun; (ii) Maschinengewehr (Germany)
MGF. Mobile Guerrilla Force (USA, 1966/7, replaced by MSF, q.v.)
MKb. Maschinenkarabiner (Germany, 1942–5)
MMG. Medium machine-gun
MNC. Congolese National Movement
MNLF. Moro National Liberation Front (Philippines)
MP, MPi. Maschinenpistole (Germany)
MPABA. Malayan People's Anti-British Army (1948–9, became MRLA, q.v.)
MPLA. Movimento Popular de Libertaçao de Angola (Angolan People's Liberation Movement)
MPLC. Mouvement pour la Liberation du Congo
MPRF. Multi-Purpose Reaction Force (USA, c.1964–6, replaced by MGF, q.v.)
MRLA. Malayan Races Liberation Army (1949–60)
MRTA. Tupac Amaru Revolutionary Movement (Peru)
MSF. Mobile Strike Force (USA, 1967–70)
MSU. Mobile Support Unit (USA)
MTT. Mobile Training Team (USA; early Special Forces units in Vietnam)
MVD. Ministerstvo Vnutrenniki Del, 'Ministry of Internal Affairs' (USSR)

NAHAL. Fighting Pioneer Youth (Israel)
NATO. North Atlantic Treaty Organization
NAVSPECWAR. Naval Special Warfare (US)

NJM. New Jewel Movement (Grenada, 1979–83)
NLF. National Liberation Front (Yemen and South Vietnam)
NOCS. Nucleo Operativo Centrale di Sicurezza (Italian CTW unit)
NPA. New People's Army (Philippines)
NPLF. National Patriotic Front of Liberia
NRA. (i) National Rifle Association; (ii) National Resistance Army (Uganda)
NRM. National Resistance Movement (Uganda)
NSA. NATO (or National) Stock Number. The US Navy and others have also used a Local Stock Number or LSN
NTK. Nittoku Metal Industries Ltd, Tokyo (Japanese arms manufacturer)
NVA. (i) National Volksarmee, 'National People's Army' (DDR); (ii) North Vietnamese Army (US abbreviation)
NWM. Nederlandsche Wapen- en Munitiefabriek NV (Dutch arms manufacturer)

OAS. Organisation Armée Secrète (Algeria, 1960–2)
ODP. Organizaçao de Defesa Popular (Angolan people's militia)
OLF. Oromo Liberation Front (Ethiopia)
OSS. Office of Strategic Services (USA)

PAIGC. Partido Africano da Independêcia de Guine e Cabo Verde (African Party for the Independence of Guinea and Cape Verde)
PATU. Police Anti-Terrorist Unit (Rhodesia/Zimbabwe)
PDP. Para-Desant Polk (USSR, paratroops)
Pepes. People Persecuted by Pablo Escobar (Colombia)
PFLOAG. Front for the Liberation of the Occupied Arabian Gulf (successor to DLF, q.v.)
PFT. Popular Front of Tazhikistan
Pi. Pistole (Germany)
PK. Pulemet Kalashnikova (Kalashnikov machine-gun, USSR)
PKK. Kurdish Workers Party (Turkey)
PKM. Pulemet Kalashnikova Modernizirovaniy (modernized Kalashnikov machine-gun, USSR)
PLF. Patriotic Liberation Front (Burma)
PLFG. People's Liberation Front Revolutionary Guards (Eritrea)
PLFP. Popular Front for the Liberation of Palestine
PLO. Palestine Liberation Organization
POP. Policia da Ordem Publicá (Angolan or Cabo Verde paramilitary police)
PRA. People's Revolutionary Army (Grenada)
PRC. People's Republic of China
PRU. Provincial Reconnaissance Unit (USA)
PUK. Patriotic Union of Kurdistan (Turkey)
PWG. People's War Group (India)

QRF. Quick Reaction Force (USA, current)

RAF. (i) Royal Air Force (Britain); (ii) Red Army Faction (West Germany)
RBMF. Red Banner Military Front (Venezuela)
RCT. Regimental Combat Team (US, Korean War)
RDF. Rapid Deployment Force (USA, current)
Red Berets. British paratroops
Red Brigade (Brigado Rosso). Italian terrorist organisation
RENAMO. Resistência Nacional Moçambicana, 'National Resistance of Mozambique'
REP. Régiment Etranger de Parachutistes (French Foreign Legion unit)
RIP. Ranger Induction Program (USA)
RMBPD. Royal Marines Boom Patrol Detachment (UK)
RMSBS. Royal Marines Special Boat Squadron (UK)
RPD. Ruchnoi Pulemet Degtyareva (Degtyarev light machine-gun, USSR)
RPF. Rwanda Patriotic Front
RPG. Rocket-propelled grenade
RPK. Ruchnoi Pulemet Kalashnikova (Kalashnikov light machine-gun, USSR)
RSAF. Royal Small Arms Factory, Enfield (British arms manufacturer); now Royal Ordnance plc, Nottingham

RT. Reconnaissance Team (USA)
RUC. Royal Ulster Constabulary (Northern Ireland)
RUF. Revolutionary United Front (Sierra Leone)

SADF. South African Defence Force
SAIQA. Special Security Company (Jordan)
SAS. Special Air Service (UK)
SAW. Squad Automatic Weapon (light machine-gun)
SBS. Special Boat Service (UK)
SD. Schalldämpfer, 'silencer' (Germany)
SDP. Steyr-Daimler-Puch AG, Steyr (Austrian arms manufacturer)
SEAL. Sea-Air Landing Teams (US Navy)
SEK. Spezial-Einsatz-Kommando (West German police CTW units)
SERE. Survival-Evasion-Resistance-Escape (USA)
SF. Special Forces (USA), the 'Green Berets'
SFG. Special Forces Group (USA)
SG. Sayeret Golani ('Golani Infantry', Israel), or Scharfschützengewehr (German for 'sniper rifle', see also SSG)
SIG. Schweizerische-Industrie-Gesellschaft, Neuhausen/Rheinfalls (Swiss arms manufacturer)
SIS. Special Intelligence Service (UK)
SKS. Samozariadniya Karabina Simonova (Simonov semi-automatic carbine, USSR, 1945)
SL. Sendero Luminoso, 'Shining Path' (Peru)
SLA. (i) South Lebanese Army; (ii) Symbionese Liberation Army (USA)
SLAM. Search-Locate-Annihilate Mission (USA)
SMG. Submachine-gun
SNSP. Serviço Nacional de Segurança Popular (national police, Mozambique)
SOCOM. Special Operations Command (USA)
SOE. Special Operations Executive (UK)
SOG. Special Operations Group (USA)
Spetznaz. Diversionary Troops (USSR Special Forces)
SPIW. Special Purpose Infantry Weapon (USA)
SPLA. Sudanese People's Liberation Army (Sudan)
SSB. Special Service Brigade (UK, Second World War)
SSG. Scharfschützengewehr ('sniper rifle' in German; see also SG ii)
SSRF. Small Scale Raiding Force (UK)
STB. Statni Tajna Bezpecnost (Czechoslovakian secret police). Replaced by FSZS (q.v.)
Sten. An acronym of Shepherd, Turpin and Enfield
StG, Stgw. Sturmgewehr
SUA. Shan United Army (Burma)
SVD. Snayperskaya Vintovka Dragunova (Dragunov sniper rifle, USSR)
SVT. Samozariadniya Vintovka Tokareva (Tokarev semi-automatic rifle, 1938 and 1940, USSR)
SWAPO. South West Africa People's Organization
SWAT. Special Weapons and Tactics
SWATF. South West Africa Territory Forces (Namibia)

TF. Task Force
THQ. Tactical Headquarters (USA)
TNA. Tamil National Army (Sri Lanka)
TPLF. Tigré People's Liberation Front (Ethiopia)

UDT. Underwater Demolition Team (USA)
UFF. Ulster Freedom Fighters (Northern Ireland)
ULIMO. United Liberation Movement for Democracy in Liberia
UN. United Nations
UNDA. Uganda National Democratic Alliance
UNEF. United Nations Emergency Force
UNITA. Uniâo Nacional para a Independência Total de Angola (National Union for Total Independence of Angola)
UNPROFOR. United Nationa Protection Force in Yugoslavia
UPSR. United Party of Socialist Revolution (Cuba)
URA. Japanese Red Army
URNG. Guatemalan National Revolutionary Unity
UVF. Ulster Volunteer Force
UW. Unconventional Warfare

VC. Vietcong (guerrilla force in Vietnam)
VNSF. Vietnam Special Forces
VOP, Vopo. Volkspolizei, "People's Police" (DDR)
VSN. Volontaires de la Securité Nationale (Haitian paramilitary forces)

WP. Warsaw Pact
WSLF. Western Somalia Liberation Front

ZANLA. Zimbabwe African National Liberation Army
ZANU. Zimbabwe African National Union
ZAPU. Zimbabwe African People's Union
ZIPRA. Zimbabwe People's Republican Army
ZNA. Zimbabwe National Army

BIBLIOGRAPHY

Anon.: *Report of the Special Subcommittee of the M-16 Rifle Program.* Deutschland Ordnance, Santa Clara California, 1968 (reprint of US government documents).
Baer, Ludwig: *Die leichten Waffen der deutschen Armeen, 1841–1945.* Journal-Verlag Schwend GmbH, Schwäbisch Hall, 1976.
Bolotin, David N.: *Sovetskoe Strelkovoe Oruzhiye.* Voennoe Izdatelstvo, Moscow, 1988.
Cook, Chris, and John Stevenson: *The Atlas of Modern Warfare.* Weidenfeld & Nicholson, London, 1978.
Craig, William: *Enemy at the Gates. The Battle for Stalingrad.* Hodder & Stoughton, London, 1973.
Datig, Fred A.: *Soviet Russian Postwar Military Pistols & Cartridges, 1945–1986.* Handgun Press, Glenview, Illinois, 1988.
Dewar, Colonel Michael: *The British Army in Northern Ireland.* Arms & Armour Press, London, 1985.
— *War in the Streets.* David & Charles, Newton Abbot, 1992.
— *Weapons & Equipment of Counter-Terrorism.* Arms & Armour Press, London, 1987.
Dobson, C., and R. Payne: *The Weapons of Terror: International Terrorism at Work.* Macmillan Ltd, London, 1979.
Dugelby, Thomas B.: *EM-2 Concept & Design* ('A rifle ahead of its time'). Collector Grade Publications, Toronto, 1980.
— *Modern Military Bullpup Rifles.* Collector Grade Publications, Toronto, 1984.
Eshel, David: *Elite Fighting Units.* Arco Publishing Co., New York, 1984.
Ezell, Edward C.: *The Great Rifle Controversy.* Stackpole Books, Harrisburg, 1985.
— *The AK-47 Story.* Stackpole Books, Harrisburg, Pennsylvania, 1985.
— *Small Arms Today* ("Latest Reports on the World's Weapons and Ammunition"). Stackpole Books, Harrisburg, Pennsylvania; second edition, 1988.
— (ed.) *Small Arms of the World.* Stackpole Books, Harrisburg, Pennsylvania; twelfth edition, 1984.
Ferguson, Tom (Jack Lewis, ed.): *Modern Law Enforcement, Weapons & Tactics.* DBI Books, Inc., Northbrook, Illinois; second edition, 1991.
Geraghty, Tony: *Who Dares Wins.* Arms & Armour Press, London, 1980.
— *This is the SAS* ('A pictorial history of the Special Air Service Regiment'). Arms & Armour Press, London, 1982.
Götz, Hans-Dieter: *Die deutschen Militärgewehre und Maschinenpistolen 1871–1945.* Motor-Buch Verlag, Stuttgart, 1974.
Hatcher, Major General Julian S.: *The Book of the Garand.* The Gun Room Press, Highland Park, New Jersey, 1977.
Hogg, Ian V. (ed.): *Jane's Infantry Weapons.* Macdonald & Jones, London, published annually.
— *Military Pistols & Revolvers.* Arms & Armour Press, London, 1987.
— and John S. Weeks: *Military Small Arms of the 20th Century.* Arms & Armour Press, London; sixth edition, 1991.
— and John S. Weeks: *Pistols of the World.* Arms & Armour Press, London; third edition, 1992.
Johnson, Melvin M., and Charles T. Haven: *Automatic Arms* ('Their history, development and use'). William Morrow & Co., New York, 1941.
Labbett, Peter: *Military Small Arms Ammunition of the World, 1945–1980.* Arms & Armour Press, London, 1980.
Ladd, James D.: *Inside the Commandos* ('A pictorial history from World War Two to the present'). Arms & Armour Press, London, 1984.
Leasor, James: *Green Beach.* William Heinemann Ltd, London, 1975.
Lewis, Jack (ed.): *Handguns '92.* DBI Books, Inc., Northbrook, Illinois; fourth edition, 1991.
Long, Duncan: *Assault Pistols, Rifles and Submachine Guns.* Paladin Press, Boulder, Colorado, 1986.
— *Combat Ammunition* ('Everything you need to know'). Paladin Press, Boulder, Colorado, 1986.
Macdonald, Peter: *The SAS in Action.* Sidgwick & Jackson, London, 1990.
Markham, George: *Guns of the Empire* ('Firearms of the British Soldier, 1837–1987'). Arms & Armour Press, London, 1990.
Millar, George: *The Bruneval Raid* ('Flash-point of the Radar War'). The Bodley Head, London, 1974.
Musgrave, Daniel D., and Thomas B. Nelson: *The World's Assault Rifles & Automatic Carbines.* TBN Enterprises, Alexandria, Virginia, c.1969.
Nelson, Thomas B., and Hans-Bert Lockhoven: *The World's Submachine Guns (Machine Pistols)*, vol. I. TBN Enterprises, Alexandria, Virginia, c.1964.
Parrish, Thomas (ed.): *The encyclopedia of World War II.* Secker & Warburg, London, 1978.
Paxton, John (ed.): *The Statesman's Year Book*, various editions. Macmillan, London; published annually.
Rivers, Gayle: *The Specialist* ('The Personal Story of an Elite Specialist in Covert Operations'). Sidgwick & Jackson, London, 1985.
Ryan, Cornelius: *A Bridge Too Far.* Hamish Hamilton Ltd., London, 1974.
Robinson, Mike: *Fighting Skills of the SAS.* Sidgwick & Jackson, London, 1991.
Smith, Graham (ed.): *Weapons of the Gulf War.* Salamander Books, London, 1991.
Stevens, R. Blake: *North American FALs—NATO's Search for a Standard Rifle.* Collector Grade Publications, Toronto, Canada, 1981.
— *UK and Commonwealth FALs.* Collector Grade Publications, Toronto, Canada, 1983.
— and Edward C. Ezell: *The Black Rifle. M16 Retrospective.* Collector Grade Publications, Toronto, Canada, 1987.
— and Jean E. van Rutten: *The Metric FAL—The Free World's Right Arm.* Collector Grade Publications, Toronto, Canada, 1985.
Skennerton, Ian: *The British Service Lee.* Arms & Armour Press, London; second edition, 1990.
Swearengen, Thomas F.: *The World's Fighting Shotguns.* TBN Enterprises, Alexandria, Virginia, 1978.
Thompson, Julian: *No Picnic. 3 Commando Bridge in the South Atlantic, 1982.* Leo Cooper/Secker & Warburg, London, 1985.
Thompson, Leroy, and Michael Chappell: *Uniforms of the Elite Forces.* Blandford Press, Poole, 1982.
— and René Smeets: *Great Combat Handguns.* Arms & Armour Press, London; second edition, 1993.
Wahl, Paul: *Carbine Handbook* ('The complete manual and guide to the U.S. Carbine, Cal. .30, M1'). Arco Publishing Co., New York, 1974.
Walter, John D.: *Rifles of the World.* Arms & Armour Press, London, 1993.
— *The Pistol Book.* Arms & Armour Press, London, second edition, 1988.
— *The Rifle Book.* Arms & Armour Press, London, 1990.
Zhuk, Aleksandr B.: *Strelkovoe Oruzhie.* Voenno Izdatelstvo, Moscow; revised edition, 1992.
— (John Walter, ed.): *The Illustrated Encyclopedia of Handguns.* Greenhill Books, London, 1995.

Prologue

What, precisely, constitutes a 'gun of the élite'? Elite units have existed throughout history – emperors' bodyguards, the Swiss Guard, Napoleon's Garde Impériale – but only rarely have they fulfilled anything other than traditional roles. Though they often carried special muskets, bayonets or swords, changes were generally cosmetic, having more to do with gaudy brass mounts and extra decoration than actual performance. A 'gun of the élite', therefore, is to be defined here in either or both of two ways: that it influenced military history in such a way that specialized units were formed to use it, or that the prior existence of specialist units made the distribution of particular guns inevitable. The introduction of rifled firearms is an example of the former; adoption of the submachine-gun, the latter.

Throughout the four centuries in which the firearm has been useful as an infantry weapon, the goals of the designers – and the users, for that matter – have stayed remarkably constant. Within the limits of the technologies of their days, each has sought maximum effectiveness (a combination of 'killing efficiency' and reliability), maximum rate of fire and maximum portability. Although battlefield criteria have changed out of all recognition during the period, these basic yardsticks were as true during the English Civil War, the campaigns against Napoleon or in the Crimea as in the two world wars, Vietnam and the Falklands.

The first handguns were cumbersome, ignited by a hand-held brand, inaccurate, short-ranged, unsuitable for infantrymen and often of utmost danger to their firer. Six hundred years after the introduction of these first firearms, it is hard to see why they were accepted so readily when accuracy and rate of fire were greatly inferior to contemporary bows. The longbow, the destroyer of the French at Crécy and Agincourt, persisted in England well into the sixteenth century; not until 1590, indeed, were the contemporary militia (the Trained Bands)

ordered to exchange their bows for guns. The English longbow shot farther, with greater accuracy and a better rate of fire, than any British military firearm made prior to the American War of Independence.

Once the gun had been accepted, however, slow but steady development through the matchlock, the wheel-lock and the flint-lock greatly improved reliability. In addition, the flintlock was comparatively cheap and easy to make, which facilitated the arming of vast numbers of men. The surprisingly rapid rise of the gun, therefore, was due to several factors. There was an acute shortage of seasoned wood; drawing a longbow required appreciable physical strength, and opponents could even fire undamaged arrows back again. Conversely, the first firearms were easy to make, required no real training to use satisfactorily, and ammunition could be made in enormous quantities. And there was such a bonus – the tremendous occult power of the first guns, which terrorized many who faced them.

The major disadvantages were limited performance and the need of adequate supplies of gunpowder, without which nothing was possible. It is probably justifiable to see any early musketeer as a member of the élite, and his weapon as a 'gun of the élite' according to the definition attempted above; the musketeer existed to make use of the gradually improving firearm, and was not subject to the same rules of engagement as archers and swordsmen a hundred years earlier.

By 1650, musket design was beginning to stabilize, though performance was still very poor; effective range was scarcely a hundred yards, and the rate of fire no more than three unaimed balls per minute. However, lighter guns were being made for cavalry and sporting use, and the value of rifling was appreciated (though with no great scientific basis) in continental Europe. Inventive gunsmiths even strove to perfect the repeating breech-loader, although the

solution to the problems – the metal-case cartridge – lay 150 years in the future.

By 1675, the firearm had ceased to be élitist and many thousands of plain military-grade guns had reached the standing armies prior to 1700. The infantry's muskets remained virtually unchanged for the best part of 150 years, though barrels were shortened and the efficiency of the locks steadily increased. Light guns were introduced for fusiliers; grenade-throwing muskets, soon abandoned, appeared in the wars between Sweden and Denmark as early as 1657; carbines were issued to the cavalry; pistols to officers. Gradually, the entire army received firearms.

Their limited range and suspect ignition still dictated the massed line-of-battle tactics, as characteristic of the battle of Waterloo (1815) as of Blenheim more than a hundred years earlier. Improvements in propellants increased certainty of ignition, but the practice of using balls of smaller diameter than the bore – without the patches favoured by many sportsmen and target-shooters on the Continent – allowed the projectiles to bounce down the barrel. Thus, the angle of departure from the muzzle became a lottery and even the best muskets shot wildly.

In 1814, Colonel Hanger said of the British Army's workhorse, the 'Brown Bess', that 'a soldier's musket, if not exceedingly ill-bored, (as many are) will strike the figure of a man at 80 yards; it may be even at a hundred; but a soldier must be very unfortunate indeed who shall be wounded at 150 yards, provided his antagonist aims at him; and as to firing at a man at 200 yards with the common musket, you may as well fire at the moon . . .' The muskets of the French, Austrian and American line infantry shot nearly as badly, saved only by less windage (the gap between the ball and the bore) and, consequently, less pronounced rattling of the ball down the barrel. However, the British muskets were among the best made, and this all but negated the differences in ammunition.

The truly 'élite' gun of the eighteenth century was the rifle, which had enjoyed a popularity on the Continent unmatched in Britain. Companies of riflemen (Jäger) had been raised in Austria and the German states as early as 1735, receiving plain versions of the sporting rifles then in vogue. These guns usually had shallow, polygroove rifling, sometimes straight rather than spiral, and fired bullets that were wrapped in tallow patches. Hammered down the bore with small mallets or unusually heavy ramrods slowed loading even more, but at least allowed the patch to grip the rifling. When the gun was fired, the grooves spun the patched ball or bullet, improving its accuracy and extending its range. Not until 1742 was the theory of rifling properly expounded by an English mathematician, Benjamin Robins, but the essence had been grasped many years previously.

By the time of the Indian Wars in the 1760s, and the campaigns undertaken by the British against the French in North America, the efficacy of the Jäger rifle and its offspring (the Pennsylvania and Kentucky rifles) was well known. And though rifles had served British irregulars for more than twenty years, the commencement of the American War of Independence (1775–83) caused the British near-apoplexy. The British Army still sought to crush the American nationalists by lines and squares – only to be faced by an enemy whose principal goal was to avoid giving the red-coated Britons such an advantage. Instead, the 'Minutemen' (so called because they could be ready to fight 'at a minute's notice') pursued a guerrilla campaign of harassment, attempting to defend strongpoints rather than be caught in the open. This policy hastened the surrender of Burgoyne at Saratoga in 1777, so alarming the British that they recruited some four thousand Hanoverian riflemen to act as scouts and ordered Jäger-type rifles from Germany as well as London and Birmingham.

Picking-off the enemy's officers so as to make his troops unmanageable was by no means a new idea, but the formation of units to achieve this aim was comparatively unusual in the British Army in 1775.

While the Board of Ordnance was seeking its rifles for the American war, the Ferguson Rifle appeared. Its principle was not new – the Frenchman, La Chaumette, had produced a similar gun sixty years earlier – but Ferguson drew attention in his patent only to his intention to keep the screwed breech-plug in the gun at all times (most earlier ones had been removable) and to groove the breech-plug screw to restrict the accumulation of powder residue.

The initial trial of the Ferguson Rifle was a sensation. Though it was a flintlock, it was appreciably less susceptible to damp than the standard muskets. The breech was exposed by turning the trigger-guard, dropping the screwed plug until a ball could be rolled directly into the chamber. Powder was then added, the plug replaced, and the gun cocked, primed and fired in the normal way. Ferguson managed to fire four shots per minute for nearly five minutes, at a target 200 yards away; fire six shots in a

Fig. 1. The early musketeer carried a cumbersome matchlock, with individual powder charges dangling in small wooden flasks from the bandolier. Though his gun was slow-firing, and accurate only at short range, possession of a firearm was sufficient to make him a member of the élite. After Jacob de Gheyn, 1607.

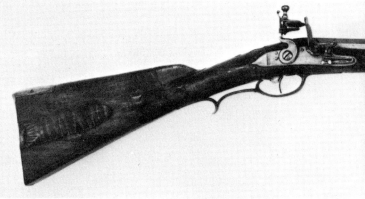

▲ 3

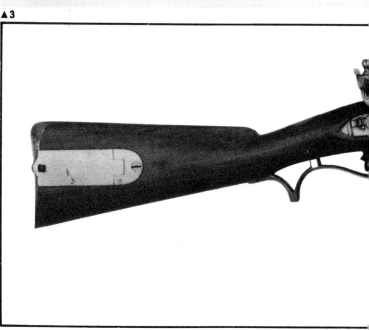

minute; fire four times per minute while advancing towards the target at a fast walk; pour a bottle of water into the pan on top of a charge, and then fire within 30 seconds; and hit the bull's-eye of a target set at 100 yards while lying on his back. Throughout the entire trial, only three shots missed the 6-foot square target in wet and windy conditions that totally defeated normal flintlock muzzle-loaders.

Here was a far more effectual design than the common musket, and Ferguson was allowed to train a hundred élite volunteers to use his rifles. At the end of 1776, he set sail for North America with his men, the rifles and the promise of special green uniforms. Despite performing well at the battle of Brandywine Hill, there were too few Ferguson breech-loaders to make much impact on contemporary warfare. Ferguson was seriously wounded at Brandywine Hill, however, and his men were eventually assimilated in the regular infantry. Ferguson fell at the battle of King's Mountain in 1780, and the Ferguson Rifle finally vanished from the scene. Some modern trials

have suggested that the rifle was at its best in damp conditions, which minimized powder-clogging, but there is no doubt that the Ferguson was much more efficient than a muzzle-loaded musket.

The success of the élite American riflemen reached heroic proportions, however, and was widely applauded even in England. One captive Minuteman was brought to London to demonstrate his skill, his marksmanship clearly indicating the superiority of his longrifle over the common musket.

Yet little was done during the remaining decades of the eighteenth century, the British Army, obsessed with defeating Napoleon Bonaparte, being satisfied with many thousands of muskets. On to this stage then came a London gunmaker, named Ezekiel Baker, with a muzzle-loading flintlock rifle of his own conception. Baker's rifle was exhibited with great success in 1800, demonstrating praiseworthy shooting at up to 200 yards, and was so obviously superior to the latest New Land Pattern Musket that it was adopted immediately. Though the Baker was less efficacious

than the breech-loading Ferguson – which fired at least as accurately when clean, and appreciably faster – it still embodied many lessons learned from the American Minuteman and the Hanoverian Jäger. Its patched ball was rammed into the bore to facilitate accuracy which, in turn, promoted the formation of the Experimental Corps of Riflemen in 1800. This truly élite unit, clothed in green and black rather than the traditional

3. During the American War of Independence (1775–83), the colonists made good use of Pennsylvania long rifles like the one shown. Longer and lighter than the European Jägerbüchsen, its 0.45in bore assisted the patched and greased ball to achieve praiseworthy accuracy at distances up to 400 yards.

4. The Baker Rifle, demonstrated in 1800, was the first rifle to achieve widespread service in the British Army, the experimental forerunner of the Rifle Brigade being raised to benefit from it. The muzzle-loading Baker was surprisingly accurate at 200 yards, though loading was painfully slow. The carbine-bore gun shown here (0.625in calibre) measures a little under 46in overall and weighs just 9lb without its massive sword bayonet. Note the 'straightline' stock, with less drop at the heel than usual in an attempt to minimize the effect of recoil.

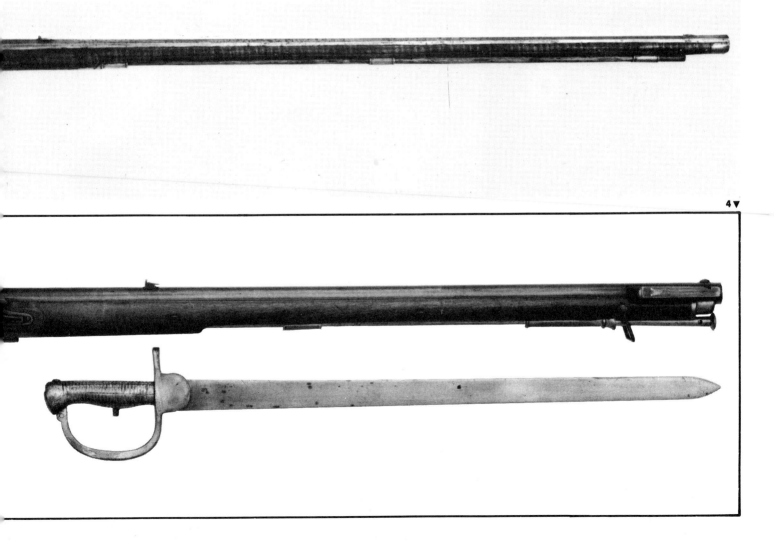

4▼

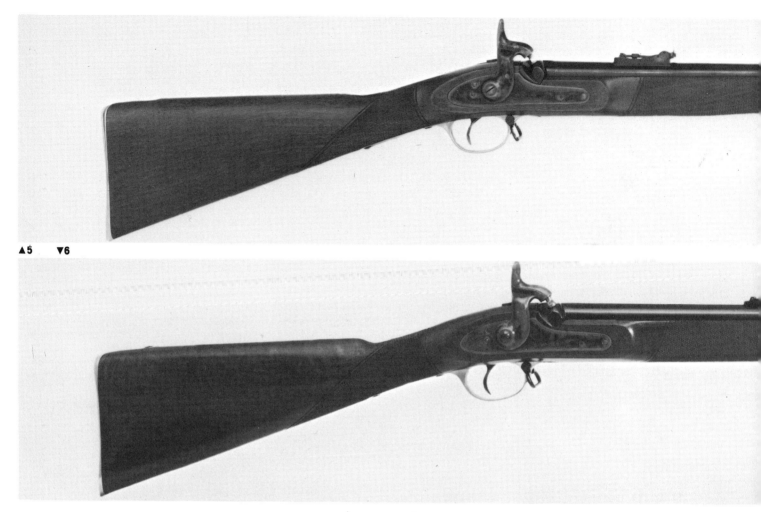

▲5   ▼6

5, 6. The perfected British muzzle-loader was the P/53 ('Enfield') approved for universal issue in 1853. These guns fired Minié-type bullets, with boxwood base plugs to assist expansion. Though performance was greatly enhanced, permitting accurate shooting at 500 yards or more, the rifle-musket was primarily the weapon of the line infantry. By the middle of the nineteenth century, the élite firearm (other than cavalry carbines) had all but disappeared. The guns shown here are modern replicas of the P/53 rifle musket (**5**) and the P/61 short rifle (**6**), made with the original production gauges. Courtesy of Parker-Hale Ltd.

gaudy red, was charged with harrying the enemy as the British had been harried in the American War. For thirty years, the 95th Regiment (renamed The Rifle Brigade in 1816) performed with great distinction.

The apogee of the flintlock – 1690–1830 – was characterized by infinitesimally slow technological advance. The Industrial Revolution had little effect other than simply to facilitate production of established designs, and the effectiveness of the guns on the battlefield remained practically unchanged until the perfection of the percussion-ignition system.

The original Forsyth 'scent bottle' percussion lock was delicate, uncertain in its action and occasionally a source of danger.

Few of the rival pill- and tube-locks offered any improvement until about 1818, when the self-contained percussion cap (developed a few years earlier) was perfected by Joshua Shaw. Within a decade, however, the cap-lock was eroding the supremacy of the flint. It had become sturdy, effectual, and had a misfire rate one-sixth that of its established rival. However, the British Brunswick Rifle of 1837 was little improved from the Baker apart from its ignition: it was still slow-firing, and accurate only to a little over 200 yards. Progress in firearms technology was still firmly obstructed by the negligible improvement in ammunition; the Brunswick belted ball still differed little conceptually from the stone balls fired by the earliest medieval cannon.

The perfection of the expanding bullet was a significant breakthrough. It is generally credited to the Frenchman, Claude-Etienne Minié, though Norton and Greener in Britain both claimed to have pre-empted him. Minié's hollow-base bullet could be dropped down the bore with minimal effort, its comparatively thin base-walls subsequently being expanded into the rifling by the violent ignition of the main charge. The

system worked surprisingly well, and was greatly improved by the discovery that an iron or boxwood plug set in the base of the bullet facilitated expansion. Ironically, the great advances being made in machine-tools and mass-production techniques at this time prevented the expanding bullet becoming the prerogative of the élite. Instead, rifles were issued to the British line infantry in time for the Crimean War (1853–6) and, typified by the British P/53 Enfield and US M1855 Springfield, had become widespread by the beginning of the American Civil War in 1861.

These rifle-muskets shot far and flat, being capable of surprising accuracy at distances of up to 1,000 yards. For the first time, battle tactics could be divorced from the geometry that had hamstrung warfare since the times of Gustavus Adolphus. But it was to be many years before the lessons were universally appreciated. Though the Crimea campaign was fought between armies of major powers, the employment of élite troops was insignificant; riflemen now had no real advantages over the line infantry, whose guns were of much the same type and could shoot just as well.

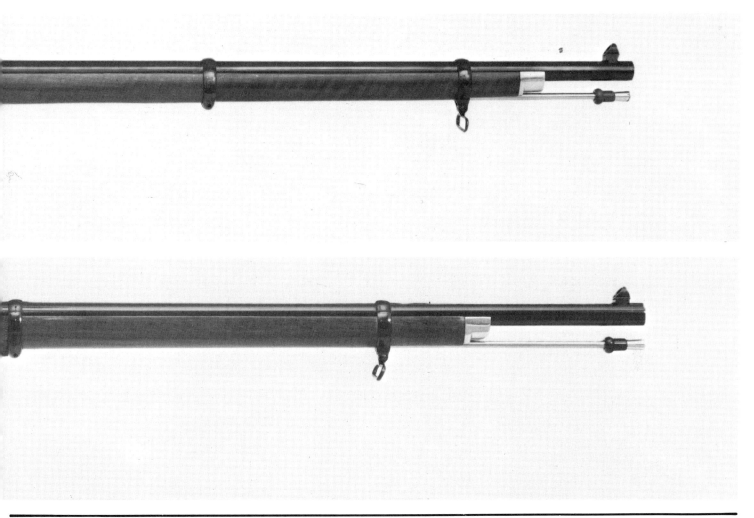

GUN PERFORMANCE, 1650–1985 – I

Gun	cal. in	weight lb	length in	mag cap	PRF rpm	Efficiency index (% hit probability) 100yd	200yd	500yd
Matchlock, 1650	.80	12.00	60.0	1	1.5	66	10	0
New Land Pattern Flintlock	.75	10.38	58.0	1	2.0	66	15	0
Baker Rifle	.62	8.88	43.5	1	1.5	90	60	2
Brunswick Rifle	.704	9.13	44.0	1	1.5	90	60	5
P/51, Minié	.702	9.50	55.0	1	3.5	95	70	30
P/53, Enfield, after 1859	.577	8.91	54.0	1	3.5	95	75	40
Snider Mk 3	.577	9.06	55.3	1	6	100	80	45
Martini-Henry Mk 1	.450	9.00	49.5	1	10	100	85	55
Lee-Enfield Mk 1*	.303	9.30	49.5	10	14	100	95	85
SMLE Mk 3	.303	8.66	44.6	10	16	100	95	85
Rifle M1 Garand	.30	9.48	43.5	8	24	100	95	85
FG.42, Krieghoff	.312	11.58†	41.0	20	30	100	95	85
MP.43/StG.44	.312	13.01†	37.1	30	35	100	95	70
AK47	.30	11.31†	34.2	30	35	100	95	70
Rifle L1A1 (FN FAL)	.30	11.10†	45.0	20	30	100	95	85
M16A1	.223	8.03†	39.0	30	35	100	95	60
SA-80 (L85A1)	.223	10.14‡	30.3	30	35	100	95	70

PRF: practical rate of fire.
†with loaded magazine; ‡with loaded magazine and SUSAT sight

GUN PERFORMANCE, 1650–1985 – II

Gun	cal. in	ball gn	round gn	rds‡	F/time §	Effectiveness index 100yd	200yd	500yd
Matchlock, 1650	.80	525	700†	64	53	8	1	0
New Land Pattern Flintlock	.75	480	620†	95	54	12	2	0
Baker Rifle	.62	320	450†	151	115	14	9	3
Brunswick Rifle	.704	557	675†	110	75	14	9	8
P/51, Minié	.702	680	820	88	26	33	26	10
P/53, Enfield, after 1859	.577	490	658	116	34	33	26	11
Snider Mk 3	.577	480	715	106	17m50	60	48	27
Martini-Henry Mk 1	.450	480	758	101	10m10	99	84	55
Lee-Enfield Mk 1*	.303	215	415	178	11m15	158	150	134
SMLE Mk 3	.303	174	384	205	12m55	159	151	135
Rifle M1 Garand	.30	150	396	184	7m45	237	226	202
FG.42, Krieghoff	.312	198	408	121	4m5	299	284	254
MP.43/StG.44	.312	125	250	131	3m45	352	334	246
AK47	.30	122	253	172	5	348	331	244
Rifle L1A1 (FN FAL)	.30	144	375	134	4m30	300	285	255
M16A1	.223	55	182	371	10m40	351	333	210
SA-80 (L85A1)	.223	62	190	307	8m40	350	333	245

†Approximately.
‡The number of rounds available after the gun-weight has been subtracted from an 'available total' of 20lb, allowing for the weight of the magazine(s).
§The notional period of fire, assuming the number of rounds deduced (above) and the continuous rate of fire from Performance Table I, expressed in minutes and seconds.

The 'misfire factor' is assumed as 1 shot in 5 for the matchlock, 1 in 7 for the flintlock, 1 in 45 for the cap-lock and 1 in 100 for the cartridge guns. The effectiveness is a notional product of the efficiency figures (Table One) and the factor resulting from dividing the rounds available by the 'minutes of fire'.

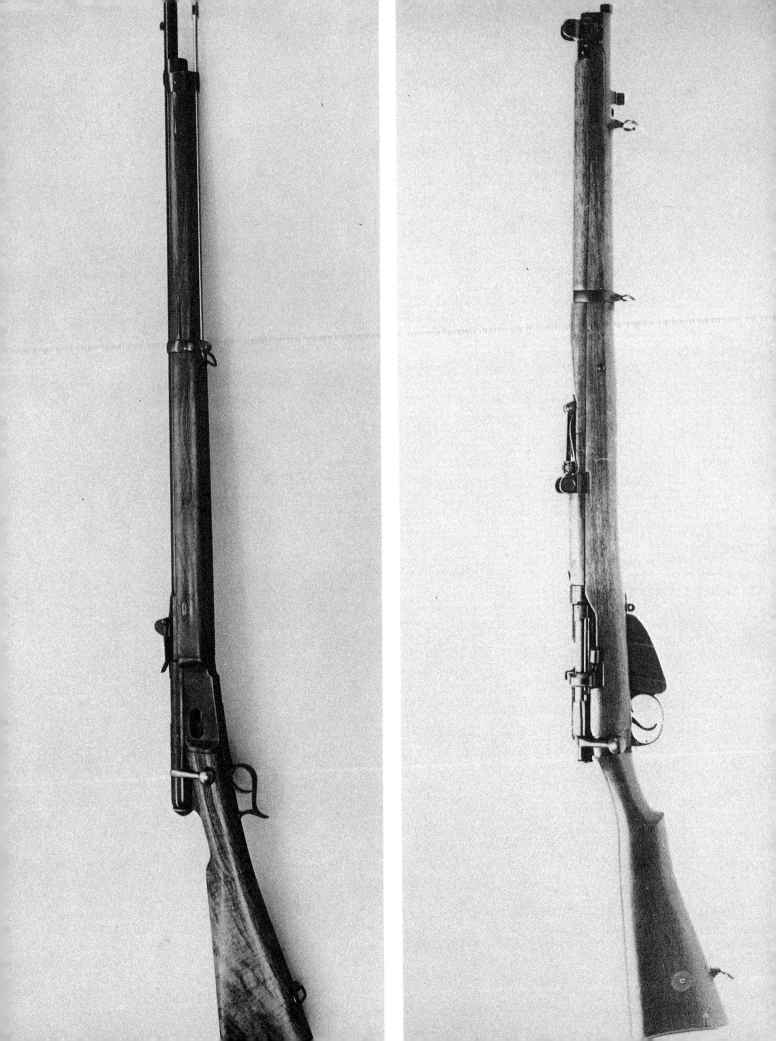

Prelude to the modern era

The American Civil War of 1861–5 furnished a proving ground for almost all the leading European rifle-muskets. However, the war also proved that poorly trained men, apt to panic in the heat of battle, were unable to determine whether their rifle-muskets had fired properly and continued to load charge upon charge in what had become a useless gun. One gun recovered from the battlefield at Gettysburg had been loaded no less than 23 times.

However, if the Civil War damaged the image of the rifle-musket, it came as a godsend not only for the breech-loading rifle but also the metal-case cartridge. These vital advances in technology were not always recognized at the time, largely because the guns tended to use unique cartridges of widely differing calibre (complicating logistics unacceptably). In addition, the ammunition often offered suspect ignition and poor-quality propellant.

Breech-loading repeaters such as the Spencer and the Henry, which could fire seven or more metal-case cartridges as fast as the trigger-lever could be thrown and (in the Spencer's case) the hammer cocked, were for the most part regarded scornfully

7. While the major European armies jockeyed to adopt perfected single-shot breech-loaders – most of which ultimately proved dead-end designs – little Switzerland, unnoticed, accepted a 10.4mm calibre bolt-action Vetterli breechloader in 1868. The Vetterli had a twelve-cartridge tube magazine under the barrel. Though the design owed much to Henry rifles used during the US Civil War, there is little doubt that the Swiss army had a tremendous technical lead at a time when the US Army was rejecting magazine systems in favour of the Allin-conversion 'Trapdoor' Springfields. The rifle shown here is the 1878-model Vetterli. Courtesy of SIG.

8. The realization that the needs of troops as disparate as cavalry, infantry and artillerymen could be satisfied with a single 'universal' rifle dawned on the British at the beginning of the twentieth century. The result was the 0.303in Rifle, Short, Magazine, Lee-Enfield (shown here: Mark 3*, 1916), the first such gun to be adopted. Though the rifle subsequently proved to be a compromise, with comparatively poor long-range performance, its bolt system allowed remarkably rapid manipulation. Pattern Room Collection, Enfield; courtesy of Ian Hogg.

by general officers brought up on single-shot muskets. Thus, breech-loaders were generally purchased by privately raised élite irregulars, militia and cavalry such as Berdan's Sharp Shooters and the Butler Brigade.

Despite teething troubles, the metallic cartridge guns had much to offer. The certainty of ignition was infinitely better than the cap-lock; a short-barrelled Burnside carbine tested at the Washington Navy Yard in 1859, for example, had fired 500 shots without a single misfire. The accuracy of the best guns was also impressive, a Spencer carbine returning a mean horizontal deviation of 13 inches at 300 yards and 16.8 inches at 500 yards – roughly half the size of groups achieved with an Enfield rifle-musket at comparable distances.

Unfortunately, the early cartridges were heavy enough to restrict the number of rounds a man could carry. As a Spencer rifle with the Blakeslee Quickloader system could easily fire twenty aimed shots per minute (six or seven times that of a rifle-musket), it was soon reduced to the status of a sophisticated club once ammunition ran out. In desperation, or away from lines of communication and supply where skirmishers and snipers were often to be found, rudimentary ammunition could always be made for a muzzle-loading cap-lock rifle – but not for most of the advanced breech-loaders. Ironically, though many magazine-loading guns had been purchased officially (including more than 100,000 Spencers), the US Board of Ordnance and Fortification subsequently chose a slow-firing 'trapdoor' conversion system for their rifle-muskets, condemning their troops to the evils of poor extraction.

The Civil War also saw widespread use of snipers, chosen from the ranks of professional hunters and skilled target-shooters. These men were truly élitist, eschewing military discipline and selecting any weapon they liked. Favourites were the heavy

Wesson bench rifles, some of which weighed more than twenty pounds, and the British-made .450 Whitworth rifle-musket. Many were even fitted with primitive telescope sights in the quest for extra accuracy. Though the Whitworth was beset by fouling problems, and supplies of its distinctive, mechanically fitting hexagonal projectile were few and far between, British official tests indicated that mean radii as small as 12 inches could be obtained at 800 yards; even at 1,100 yards, 30 inches could be bettered.

In the brief Seven Weeks War of 1866, the Prussians had comprehensively outshot the vaunted Austrian army that was armed with conventional Lorenz rifle-muskets. The Prussians had armed themselves with a crude, bolt-action 15.4mm calibre needle gun. The breech leaked gas, averred the experts, and the high, looping trajectory of the slow-moving bullet undeniably contributed range-gauging problems. The Prussian inventor, Dreyse, had even buried the percussion igniter immediately behind the bullet, forcing the firing needle to run through the charge before reaching the cap. When the cap fired the main charge, the needle, amidst the combustion, speedily corroded. Prussian soldiers even carried spare needles, noted the experts.

But the experts failed to appreciate that the bolt system facilitated loading, particularly when the firer was prone or behind cover: factors which contributed greatly both to Prussian success and a lower than expected casualty rate. By 1866, Dreyse Zündnadelgewehre had been issued throughout the Prussian army. There was a special rifle for the élite, the Jägerbüchse M 1865, but only its trigger, sights and bayonet differed substantially from those of the standard infantry rifle. The Jäger were distinguished more by their employment as scouts and skirmishers than by the efficacy of their firearms.

The success of the needle gun persuaded the French to adopt a variant, firing a smaller bullet (11.43mm) at a higher initial velocity to give a flatter trajectory. The Chassepot would have been an improvement on the Dreyse had not the French, in their wisdom, used an indiarubber obturating washer to seal the breech. After a few shots, the heat of combustion destroyed the elasticity of the washer and the breech seal failed; at least the all-metal cone-seal Dreyse continued to work, despite its occasional back-blast. The needle gun was doomed by the inefficiency of its ammunition and had no lasting effect on firearms history, apart from adding further testimony to the potential of the bolt-action.

By the 1870s, the single-shot breech-loader was well established and most armies had replaced their rifle-musket conversions. Little Switzerland had even adopted the 10.4mm Vetterli bolt-action repeating rifle in August 1869 and the way ahead was plainly signalled. The Vetterli infantry rifle had a twelve-shot tube magazine under the barrel and could carry a thirteenth on the cartridge elevator. Though long and heavy, it conferred a considerable advantage on the Swiss infantryman. No real attempt was made to provide an 'élite' version of the Vetterli, though the Repetierstutzer, introduced in 1871, had a special set-trigger in the tradition of the Austro-Prussian Jäger-büchsen.

By this time, élite units were indistingishable from the rank-and-file. Virtually everyone had rifles of comparable effectiveness, and emphasis had switched to the cavalryman. Show and spectacle ruled the day rather than 'killing power', as cavalry and advanced firearms were not necessary corollaries: lances, sabres and single-shot carbines sufficed. However, an incident during the Russo-Turkish War of 1877–8 indicated not only that the single-shot breech-loader was doomed, but that outnumbered (but well-protected) riflemen could still defeat infantry and cavalry advancing across open ground.

At the beginning of the First Battle of Plevna (Pleven), on 20 July 1877, more than six thousand men, the vanguard of the Russian Army, rashly stormed well dug-in Turkish defenders. Attackers, armed with Berdan bolt-action rifles – typical single-shot 11mm rifles of their day – were pitted against defenders firing block-action Peabody-Martini rifles of similar efficiency. But when the Russians were within 300 yards of the Turkish positions, the Turks countered with fire from Winchester lever-

action repeaters. The Russian Army simply withered away, retiring with the loss of a third of its strength; in a second assault, 30,000 Russians were repulsed with losses exceeding seven thousand. On 11/12 September the attackers tried again, fielding no fewer than 95,000 men; once again, the Turks exacted a terrible toll, felling 20,000 Russians at a cost of a quarter of that number. Only in the final stages of the campaign, when Osman Pasha attempted to break out of the town, did the Russians finally gain an upper hand. Plevna remains the classic nineteenth-century demonstration of the superiority of the breech-loader and an illustration of the argument engaging even post-1945 designers: the necessity to balance long-range effectiveness against close-range firepower.

The fighting for Plevna was contemporaneous with British colonial campaigns in Africa and on the North-West Frontier, where the need for firearms suited to a wide range of climatic conditions was emphasized. Colonial powers often discovered that guns that worked perfectly on home service fell short of perfection abroad. The Martini-Henry was no exception, encountering such severe extraction troubles in the heat, sand and dust of Suakin and Tell el-Kebîr that the problems could no longer be suppressed. After an outcry in the Press, and a government inquiry, the culprit was found to be the 0.450in coiled-case cartridge, which unwound under the African sun, leaving the separate case-head to be torn away by the extractor as the breech was opened.

By 1887, the French had introduced the first serviceable small-calibre military rifle, firing an 8mm cartridge loaded with smokeless 'Poudre B'. The French Lebel rifle had an archaic, potentially dangerous tube magazine in which premature ignition could be caused even by slamming the butt hard on the ground – allowing the nose of a cartridge to smash into the primer of the round ahead of it. But though the rifle offered no real advance on the contemporary 11mm clip-loaded Mannlicher, its cartridge represented a huge advance in efficiency. No less lethal than the big blackpowder patterns that it replaced, it performed far better at long ranges and was so much lighter that many more cartridges could be carried for a given weight. Where the French led, everyone else followed.

The Spanish-American War (1898) and the Boer War (1899–1902) both found the

vaunted firearms of major powers lacking. The Americans found the Norwegian-designed Krag-Jørgensen very inaccurate, problems eventually traced to poorly made barrels and inefficient bedding, while the British were comprehensively outshot in South Africa by Mauser-carrying Boers. The Boers, it is true, were experienced fieldsmen and had a considerable advantage with their modern rifles against the obtrusively red-coated British; and their commando tactics so influenced the development of irregular warfare that the British, in particular, were to make good use of the lessons forty years later.

By the time of the First World War (1914–18), revisions had been made to the bolt-action rifles used by Britain and the United States of America. The British had simply chopped five inches off the barrel of the Long Lee-Enfield, revised the sights and fitted guides which enabled the contents of two 5-round chargers ('stripper clips' in US parlance) to be fed into the magazine, while the US Army had replaced the Krag with a modified Mauser known colloquially as the Springfield.

The Rifle, Short, Magazine, Lee-Enfield (SMLE) was particularly vulnerable to criticism from the target-shooting fraternity, particularly after the politically inspired adoption of the Ross rifle in Canada. The Canadian Army had previously taken nothing but the standard British rifles. The Ross was everything the SMLE was not: long, very accurate and thus revered by target shooters. Agitation was such that the British War Office even promoted an experimental modified Mauser, the 0.276in Rifle Pattern 1913 (P13), to deflect criticism from the National Rifle Association, the gun trade and even its own experts. By August 1914, the SMLE, it had been decided, would be replaced with a rifle based on the P13. However, war caused the plans to be changed; not only was production of the SMLE accelerated, but the P14 – the P13 chambering the rimmed 0.303in cartridge – was ordered into production as well.

The contrast between the comparatively short and handy SMLE and the long, cumbersome Ross Mk III and P14 highlights another recurrent theme in military weapon design. In the pursuit of maximum effectiveness – the combination, as we have seen, of reliability and 'killing power' – compromises must be made. The target shooters' ideal is rarely suitable for mass distribution to untrained men, and new or 'revolutionary' weapons rarely reach service status without protracted development. During the opening phases of the First World War, the time-proven SMLE performed unusually well in the hands of troops trained in rapid-fire. The British Expeditionary Force, that 'contemptibly small army' grudgingly admired even by the Kaiser, turned and held the Germans on the Marne. Each Tommy, the Germans believed, had a machine-gun. Rapid fire had not been taught to the partially conscripted German armies, and they were caught very much by surprise by disciplined regulars.

Quite apart from the potentially lethal chance of reassembling the bolt without the lock-piece, the vaunted Ross ultimately proved a disaster in the mud of the Western Front – just as British trials has suggested it would be. Surviving Ross rifles were withdrawn from the dispirited Canadian troops in 1916 and replaced by the SMLE Mk III. Some remained in the hands of snipers, however, who appreciated their shooting qualities and could clean them as and when necessary out of the line. Before the war was over, though, most of the Rosses had been replaced by the P14 – heavy and unwieldy but with a stronger bolt system than the

SMLE – which proved especially popular among British snipers.

Many senior British Army officers initially regarded sniping as 'Bad Form': ungentlemanly, and therefore not to be considered by a civilized power. However, once the First World War had stretched past 1915 with no immediate end in sight, the British, having had a change of heart, found themselves impossibly short of suitable rifles. Commandeered Mannlicher, Mauser and Ross sporting rifles, as well as Long Lee-Enfields, received a curious selection of commercial optical sights until sufficient supplies of P14 and the otherwise temperamental Canadian Ross Mk III had been assured. The P14 usually received 4× Aldis optical sights; the Ross, American-made 6× Warner & Swazey Telescopic Musket Sights of 1908 and 1913. Though the performance of the Warner & Swazey sights, in particular, was surprisingly poor, they came as a revelation to shooters used to nothing but open sights. The Germans were rather better equipped, fitting selected (but otherwise standard) Gewehre 98 with excellent Zeiss, Goerz and Ajack optical sights. German snipers were élitist, and lessons learned from their activities promoted the sniper to a value that is appreciated today.

The First World War brought the first increase in élite forces in several decades. This was partly due to the increasingly stagnated nature of the trench war, which promoted sniping, and the success of the machine-gun. The crews of the German Maxim and British Vickers guns rightly judged themselves as élite units, though the subsequent issue of lightened guns to infantry machine-gun companies removed some of the gloss. By 1918, machine-guns had appeared on tripod mounts to provide sustained fire, on light bipods for close-quarter infantry support, as 'machine rifles' and in the air. The machine-gun had truly arrived.

The classic designs of this period were the water-cooled Maxim and Vickers guns that exacted a dreadful toll on the Western

9. The classic élite weapons of the First World War were the machine-guns, particularly the German Maxim MG.08 and its British near-relation, the Vickers Gun. A Vickers is shown here traversing German communications trenches at night, Cambrai, 14 June 1918. Note the flare-tracks in the sky. Courtesy of the Trustees of the Imperial War Museum (negative Q 6969).

9 ▼

Front. However, these guns were very heavy – the standard German Maschinengewehr-Gerät 08 (System Maxim) weighed 132lb (62kg) – and required several men to manage them. The emerging pattern of trench warfare soon indicated that while these heavy machine-guns were excellent for static use, built into strongpoints in the defence system, lighter guns were needed to support the troops during advances across no man's land and into the ground commanded by the opponents' machine-guns. The Germans simply lightened the MG.08, producing the MG.08/15, but this was still water-cooled, clumsy, weighed 40lb (18kg) without the coolant, and was usually serviced by four men.

Strangely the Germans ignored the contemporary air-cooled Bergmann light machine-gun, weighing a little under 29lb without its small tripod, and restricted the efficient Parabellum to aerial use. The young Erwin Rommel, famous for his role in a later war, commanded a Württemberg mountain unit on the Italian Front during this period. Among the guns especially favoured by his unit was the Madsen light machine-gun, purchased in Denmark, which provided an effective combination of mobility and firepower some years ahead of its time. With their top-mounted magazines, these Madsens proved to be far better machine-rifles than the MG.08/15, and were greatly prized.

At the outset of war, the British had acquired small numbers of Lewis light machine-guns, designed by an American, Colonel Isaac Lewis, but made by BSA. Though the Lewis was very prone to jamming, because of its spring-operated pan magazine and rimmed cartridge, it weighed only 26lb and could be carried in the manner of a large rifle. Despite its weaknesses, six Lewises could be made for each Vickers Gun, and they were to provide indispensable infantry support.

In 1915, the French adopted a light machine-gun (a Fusil Mitrailleur, or automatic rifle) known as the CSRG or Chauchat. Despite its poor performance, the Chauchat was well suited to the French technique of firing from the hip while advancing. Converted for the powerful US .30-06 round, whereafter it performed even worse than the original, the Chauchat was adopted to alleviate shortages of machine weapons when the US Army entered the First World War.

The failure of the Chauchat in US service, however, inspired John Browning to develop the Browning Automatic Rifle – now often considered to be the true prototype assault rifle. The BAR is a large gun, weighing about 16lb in its original form, but sufficiently light to be used from the shoulder by the specially selected men to whom they were issued. A 20-round detachable box magazine, protruding beneath the receiver, provided more than adequate firepower in 1918. Though manufacturing problems were experienced with the early BAR – which is hardly surprising, considering the haste in which it had been readied for service – the rifle was well liked. In the post-war period, however, its role was scrutinized, a bipod added (increasing the weight by more than two pounds) and the BAR became more of a light machine-gun than a true automatic rifle. Lacking a quick-change barrel, the modified Browning Automatic Rifle was tried and found wanting against guns such as the Madsen, the Czech ZB vz/26 and the Bren – though derivations were made in Belgium, Sweden, Poland and elsewhere during the 1930s.

THE STURMTRUPPEN

During the First World War, the Germans and Austro-Hungarians also evolved the concept of the Sturmtruppen ('storm troops'): heavily armed raiding parties who carried minimal equipment other than their firearms and grenades. As close-quarter fighting required special solutions (such as trench daggers, clubs and sharpened spades), the Germans initially issued the long 'Artillery Lugers' with 32-round drum magazines. These semi-automatic pistols were scarcely ideal, as the magazines jammed too easily and projected clumsily below the gun-butt. In 1918, therefore, the first true Bergmann submachine-gun appeared. The MP.18,I retained the cumbersome drum magazine associated with the artillery Lugers, but could fire fully automatically at

◄ 10. Though the heavy water-cooled machine-guns were held in awe in the trenchscape of the First World War, mobility had been sacrificed to the god of firepower. As a result, guns such as the jam-prone American-designed BSA-made Lewis Gun were introduced to keep pace with an advance. Here, Lewis Guns are being carried by Portuguese infantrymen at the infantry training school, Marthes, France, in June 1917. Courtesy of the Trustees of the Imperial War Museum (negative Q 5534).

11, 12. As even automatic rifles and light machine-guns were unsuitable for trench warfare, the Germans pioneered the light automatic carbine – first with the long-barrelled Luger pistol, the LP.08 (**11**), and then with the Bergmann MP.18,I, the first true submachine-gun (**12**). Author's collection.

11▲

12▼

600 rounds per minute. Though perhaps less than 50,000 were made prior to the armistice, the MP.18,I was later to have an impact disproportionate to its numbers.

BEYOND THE ARMISTICE

It was thought that the period after 1919 would be one of peace, and very little fire-arms development reached fruition. Most of the efforts were devoted to perfecting machine-guns and large-calibre cannon, but the US Army took the opportunity – after trials lasting more than a decade – to introduce the Rifle Caliber 0.30 M1, better known as the 'Garand' after its inventor.

The Garand was the first self-loading rifle to be approved for universal issue, though this had not been completed by the time the US Army entered the Second World War in December 1941 and many units went to war armed with the bolt-action Springfield.

The Garand was another of the many designs that attracted considerable criti-cism; it even failed the standard British dust and mud tests. The worst feature of the rifle was its idiosyncratic clip-loaded magazine, which prevented the action being loaded with loose rounds. The magazine capacity (a

mere eight) was also subsequently found to be too small. But in terms of rate of fire and, more importantly, ease and comfort of firing, the Garand was deemed a vast improvement on its bolt-action predeces-sors, as it eliminated the considerable physical effort expended on manipulating the bolt-action rifles and minimized fatigue, muscle tremors, increases in blood pressure and consequent deterioration of accuracy.

In the early 1930s, the rise of Germany panicked many European countries into developing new light machine-guns. During this period, the tactical employment of machine-guns was dissected, to be analysed over and over again even though most armies remained convinced by pre-1918 dogma: heavy support guns, generally water-cooled, reinforced by box-fed light guns for close-quarter fire support when mobility was the prerequisite. By 1939, Britain had the Vickers and Bren Guns, while Russia had the Maxim and the light, pan-fed Degtyarev. The French, going a stage further, had adopted the box-fed Fusil Mitrailleur Mle 24/29 ('Châtellerault') for widespread issue, and a curious drum-fed MAC31 for static use in the Maginot Line and in aircraft. Once again, war was to provide conditions under which peacetime developments were to be judged.

The period between the wars also saw the birth of the paratroops, a type of warfare that appealed – particularly – to the Rus-sians and Italians. The Russians had some of the world's largest aircraft and could make spectacular mass drops; there was even talk of dropping men, at low level but without parachutes, into banks of soft snow. The Italian Arditi ('bold ones') showed characteristic artistry, preferring the so-called 'angel leap' to the traditional upright body position and unusually controllable chutes.

Initially, few concessions were made to the armament of paratroops, though many of the light machine-guns introduced in the 1930s where easily dismantled into ideal loads. The Italians' Mo.91/38 infantry rifle was comparatively short, like the SMLE, and could be carried easily in a 'bucket' attached to the paratroopers' ankles. The Russians and Germans were not so lucky, and efforts were made to develop suitable submachine-guns to replace the clumsy infantry rifle. Among the results were the German MP.38 ('Schmeisser') and the Italian Moschetto Automatico Beretta, or 'MAB'. The Italian design was efficient enough to be prized by German units as well as the Arditi, and modified variants were still being made into the 1970s.

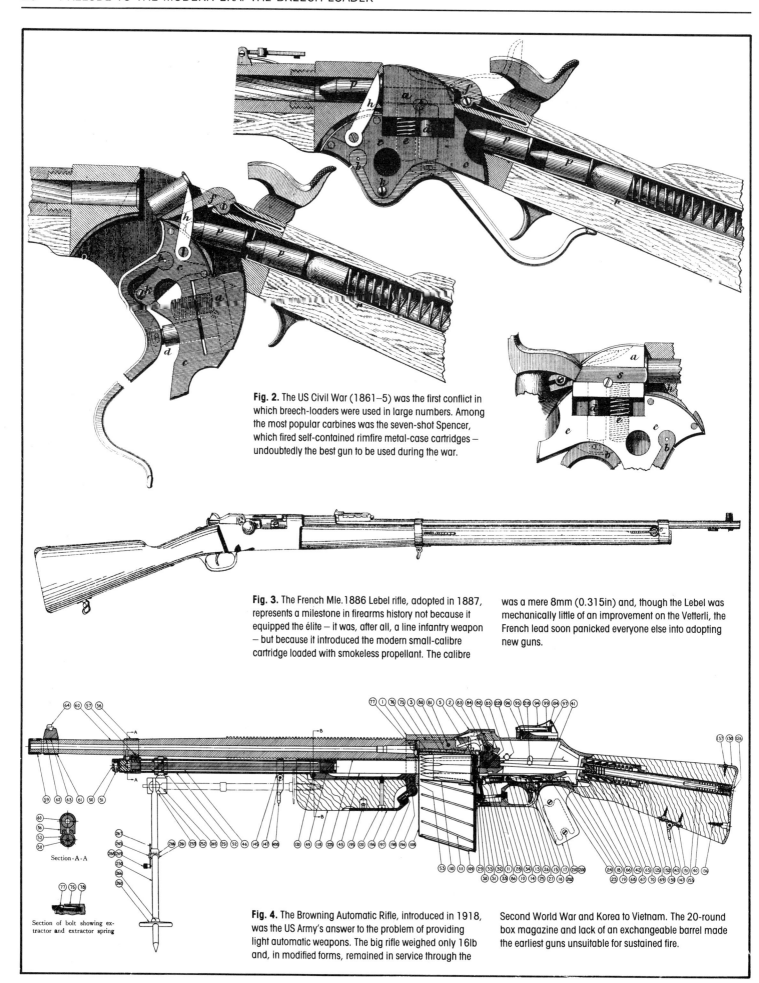

Fig. 2. The US Civil War (1861–5) was the first conflict in which breech-loaders were used in large numbers. Among the most popular carbines was the seven-shot Spencer, which fired self-contained rimfire metal-case cartridges — undoubtedly the best gun to be used during the war.

Fig. 3. The French Mle.1886 Lebel rifle, adopted in 1887, represents a milestone in firearms history not because it equipped the élite — it was, after all, a line infantry weapon — but because it introduced the modern small-calibre cartridge loaded with smokeless propellant. The calibre was a mere 8mm (0.315in) and, though the Lebel was mechanically little of an improvement on the Vetterli, the French lead soon panicked everyone else into adopting new guns.

Section - A - A

Section of bolt showing extractor and extractor spring

Fig. 4. The Browning Automatic Rifle, introduced in 1918, was the US Army's answer to the problem of providing light automatic weapons. The big rifle weighed only 16lb and, in modified forms, remained in service through the Second World War and Korea to Vietnam. The 20-round box magazine and lack of an exchangeable barrel made the earliest guns unsuitable for sustained fire.

The Second World War

Considerable experimentation between the wars had improved the quality of smallarms almost universally, but had had little effect on the design of the weapons of the rank and file. Thus, the initial Wehrmacht successes during the early campaigns of the Second World War owed as much to mechanization – the Panzers, particularly – and the perfection of aerial dive-bombing against lightly defended positions as to improved smallarms design.

Apart from the adoption of the Garand by the US Army in 1936, which had excited much controversy, the Allies had achieved little; the British Army had the new, highly efficient Bren Gun, but the infantry rifle was still the bolt-action Rifle, Short, Magazine Lee-Enfield. Only the Russians had much progress to show for the experiments with automatic rifles that had obsessed most European armies in the 1930s: the majority view was exemplified by the British, who still regarded them as wasteful of ammunition and lacking in durability.

THE RUSSIAN FRONT: THE SNIPER COMES OF AGE

The Red Army had tried the Simonov-designed AVS in Manchuria, where Japanese incursions were comprehensively rebuffed, but such a lightweight rifle – it weighed a little under 9lb unladen – was too flimsy to sustain automatic fire with the standard 7.62mm cartridge, quite apart from the maltreatment associated with service conditions. Throughout firearms history, this has been a recurrent theme: often, promising designs have failed merely because they were insufficiently strong. Surviving Simonovs were expended in Finland during the Winter War, the complicated, rather fragile guns being superseded in 1938 – after protracted trials – by the Tokarev-designed SVT. Adopted in February 1939, the pre-production SVT shared some of the weaknesses of the

Simonov. Procurement was soon suspended while an improved AVS was tested, but Simonov was less acceptable politically than Tokarev and the first true SVT rifle was assembled in July 1939. Experience in the Winter War against Finland indicated so many weaknesses that the SVT38 was withdrawn, to reappear in April 1940 as the 'SVT40'. Huge quantities of Tokarev rifles were made (more than a million in 1941 alone), but production was bedevilled by constant problems.

During the Winter War against the Finns, in 1939/40, the Russians had learned from bitter experience the value of well-trained snipers. One thorn in their flesh was Simo Hähyä, a farmer who had won many pre-war marksmanship trophies. Attached to a unit on the Karelia Front, Häyhä, firing an open-sighted Model 1928 rifle (a Finnish Mosin-Nagant), killed more than 500 Russian soldiers in fifteen weeks. As a result of experiences in Finland, the Russians selected the most accurate

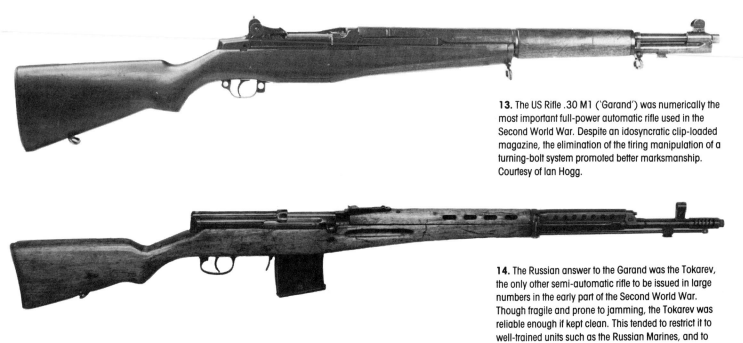

13. The US Rifle .30 M1 ('Garand') was numerically the most important full-power automatic rifle used in the Second World War. Despite an idosyncratic clip-loaded magazine, the elimination of the tiring manipulation of a turning-bolt system promoted better marksmanship. Courtesy of Ian Hogg.

14. The Russian answer to the Garand was the Tokarev, the only other semi-automatic rifle to be issued in large numbers in the early part of the Second World War. Though fragile and prone to jamming, the Tokarev was reliable enough if kept clean. This tended to restrict it to well-trained units such as the Russian Marines, and to snipers. The gun shown here is an SVT-40. Pattern Room Collection, Enfield Lock.

▲ 15   16 ▼

15. The Russians made extensive use of snipers during the Second World War, perhaps to a greater degree than any other army. Here, left-handed Komsomol member Lyuba Makarova is seen practising her art. Firing a Mosin-Nagant rifle, Miss Makarova had killed 30 Germans by the time this picture was taken on the Kalinin Front in 1943. Courtesy of Novosti Press Agency.

16. The standard Russian PU telescope sight, mounted on an obr.1891/30 Mosin-Nagant rifle. Pattern Room Collection, Enfield Lock.

Tokarev rifles for snipers' use, fitting them with telescopic sights, but the SNT40 proved appreciably less reliable than the solid Mosin-Nagant bolt-action 1891/30. The latter was ordered back into production in 1942 and remained the standard Eastern Bloc sniping rifle until 1963.

The best of the Russian snipers preferred the 1891/30 to the semi-automatic for reasons that are as relevant today as in 1941: the manually operated rifle was more reliable, less prone to structural failure and had no mechanical noise in the action. This was particularly important when silence was essential – the ejection-reloading cycle of the SNT was accompanied by considerable clatter. The great Vasiliy Zaitsev almost always fired Mosin-Nagants, and left-handers such as Lyuba Makarova found that the SNT ejected fired cases too close to their faces for comfort.

Despite the troubles originating from the disruption of manufacture after the German invasion of Russia in June 1941, the Tokarev was by no means a failure. Poor equipment would not have been tolerated by the Soviet snipers, who were rightly respected by their opponents and extracted a terrible price for the German invasion. Provided it was kept reasonably clean – a stricture still applying to automatic weapons – it functioned satisfactorily enough in the hands of good-quality troops such as the Russian marines.

'The Russians backed out of their trench. Anxious to put the German sniper in a maximum amount of blinding sunlight, they followed the irregularly curving front line until they found a spot where the afternoon sun would be at their backs . . . Aware that the sun would reflect on their scopes, they waited patiently for it to go down behind them. By late afternoon, now wrapped in shade, they had Konings at a disadvantage. Zaitsev focused his telescopic sight on the German's hiding-place. A piece of glass suddenly glinted at the edge of the sheet. Zaitsev motioned to Kulikov, who slowly raised his helmet over the top of the parapet. Konings fired once and Kulikov rose, screaming convincingly. Sensing triumph, the German lifted his head slightly to see his victim. Vassili Zaitsev shot him between the eyes . . .'*

Snipers also made their presence felt in the Pacific, where the Japanese not only became past masters in the art of concealment, but also had a degree of fanaticism sufficient to persist long after most Western marksmen would have prudently withdrawn. The lessons were not lost on the Americans, while, even at Arnhem, the Germans feared British snipers largely because the latter were taught to aim only at the head if circumstances permitted.

*William Craig: *Enemy at the Gates – The Battle for Stalingrad.* Zaitsev, credited with killing 242 Germans in Stalingrad before being injured by a landmine, became a Hero of the Soviet Union.

A NEW GOAL: SIMPLICITY

17, 18. The German MG.34 was the first truly successful general-purpose machine-gun, a genre that is now in vogue. The gun, which weighed a little under 27lb with its bipod (**17**), could also be mounted on a special buffered tripod (**18**). Author's collection.

At the start of the war, the Germans, despite their spectacular successes, were lacking in advanced smallarms. The standard infantry weapon was the strong, accurate but somewhat cumbersome Mauser-type bolt-action Kar.98k, 45.6in overall, weighing 8.85lb and taking five 7.9mm rounds in its magazine. This was supplemented by a comparatively new air-cooled medium machine-guns, the MG.34, developed clandestinely in Switzerland in the early 1930s and adopted after experiments in Hungary and elsewhere. The belt-fed MG.34 was appreciably lighter than most of its predecessors, very well made and efficient under normal conditions, but when the Germans became bogged down in Russia and the Western Desert, demonstrated a tendency to jam, its excellent manufacturing standards and minimal tolerances proving an unexpected Achilles' heel. While the MG.34 jammed, the archaic-looking Russian Degtyarev light machine-gun, so crude by German standards, proved extremely reliable under adverse conditions. That impeccable quality did not guarantee efficiency was not lost on the Germans, however, and had a lasting effect on firearms development.

19. The replacement for the venerable Bergmann submachine-gun in the Wehrmacht had been the Schmeisser-designed MP.38 and MP.40 (the latter being shown here). The 'Schmeisser' has become associated with the German army of the Third Reich period in much the manner that the Thompson is associated with the Chicago mobsters of the Roaring Twenties! However, it was popular with the Allies during the Second World War, and some were being used by the SAS in Yemen as late as 1963. Pattern Room Collection, Enfield Lock.

The German armies also had the Schmeisser MP.38 and MP.40, sub-machine-guns providing a considerable volume of fire at the expense of firing a pistol cartridge with limited effective range. The Germans used their automatic weapons to good effect in the early campaigns, including the daring capture of Fort Eben Emael in Belgium in May 1940. However, the impetus for the development of special forces was soon to swing to Britain, desperately facing up to the threat posed by German troops in the Pas de Calais and haunted by the bitter memories of the near-débâcle at Dunkirk.

THE FIRST SPECIAL FORCES

Penned back into the home islands, the British were nothing if not inventive – particularly where coast defence was concerned – and many military personnel retained faith in the maxim that attack is the best form of defence. While the RAF was battling the Luftwaffe, the first commando units were being formed. There was nothing particularly revolutionary about the concept. While walking home from the War Office in Whitehall, Lieutenant-Colonel Dudley

Clarke, mindful of historical lessons, pondered controlled aggressive action by small well-trained bands acting independently of centralized command. Searching for a name for his irregulars, he seized on 'commando' – the Boers that had plagued the British army forty years earlier in the South African War. Dudley Clarke's superior was Field Marshal Sir John Dill, Chief of the Imperial General Staff, who could have been expected to oppose the idea of an army within the army; but Dill was also concerned by rock-bottom army morale and the need for achievement. He explained the matter to the Prime Minister, Winston Churchill, and within a day the Commandos were born.

Their role was to disrupt the communications, efficiency and nerve of the Wehrmacht in 'shoot 'n scoot' missions, seeking to cause as much trouble in the shortest time possible, then retire in the confusion. If the defenders reinforced the position, or moved fresh troops into the area, the next strike could be made whence they had come. And so it continued in occupied Europe, North Africa, the Mediterranean and the Aegean, the Commandos spawning a dozen or more offshoots such as the US Rangers and the ANZAC Independent Companies.

Many early raids were fiascos, apparently confirming worst fears of the military. In July 1940, however, the hero of the legendary Zeebrugge Raid in the First World War, Admiral Sir Roger Keyes, was appointed to direct the Commandos. Things improved. By October 1940, two thousand men had been recruited into the 'Special Service Brigade' and divided into commandos numbered 1–12. Unbelievably

rigorous training programmes began in the surf and on the beaches of the Western Highlands, the Combined Training Centre eventually being founded at Achnacarry. Here trained not only the British Commandos, but also the US Rangers and the Royal Marine commando detachments formed in 1942. Training was often very dangerous – undertaken with live ammunition – and forty men were killed at Achnacarry during the war. In terms of the successes achieved by the Commandos, this price was small. But the deaths, and mock gravestones in the camp labelled THESE MEN BUNCHED or THIS ROYAL MARINE WALKED IN FRONT OF HIS PAL'S RIFLE punched the message home: brains as well as brawn were required for Special Service.

After the initial reverses, the Commandos' fortunes improved on the strength of spectacularly successful raids on the Lofoten Islands, in March 1941, and on Vagsoy and Maloy in December, by which time Keyes had been replaced by Captain Lord Louis Mountbatten. The best was yet to come. A suspicious building had been spotted during a routine sweep over the village of Bruneval, near Le Havre, and a photo-reconnaissance Spitfire ultimately brought back one of the classic air-reconnaissance photographs of the war: a perfect oblique view of the cliff-top villa and the dish antenna of a German Würzburg radar. In a daunting, unbelievably ambitious raid, the Commandos not only silenced the defences, but also stole the entire radar dish – an exploit matched in its conception only by the seizure of a Russian-made radar station by the crack Israeli NAHAL paratroops from Ras Gharib in 1969.

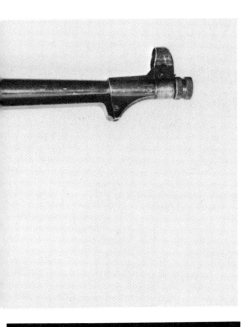

SPECIAL FORCES OPERATIONS: TAKE NOTHING FOR GRANTED

Large-scale clandestine activities are never guaranteed successes, as proved by the loss of six hundred highly trained Commandos covering the British withdrawal from Crete in May 1941. By the end of the year, success was needed to restore flagging spirits and a spectacular coup was planned – the assassination of Erwin Rommel, officer commanding the Afrika Korps, in his headquarters at Beda Littoria in Libya.

Proposed by youthful Lieutenant-Colonel Geoffrey Keyes, son of the former Director of Combined Operations, its chances of success were adjudged as practically nil. Keyes persisted, however, and the gimcrack scheme was eventually approved for the night of 17 November 1941 – one day prior to the start of a British offensive seeking to relieve Tobruk.

A small party was detached from the main force on the perimeter of Beda Littoria to cut communications between the headquarters and Cyrene, while the remaining 22 men, their faces blacked, proceeded stealthily into the deserted marketplace a mere hundred yards from a large house which, they were told, served as Rommel's headquarters. The building would be stormed by six men led by Keyes, while the remainder were to guard the approaches to the building.

Keyes led his party around the building to begin the assault at the main door. Things went wrong: the German sentry seized the muzzle of Keyes' Colt revolver,

trying to wrest it away, and retreated against a wall using Keyes as a shield before being shot. A burst from a Thompson sub-machine-gun discouraged a soldier about to descend the stairs. Keyes pointed to light shining under the guardroom door, which opened to reveal eleven dumbstruck German soldiers. Captain Campbell lobbed a No. 36 grenade into the centre of the room as Keyes opened the door for the second time. A rake of submachine-gun fire prevented the Germans replying, but a single shot felled Keyes as the British closed the door. After the grenade had done its job, and a fruitless search of the house had been made, Campbell forgetfully emerged from the back door and was promptly shot by one of the Commando sentries. And there had been no sign of Rommel at all.

The Beda Littoria raid, a heroic failure, gained Keyes a posthumous Victoria Cross but achieved little else. Yet its lightning attack with grenades, light firearms and explosives was typical of the many independent operations carried out during the Second World War.

During 1941, the Commandos had been joined by the Long Range Desert Group (LRDG), a mobile reconnaissance group drawing inspiration from the Arab nomads in the trackless sands, and David Stirling's 'L' Detachment – the precursor of the Special Air Service (SAS).

THE BIRTH OF THE SAS

Tony Geraghty, in *Who Dares Wins*, explains that 'Stirling drafted a long memorandum . . . wherein he argued that strategic raids – that is, deep penetration behind enemy lines – did not require the ponderous naval back-up of full-blown Commando assaults . . . Instead, Stirling proposed using parachutist saboteurs to inflict a level of damage on enemy airfields equivalent to that of a Commando force twenty times greater.'

Stirling had been injured in a parachuting accident and was confined to a hospital bed. He realized that his submission would not get past the junior officers at GHQ, Cairo, and decided upon action in keeping not only with his ideas but also with the subsequent exploits of the Special Air Service. 'A high wire fence surrounded the headquarters area,' says Geraghty. 'Leaving his crutches outside the fence, Stirling hauled himself

painfully over, and dropped into the compound. He then walked gingerly into the main administrative block, bumping into various offices and their occupants, before discovering that Auchinleck was out. By now, the internal security staff had been alerted to his presence. Stirling found the Deputy C-in-C, Lieutenant-General Neil Ritchie, just before they found him . . . Ritchie scanned the paper and subsequently recalled Stirling for a discussion of the scheme with Auchinleck. Soon afterwards, in his new rank of captain, Stirling was given permission to recruit 66 men from the remains of Layforce Commando.'

The SAS was confined largely to North Africa during this period, successfully sabotaging Axis airfields at comparatively little cost. Success bred success; the Commandos, the LRDG and SAS were soon joined by the Special Boat Service (SBS), the Royal Marines Boom Patrol Detachment, the Combined Operation Pilotage Parties (COPPs – specializing in beach reconnaissance) and a host of other special purpose forces.

As the war ran its course, other special units appeared. Popski's Private Army was formed by a Belgian businessman of Russian origin, Vladimir Peniakoff, whose company size reconnaissance and raiding force was active in North Africa and later in Italy. Merrill's Marauders, officially the 5037th Composite Unit of the US Army, was organized in October 1943 under Brigadier-General Frank Merrill and trained specifically in jungle fighting for service in Burma. The Chindits, alias the Long-Range Penetration Group or 77th Indian Infantry Battalion, were raised by Orde Wingate in the summer of 1942 and successfully harried the Japanese for two years. *The Encyclopedia of World War Two* aptly sums up a popular official feeling to such units by saying of the Chindits, '[they] were as controversial as their tactics. Many staff officers regarded them as eccentric and undependable. But despite their detractors' claims, they played an important role . . .'

The Germans had the Brandenburgers, who specialized in infiltration but ultimately fell foul of politics and paved the way for the personality cult of Otto Skorzeny and his commandos. Despite the diversity of these units, however, most were satisfied with standard firearms. The designers' ingenuity was reserved more for assassination weapons, clandestine radio-communication equipment and cryptology.

THE FIRST SPECIAL FORCES FIREARMS

Initially, the British special forces had to make do with standard firearms and grenades. This was not disastrous, because the basic smallarms, if somewhat unadventurous, were reasonably effective. Though the bolt-action SMLE was not ideal in a fire-fight, it could be operated quicker than most comparable guns and carried twice as many cartridges as rival designs. The Bren Gun was portable, extremely accurate and well liked, and could be used to pick off key targets with single shots while providing appreciable extra firepower when required. Handguns varied: the standard 0.38in Enfield (Webley) revolver, the .38/200 Smith & Wesson and various Colts – including the US Government M1911A1 pistol – all saw use early in the war. However, none of the smallarms provided what the special forces sought most: the combination of handiness and firepower that had defeated most pre-1939 inventors.

An early favourite was the Thompson submachine-gun, made by Colt for the Auto-Ordnance Corporation and revered by police and mobsters alike during the Roaring Twenties. The Thompson fired the .45 ACP pistol cartridge, widely recognized as a good manstopper, but was particularly cumbersome – with its loaded 50-round magazine, it weighed 15lb – and many doubted the integrity of its locking mechanism. Ordinarily quite reliable, the Thompson was prone to jamming when

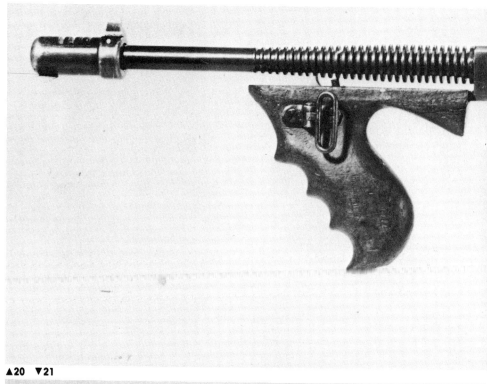

▲20 ▼21

20. The classic submachine-gun of the SAS, Commandos and other special forces in the early days was the Thompson. Despite the awe in which the Thompson was held – a legacy of its exploits during Prohibition – the M1928, shown here, was heavy, complicated and prone to jamming unless properly lubricated. The simpler M1, with a 30-round box magazine, was preferred by the troops.

21. The legendary Bren Gun, adopted by the British Army in 1936, is one of the all-time classic light machine-guns. Despite chambering the rimmed 0.303in round (not ideal for an autoloader), the 22lb Bren provided a good blend of accuracy and firepower. Converted to handle 7.62mm NATO ammunition in the 1960s, Brens have proved particularly useful in theatres where their mobility, exemplary single-shot accuracy and comparatively light weight have the edge on the belt-feed L7 GPMG. During the Falklands conflict, L4A4 Bren Guns were withdrawn from service in Norway and elsewhere and shipped to the South Atlantic, where they were received with enthusiasm. The gun pictured is one of the original 7.92mm examples made for the Chinese by Inglis of Toronto.

inexpertly lubricated and this was a distinct liability in the desert.

Supplies of the improved blowback Thompson M1, with a 30-round box magazine, appeared in 1942. The M1 was greatly appreciated by the British Commandos and the US Rangers, who preferred it to the later M3 'Grease Gun'. But the basic Thompson design remained too complicated and too expensive to mass produce. The British developed the Lanchester instead, simply by copying the German MP.28 (Bergmann), but then graduated to the Sten Gun. Credited to Major Richard V. Shepherd and Harold Turpin, pilot models of the Sten were made in 1941. A whole new BSA factory was erected at Tyseley, on the outskirts of Birmingham, and volume production began in the summer. As the Lanchester production line had also been completed, supplies of this otherwise obsolescent design were diverted to the Royal Navy so that the Stens could be supplied to the army.

By the end of the war, millions of Stens had been made in a variety of 'Marks'. The unbelievably basic 'Woolworth Wonder' or 'Stench Gun' eventually cost no more than 7s 6d (37½p) for what were reputedly its main components – a pipe and a bedspring. Yet this horror worked surprisingly well. Lubrication was practically unnecessary and, as accuracy was not prerequisite, bullets could be sprayed far and wide with impunity.

The Sten supplemented the Thompson in the hands of the special forces, its

▲ 22

22. Familiarity with opposing weapons is an indispensable part of special forces training. Here, HRH Duke of Gloucester inspects men of the SAS at the Paratroop Training School, Kabrit, Egypt, in 1942. Visible are three Italian Mo.30 light machine-guns, one heavy machine-gun tripod, an MP40 and a Beretta Mo.38 submachine-gun. Courtesy of the Trustees of the Imperial War Museum (negative E 12971).

23. The British answer to the problems of the Thompson was the cheap, crude Sten Gun Mk 1 – which, though prone to feed jams, was available in vast numbers and usually continued to operate with minimal lubrication. The success of the Sten was such that attempts were made to provide 'luxury' variants (such as the Mk 5) for paratroops. Courtesy of Ian Hogg.

24. The Australian Army preferred the extraordinary-looking Owen submachine-gun, the Mark I/43 being shown here. Notwithstanding its strange appearance and crude construction, the top-mounted magazine gave the Owen an unusually reliable feed. The gun was greatly favoured by the Australian SAS, who preferred it to the Thompson, the Sten, the Austen and the US M3. Owens were also widely distributed to the re-activated SAS units during the Malayan Emergency. Courtesy of Ian Hogg.

23 ▲

24 ▼

dreadful finish coming as something of a shock after the good manufacturing quality of its predecessor. Efforts were eventually made to improve the Sten, a special compact gun being developed experimentally in 1943–4. The final Mk V, with a wood butt, a handgrip and a bayonet lug, was developed in time for Operation 'Market Garden' – the ill-starred drop at Arnhem, related in Cornelius Ryan's epic *A Bridge Too Far*. The Sten Mk 2S had a special Maxim-pattern silencer surrounding the barrel, giving it a peculiarly bulky appearance compared with the standard gun; but it was very effective as long as only single shots were fired, and inspired the current L34A1 silenced Sterling.

Apart from the appearance of the Sten and the Rifle No. 5 (a 'jungle carbine' variant of the SMLE), and increasing enthusiasm for the US Carbine M1 as the war progressed, few basic changes were made in the smallarms issued to the SAS and other British Special Forces, though the Canadian-made Pistol GP Browning No. 2 Mk 1 gradually achieved wider distribution. A much-appreciated predecessor of the pistol adopted by the British Army in 1957, this had the unique distinction of being manufactured for both sides' special forces concurrently – German paratroops favoured the guns being made in the occupied ex-Fabrique Nationale factory in Herstal while Anglo-Canadian guns were being made by Inglis in Toronto.

Various special-purpose guns appeared, including the Welrod and the Projector, Arm Mk 1 – and the silenced High Standard Model B pistol procured for the OSS – but their distribution was rarely significant and few had lasting effects on post-war developments.

A MISSED OPPORTUNITY?

The US M1 Carbine deserves to be considered as a landmark in military weaponry, though its value passed largely unnoticed at the time. Its origins are traceable to an experimental Winchester rifle unsuccessfully tested by the US Marine Corps in 1940, competing against the Garand and the Johnson. The Winchester was prematurely adjudged a failure; but it embodied an excellent short-stroke gas piston system, designed by David M. 'Carbine' Williams, and could have been developed to rival the Garand had it not appeared at an inopportune moment in history.

Three years previously, however, the Chief of Infantry, Major-General George Lynch, had highlighted a need for a light semi-automatic personal weapon more powerful than the .45 ACP pistol but with an effective range at least ten times the 25 yards of the M1911A1 Colt-Browning. As considerable opposition came from the Ordnance Department, the project foundered until a draft specification was circulated to interested parties in October 1940. This called for a weight of less than five pounds, provision for full-automatic fire and a 50-round detachable box magazine.

Winchester designed a straight-sided 0.30in cartridge, adapted from the commercial 0.32in WSL ('Winchester Self Loading'), and nine carbines arrived for trials. The undesirability of the fully-automatic feature and the large magazine was soon noted, and both these features were dropped. Winchester then entered the gun competition by adapting the Williams short-stroke piston system and scaling down the USMC trials rifle, producing the first prototype in an incredible thirteen days. After a successful demonstration at Aberdeen

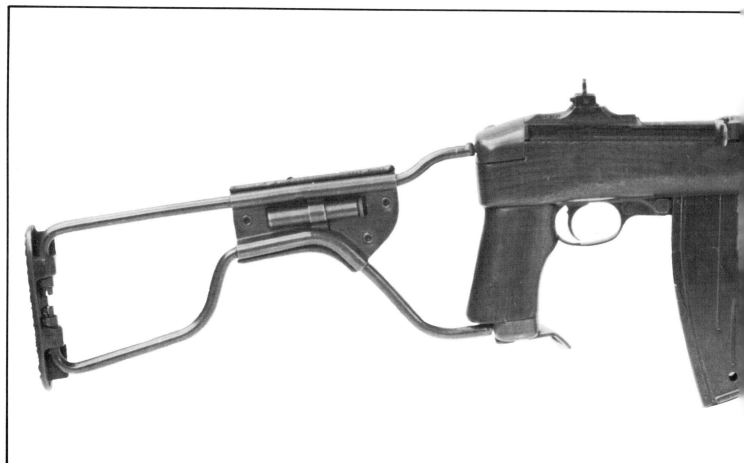

Proving Ground, the entire trials were postponed while a second Winchester carbine was made. A mere 34 days later, the gun was dispatched to Aberdeen. Amazingly, the Winchester defeated the Garand and Hyde guns, victors of previous trials, and was ordered straight into production as the 'Carbine, Caliber .30, M1'.

Its combat début was eagerly awaited, but anticipation was soured when the first reports filtered back from the Ordnance Department 'experts'. The carbine had many attractive features: it was reliable, handled well and was quite accurate at short range, but the .30in bullet was, rather stupidly, adjudged a poor manstopper by the criteria of the standard M2 Ball used in the Garand. Most armchair soldiers conveniently forgot that the carbine was specifically designed to be effective *only out to 300 yards* (my italics), but their lack of enthusiasm was rarely shared in the field and the eventual production of more than six million guns made the point. The special forces, British and American alike, relied greatly on M1 (semi-automatic) and M2 (fully automatic) Carbines in jungle theatres where their handiness, light weight and good rate of fire were advantageous.

Had the M1 Carbine chambered a more effective round, it might have been an even greater success. The post-war commercial version chambering the 5.7mm Johnson Spitfire cartridge – not unlike the current 5.56mm M193 in terms of power – could have had a far-reaching effect on firearms technology had it appeared in 1941, pre-empting the AR15/M16 by sixteen years.

It is ironic that the so-called Pig and Goat Boards, appointed to investigate the lethality of cartridges under consideration for the Garand in the 1930s, had shown what was necessary – a long and relatively unstable projectile which set-up on striking the target and caused serious wounds. The most lethal performer in these trials at short-range had been the Japanese 6.5mm pattern.

THE FIRST ASSAULT RIFLE

The problems that beset the M1 Carbine highlighted the dilemma that had faced most military firearms designers since the end of the First World War. The urge to lighten and simplify weapons, and particularly to develop lightweight infantry rifles, was inevitably rejected by senior officers who had seen active service many years previously. Infantry rifles, they said, should be capable of engaging targets out to 1,000 yards or more.

Anyone who has fired a military rifle at a conventional 500- or 600-yard target, six feet square, will realize the inherent difficulties of engaging a moving man-size target with sights developed more for their durability than precision. Imagine placing a football on the ground, walking four pitch-lengths away and then trying to hit it with an open-sighted rifle. In man-to-man combat, the chances of a successful long-range hit are comparatively low. Why, then, was it necessary to engage targets with an infantry

25. The US M1 Carbine, shown here in its folding-stock M1A1 form, was conceived as a light automatic for officers, artillery and other personnel who were not front-line infantrymen. Limitations on weight and size, plus tactical restrictions to a maximum effective range of only 300 yards, gave the M1 Carbine an underpowered cartridge that proved to be a poor manstopper. This now tends to overshadow the fact that in excess of six million Carbines were made, and that they served effectively in every theatre during the Second World War, on into Korea and Vietnam, and with special forces such as the SAS. Courtesy of Ian Hogg.

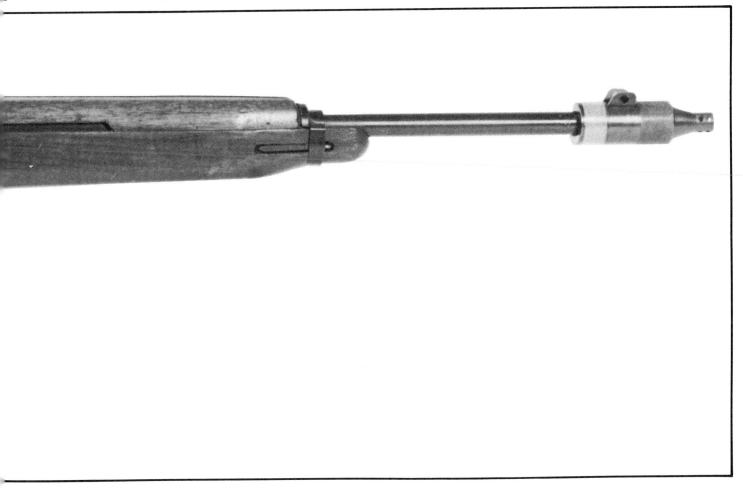

rifle at a thousand yards when this was surely better left to the machine-gunners?

German designers, having apparently examined work undertaken in Switzerland in the 1920s, set out to investigate the relationship between range, power and hit probability at a time when the US Army – prodded by Douglas MacArthur – had rejected the promising 0.276in cartridge developed for the experimental Pedersen and Garand rifles in the late 1920s. In 1935, the British had even framed a specification calling for a bolt-action infantry rifle capable of defeating 14mm armour plate at 100 yards; one trial cartridge exceeded 4,000fps with a 104-grain bullet.

The successful German paratroop invasion of Crete in 1941 was accompanied by such an excessive casualty rate that the Wehrmacht never again contemplated airborne attacks on such a large scale. Many survivors of the drop believed that the Schmeisser submachine-gun and Mauser bolt-action rifles could not provide sufficient firepower to overcome tenacious defenders. The Fallschirmjägergewehr 42, as its name suggests, was developed specifically to provide German paratroops with a portable selective-fire rifle firing the standard full-power rifle cartridge to maximize effective range. Guns were submitted by Krieghoff, Mauser and Rheinmetall, the successful design being credited to Rheinmetall engineer Louis Stange, but most guns were made by Krieghoff (code 'fzs').

The earliest guns were just 37in long, weighing 9.93lb unladen, with an integral bipod and a lateral-feed detachable 20-round box magazine protruding from the left side of the receiver. The gun locked with a rotary bolt and had a straight-line layout to minimize climb in automatic fire, though this required sights raised well above the gun. Many stampings and pressings were used in an attempt to simplify production, but very few rifles were made because of production problems and a lack of raw material. Despite being used by Otto Skorzeny's Commandos during the highly successful release of Mussolini (September 1943), the earlier FG.42 was insufficiently robust; the later variant is longer and heavier, with a laminated wood butt and the bipod moved to the muzzle from around the gas-port assembly. It also has a different muzzle brake, an adjustable four-position regulator and various detail differences.

FG.42 were used with great success at Monte Cassino, impressing Hitler so greatly, it is said, that he decreed that they be distributed to the élite troops of the Wehrmacht to replace the ageing bolt-action Karabiner 98k. Unfortunately, production never matched demand – by no means an unusual event in German small-arms circles.

THE MASCHINENKARABINER

This gun apparently arose out of a requirement similar to that for the M1 Carbine in the USA, seeking to replace the Schmeisser machine pistol with a more powerful semi- or fully-automatic weapon without sacrificing high fire rate. After protracted experiments, beginning in the mid 1930s, the German ammunition technologists had settled on the 7.9mm Kurz cartridge. This combined a lightweight bullet (125 grains compared with 198 for the standard sS ball) with a short case, but was appreciably more powerful than the 9mm Pist.Patr.08 and the US M1 Carbine round. It was, however, markedly less effectual than the standard German 7.9mm service rifle cartridge beyond 400 metres and ideally suited to the light automatic 'Maschinenkarabiner'.

Mindful of the billions of full-power 7.9mm cartridges that had been stockpiled by 1939, Hitler was initially firmly opposed to the light automatic. Once the Wehrmacht had advanced into Russia, however, the situation changed; not only was the vaunted German army short of motor transport, but also still relied heavily on the bolt-action infantry rifle. Consequently, the Russian PPSh submachine-gun, crude by German standards, left an indelible impression on the invaders. Issued on a tremendous scale, the PPSh was accompanied by a 71-round drum magazine which gave awesome firepower.

Although the Führer was insisting that production of the obsolescent Kar.98k should be accelerated even as late as March 1943, experimental Maschinenkarabiner (MKb) had been submitted a year previously and the HWaA had accepted the Haenel prototype at the expense of its Walther rival. Encouraging field trials were undertaken by SS Division 'Wiking' in the spring of 1943, more than half the troops reporting that the rifle was a suitable replacement for the Schmeisser submachine-guns and the Mauser infantry rifles. One man in ten had even opined that the Maschinenkarabiner could replace all the infantry weapons up to the MG.34 and MG.42.

The MKb.42 (H) became the MP.43 and limited production began. By the autumn of 1943, discouraged by accuracy/reliability problems with the new Gew.43 and troubled by the reverses in Russia, Hitler finally accepted that the MP.43 should replace the MP.40. However, production problems and overly optimistic delivery predictions prevented the MP.43/StG.44 achieving the anticipated universal distribution, and production of the Kar.98k and Gew.43 continued until the end of the war.

The use of an intermediate cartridge should have permitted a reduction in the weight of key components, yet the MP.43 was surprisingly heavy; at over thirteen pounds with a loaded 30-round magazine, it was heavier than the full-power FG.42. This was largely due to use of stampings, pressings and other advanced sheet-metal forming techniques still in their infancy. The German designers erred towards caution, subsequent experience indicating that weight could be reduced appreciably. However, the excessive weight and straight-line configuration made the gun controllable in burst fire and, being much more powerful than the standard submachine-guns, the troops of the beleaguered Kampfgruppe Scherer (to whom some of the first production guns were air-dropped) were sufficiently happy with it to fight their way out of encirclement at Kolm.

The term Sturmgewehr, in its English translation 'assault rifle', has since been adopted as a generic term. Whether either the FG.42 or the MP.43 owes its modern reputation to anything more than luck, how-

26. The German FG.42 paratroop rifle was a most successful attempt to combine the attractive long-range performance of a full-power infantry rifle cartridge with the firepower of a light automatic. Two variants of the FG.42 are known, one weighing less than 10lb! The straightline layout pioneered by the MG.30 and MG.34 light machine-guns was adopted to minimize the tendency to rotate the muzzle upwards around the pivot provided by the firer's shoulder. The FG.42 (final version, 26) had considerable impact on post-1945 designs, the Swiss StGw.57 being most notable. Author's collection.

27, 28. The culmination of German experiments with sub-power 'intermediate' cartridges, based on the doctrine that most engagements take place at less than 500 yards, was the development of experimental Maschinenkarabiner in 1941–2. The successful Haenel prototype became the MP.43 (27). Picture 28 shows German soldiers killed by a mine near La Roche, 1944. Two MP.43s are clearly visible. 27: Author's collection. 28: Courtesy of the Trustees of the Imperial War Museum (negative B 1733).

26 ▲

27 ▲   28 ▼

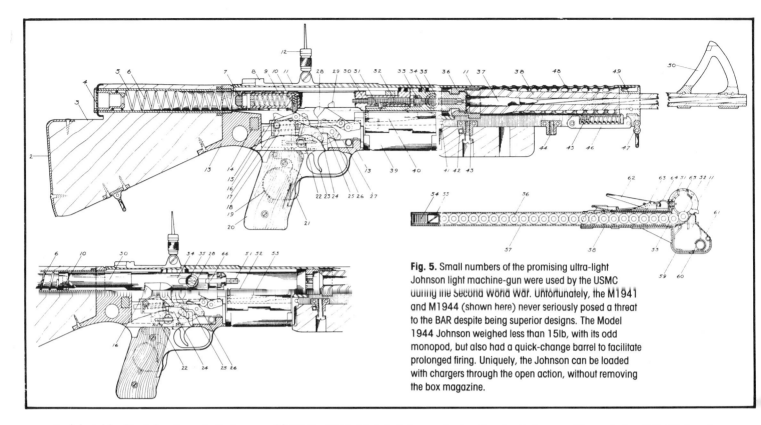

Fig. 5. Small numbers of the promising ultra-light Johnson light machine-gun were used by the USMC during the Second World War. Unfortunately, the M1941 and M1944 (shown here) never seriously posed a threat to the BAR despite being superior designs. The Model 1944 Johnson weighed less than 15lb, with its odd monopod, but also had a quick-change barrel to facilitate prolonged firing. Uniquely, the Johnson can be loaded with chargers through the open action, without removing the box magazine.

ever, is debatable. Each has been hailed as a masterpiece, but several questions remain unanswered. The layout of the FG.42 clearly owes something to the Solothurn MG.30 – the predecessor of the MG.34 – but, one wonders, had its designers examined the Johnson light machine-gun of 1941? By 1944, Melvin Johnson had refined the latter to provide an efficient light support weapon weighing just 12.8lb. The US Marine Corps and Rangers were sufficiently impressed to use Johnson machine-guns for special purposes during the Second World War.

There seems little evidence that, despite the efforts of the Heereswaffenamt, the Wehrmacht command ever seriously considered the MP.43 as a universal replacement for the full-power rifle. Had Hitler had his way, the MP.43 might simply have remained the German equivalent of the M1 Carbine – with the Gew.43 as the standard

29. This typical 1943-vintage SAS Jeep shows its teeth – twin Vickers K guns aft, a single K forward . . . and a 0.5in Browning. The Vickers K was originally adopted by the RAF as an observer's gun, but proved to be ideally suited to vehicle mounts. The two-tier pan magazine offered a much greater capacity than the Bren's box pattern. Courtesy of the Trustees of the Imperial War Museum (negative NA 677).

infantry rifle and the FG.42 for the paratroops. By the end of the war, however, sufficient MP.43 and StG.44 had been captured to cause the Allies to consider their future armament requirements; and the Germans, realizing that the StG.44 fell short of perfection, had issued specifications for the lightened 'StG.45'. Designs had been submitted by Mauser, Gustloff-Werke and others, but were still under examination when hostilities ceased. The promising Mauser StG.45 prototype, also known as Gerät 06, provided the basis for the modern CETME and Heckler & Koch systems.

Post-war developments

No sooner had Germany capitulated than Allied weapons experts seized their chance to interrogate their opponents. Secretly, many Anglo-American specialists were prepared to admit that there was much to learn. In addition to the FG.42 and the MP.43/StG.44 series, not forgetting the incomplete StG.45 and the highly-rated MG.45V light machine-gun, there were countless interesting projects to examine.

THE OPENING GAMBIT

The Russians were the first to act. They have claimed that their experiments with 'intermediate' cartridges began before the Second World War, which is undeniably true. However, these appear to have concerned pistol-type cartridges, and the inference is that the Simonov and other carbines were directly comparable with the US Carbine M1 rather than the MP.43. Too many modern writers have swallowed Soviet propaganda that they had outguessed the Germans!

The MP.43 had shown the Russians that their policy of mass attack, based around the crudely effective PPSh-41 submachine-gun, would be improved greatly by an assault rifle. Shortly before the war ended, the Russians had produced an adaptation of the German 7.9mm Kurz cartridge known as the Model 43, but had been unable to produce an effective gun. The trials, however, had produced promising gas-operated Simonov and Kalashnikov prototypes. Both

30▲ 31▼

30. Service in unusual theatres often involves alien equipment. When the British Commandos were despatched to Korea in 1950, they were equipped with standard US smallarms such as the Garand and – as shown here – the M1 Carbine and M1919A4 Browning machine-gun. Courtesy of the Royal Marines Museum, Eastney.

31. An SAS patrol returns to its base, having traversed the border of Brunei and Sarawak for several weeks. Note the standard L1A1 rifles. Courtesy of the Trustees of the Imperial War Museum.

were ordered into limited production, probably with a view to undertaking mass trials in the manner popularized by the Germans. Simonov's SKS entered service in 1945; Kalashnikov's more radical AK, two years later. The first field trials confirmed that the Kalashnikov required more development, and the appreciably more conventional SKS was ordered into mass production as an expedient. Though discontinued in Russia in about 1952, it proved so popular elsewhere that production continued in the People's Republic of China and other satellites for many years. Once the AK-47 had been perfected, however, the Soviet Army retained the SKS only for ceremonial duties.

The Kalashnikov remains most people's concept of an assault rifle. In excess of forty million have been made in several countries, receiving so much media exposure in the hands of guerrillas, urban terrorists and 'freedom fighters' that their silhouette is easily recognizable. The original AK was a short and rather clumsy gun, comparatively heavy at 10.5lb laden, but its efficiency belied its crude construction. The Kalashnikov is simply the latest in a long line of smallarms embodying the post-1917 Russian development philosophy that nuances of construction or finish are irrelevant, provided that the gun works efficiently and is sufficiently robust for service.

The gas-operated AK, locked by a turning bolt, fires its 122-grain bullet from the M43 intermediate cartridge at about 2,460fps. It is acceptably accurate and, particularly when fitted with the perfected compensator, surprisingly stable in the automatic mode. Since its inception nearly forty years ago, however, changes have been made: the improved AKM, introduced in 1959, was much lighter, and recent reductions in calibre (to 5.45mm) have flattened the looping trajectory of the original 7.62mm cartridge.

THE NATO RIFLE

Though the Russians were quick to follow the German lead, the remaining Allies were much more sceptical. Once again, the old problem of maximum effective range took precedence. Though analysis of the German 7.9mm Kurz cartridge, the MP.43 and the other experimental Sturmgewehre

showed their merits, the US Army, particularly, refused to countenance cartridges whose maximum effective engagement range was only 400–500 metres. Immediately after the war, using a mixture of German, Polish emigré and indigenous research, the British produced the EM-1 (Thorpe) and EM-2 (Janson) rifles around a special 0.280in cartridge. The roller-locked EM-1 was soon discontinued in favour of the EM-2, which had a modified Kjellman flap-lock. The 0.280in bullet, which weighed 140 grains, reached a muzzle velocity of 2,535fps; less powerful than the US .30-06, but better than the lighter German 7.9mm Kurz.

The British government optimistically entered the EM-2 in the NATO trials of 1951–2. The rifle had several obvious

advantages: its 'bull-pup' design, with the magazine behind the pistol grip, permitted a standard-length barrel in an otherwise compact design. Minor, but by no means insoluble problems appeared during the trials – the gun was not particularly accurate, and had an assortment of teething troubles – but the US Army was so opposed to the EM-2 that the project foundered amid recriminations and allegations of deliberate bias. Even though some later EM-2 rifles chambered the 7.62mm T65 (the precursor of the 7.62×51mm NATO) and even the bigger US .30-06, the design disappeared into history. The US Army adopted the Rifle M14, little more than an updated Garand, most remaining NATO powers taking variants of the FN-designed Fusil Automatique Léger (FAL). The British accepted the Belgian gun in the interests of standardization, production of the slightly modified Rifle L1A1 beginning in the Royal Small Arms Factory and at BSA Guns Ltd in 1956.

THE SOLDIER AND THE FREEDOM FIGHTER

The Korean War of 1950–3 was fought on comparatively conventional lines, with the smallarms that had served since the Second World War. In addition, most of the special forces that had performed so well prior to 1945 had been stood down or disbanded. After Korea, however, a perceptible change in warfare occurred. Gone was the classic large-scale confrontation between major powers; instead, the fragmentation of the great colonial empires promoted the 'freedom fighter' – a guerrilla, often but not inevitably Communist-motivated, determined to overthrow the existing order and then impose his ideology to bring order from the resultant chaos. Nowhere was this more obvious than in poor countries where no attempt had been made to educate the population, or where national borders had

32. The post-war era was one of intense experimentation, often based on incomplete German research. One exception to this rule was the Fusil Automatic Léger ('Light Automatic Rifle') developed by the FN engineer Saive from the SAFN rifle, which had pre-1939 origins. The FN/LAR has been adopted in more than fifty countries, including Britain (Rifle L1A1). The modern light automatic has to cope efficiently with all kinds of conditions from sand and heat to mud and snow, and to accept accessories such as the British Pilkington Pocketscope sight shown here. Courtesy of Pilkington PE Ltd.

been drawn with little regard for tribal demarcation.

Though small-scale 'traditional wars' arose in the Middle East and the Indo-Pakistan sub-continent, the involvement of the Great Powers has been comparatively limited; most of the conflicts have been between opposing guerrillas, guerrillas and local authorities, or guerrillas and supposedly powerful Western nations. One outcome of the change in warfare has been the erosion of traditional industrial supremacy, which is rarely capable of defeating guerrillas who can carry the sympathy of the people with them. Confrontations between the French and the Viet Minh in the First Indo-China War (1946–54), for example, showed that Western strategists often underestimated their comparatively weakly armed opponents, hastening the ignominious French withdrawal from Indo-China. Many of the lessons were lost on the Americans, whose embroilment in Vietnam (1961–73) never wholly subdued the Vietcong in fighting that was brutal and bloody in the extreme.

The US Special Forces – the 'Green Berets' – strove hard to form teams of local irregulars (CIDG) to help rebuff the advances of the Vietcong. Worried by the success of the 'Hearts and Minds' campaigns, even on a limited basis among anti-Communist tribesmen, the North Vietnamese gave priority to attacks on SF/CIDG bases such as Lang Vei, near Khe Sanh. In February 1968, the numerically insignificant base was attacked by regular units of the North Vietnamese Army (NVA) supported by PT-76 light tanks. Though some of the tanks were knocked out, the remainder penetrated the camp perimeter and the NVA poured through the breach. Encircled, the CIDG fought back desperately for the remainder of the day; and, after darkness had fallen, the survivors broke out to reach the heaven of Khe Sanh. More than half their number were dead, wounded or in the hands of the North Vietnamese, but they had made the point that the guerrilla fears nothing so much as a rival guerrilla.

For all the millions of tons of bombs, defoliant chemicals, shells and smallarms ammunition expended during the conflict – and the loss of more than fifty thousand American lives – the Communists eventually gained not only Vietnam, but also neighbouring Cambodia. Nor could the Portuguese halt nationalism in Angola or

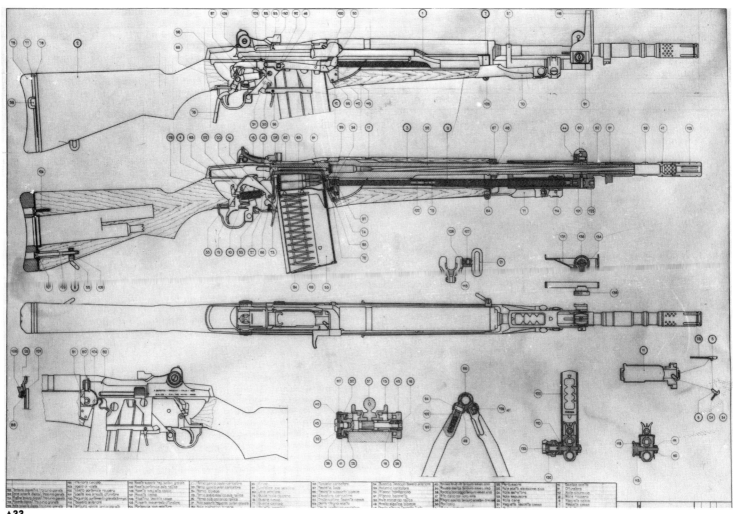

▲33

Mozambique, and the Belgians were panicked into withdrawing from the Congo. Experience in the Yemen, Central America and Afghanistan makes the point over and over again: guerrillas are rarely conclusively defeated solely by the non-nuclear military might of even the most powerful industrialized nations (whose politicians are rightly wary of all-out war).

HEARTS AND MINDS: SUCCESS IN COUNTER-TERRORISM

Among the few highlights in a catalogue of misfortune are the British exploits in Malaya (1948–60) and the rebuttal of Indonesian infiltration in Borneo (1963–6), where emphasis was put on fighting irregulars on their own terms – but with all the sophisticated back-up available to a modern soldier. The initially inauspicious reactivation of the SAS during the Malayan Emergency heralded the re-emergence of the classic Special Force.

The British campaigns in Borneo placed a premium on skills more suited to a hunter

– the art of concealment, endurance, determination, a tracker's skill, local knowledge and perfect confidence in issue weapons.

'Turnbull . . . achieved an eye for spoor as accurate as [his native tracker's] . . . reading the splayed toe-prints of an aborigine for what they were; the terrorist's footprint, which invariably revealed cramped toes that had once known shoes; and spotting a fine human footprint imposed by the more canny walker on an elephant footmark in an attempt to blur the trace. Turnbull once followed the tracks of four men for five days, until he spotted the hut they were occupying. He then waited for an impending rainstorm to arrive, correctly guessing that the sentries would take shelter, and drew to within five yards of the hut before killing the four guerrillas . . . According to one officer who served with him, Turnbull used a repeater shotgun with such speed and accuracy that it would "fill a man with holes like a Gruyère cheese" . . .'*

*Tony Geraghty, in *Who Dares Wins*, describing the exploits of Sergeant Bob Turnbull, 22 SAS.

33–6. During the late 1950s, the US authorities experimented with several rifle designs. Although the American-designed .30 T65E3 cartridge had been standardized as the 7.62mm NATO in 1955, and the M14 (a modified Garand) adopted in 1957, trials with the 7.62mm Armalite AR-10 rifle led to the 5.56mm AR-15. Shown here are an Italian Beretta BM-59 (**33, 34**), a minor derivative of the M1; an AR-10 in its light machine-gun configuration (**35**); and a CAR-15 with a British Davin MH218 Compact Rifle Sight (**36**). Courtesy of Pietro Beretta SpA, Davin Optical (UK) Ltd and Ian Hogg.

CHANGING WARFARE: THE EMERGENCE OF THE SMALL-CALIBRE RIFLE

The increase in the type of fighting encountered in Malaya and Borneo gradually changed attitudes to smallarms. During the 1950s, most NATO-aligned armies had adopted the comparatively cumbersome FN rifle, the FAL, which weighs about 11lb loaded and measures 44in overall. Despite its undoubted power, impeccable reputation and suitability for long-range fire, the FAL was no more appropriate for jungle warfare

34▲

35▲   36▼

▲37 ▼38

than the equally large and powerful US Rifle M14. During the mid 1950s, the US Army – such a strong advocate of power in the trials that caused the demise of the British EM-2 rifle – suddenly decided to seek a smaller gun firing a lighter, handier cartridge. As the wood of the M14 stocks rotted in the tropics, the new gun was also to feature a synthetic butt and fore-end. After protracted testing, the Armalite rifle, designed by Eugene Stoner, became the Rifle M16. Built around the commercial 0.222in Remington sporting rifle cartridge, which had proved itself against thin-skinned game, the M16 represented a great reduction in rifle weight and allowed the soldier to carry more of the appreciably lighter cartridges (182 grains compared with 396 for the standard Cartridge, 0.30, Ball M2). The finalized M16, together with its loaded 30-round magazine weighed a mere 8.7lb!

The M16/M16A1 series has been purchased for Limited Theatre use by the British Army, and was particularly popular in Borneo. The worst problem has concerned the American 5.56mm M193 bullet which, though undeniably very destructive at short range, is not especially effective beyond 400 metres and is readily deflected by branches and obstructions. The European compromise is a heavier, slower moving bullet (the SS109) and a faster rifling twist to improve stability. Although this improves carrying properties appreciably, lethality is reduced compared with the M193.

THE CASE FOR FIREPOWER: CONVENTIONAL WARFARE IN THE MODERN ERA

After an inauspicious beginning, experience in Vietnam showed that the intermediate cartridge and (ultimately) the small-diameter bullet were suitable for combat use, indirectly confirming the advocacy of the Germans during the Second World War and the Russians thereafter. However, most of the 'traditional' wars contested by highly industrialized nations have none the less featured full-power cartridges. These have

37, 38. Counter-terrorist warfare has become a primary concern for many of the world's security forces, whether threatened by urban guerrillas or cross-border incursions. These Rhodesian ZAPU soldiers (**37**), photographed before the emergence of independent Zimbabwe, display a collection of AKM and AKMS rifles. Their adversaries included men of the South African Army (**38**), seen here with a heavy mortar and R4 (modified Galil) rifles.

included the continuing conflict between Iraq and Iran, and the brief (but all too conclusive) confrontation between Britain and Argentina in the South Atlantic in 1982. Ironically, both armies were armed similarly: both, for example, used FN-designed infantry rifles, general-purpose machine-guns and pistols. The principal difference lay in the light machine-guns, where the British Bren proved more serviceable than the Argentine heavy-barrelled FAL, and in support weapons. The British were particularly keen to capture the Argentinian 0.50in Brownings, which were speedily turned against their former owners.

The open treeless expanse of the Falkland Islands proved to be more suited to the traditional concepts of infantry confrontation than, for example, the tropical jungles and sub-tropical rain forests of Malaya, Vietnam or Borneo. The fighting also reflected a traditional role.

'Corporal Hunt, a section commander in Z Company, was scanning through his IWS, as were all who were equipped with them, and spotted enemy movement on the skyline above them . . . 8 Troop skirmished forward again, taking a newly acquired [ex-Argentinian] .50 inch heavy machine-gun with them. Clearing enemy positions as they went, they arrived at the limit of their objective . . . Dytor [Troop Commander, Z Company], reorganizing on his Company objective, could clearly see the enemy fire which was coming from positions immediately to his front and about 200 metres away. He at once started the Troop forward with their .50 heavy machine-gun, three GPMGs and three Bren LMGs to engage this fresh target.'*

Apart from the reference to the Individual Weapon Sight (IWS) and the substitution of the GPMG for the Vickers Gun, this could have described an action during the Second World War. Issued in surprisingly large quantities, the Sight, Infantry Weapon, L1A2 (Rank Pullin SS20) was a cumbersome first-generation image-intensifying sight issued in conjunction with the L1 infantry rifle or the GPMG. Many of the photographs taken in the Falklands show these sights to good advantage. Interestingly, despite the relative industrial strengths of the participants (and the parlous state of the

*Brigadier Julian Thompson, Officer Commanding 3 Commando Brigade, describing the night attack on Mount Longdon and Two Sisters on 11/12 June 1982, in *No Picnic: 3 Commando Brigade in the South Atlantic, 1982.*

contemporary Argentine economy), the defenders had supplies of second-generation French Sopelem and American Varo AN/PVS-4 StarLight image-intensifiers and excellent night-vision systems. Improved night vision was particularly useful in the Falklands, where dusk fell shortly after four o'clock local time.

Photographs taken by the British Press photographers (as well as official representatives of the Ministry of Defence) reveal that the US M16 rifle was popular with many Commando officers and the men drawn from the Mountain and Arctic Warfare Cadre, who usually trained the Commandos' specialized instructors but served in the Falklands as 3 Commando Brigade Reconnaissance Troop. Lee-Enfield type L42A1 sniper rifles were also in evidence.

COUNTER-TERRORIST WARFARE

Fighting guerrillas on their own terms, dealing with urban terrorism on politically acceptable terms, has brought the greatest changes in the guns of the élite. Virtually any weapon needed to fulfil a specific task will now simply be brought in. SAS personnel, for example, have been seen carrying M16/M16A1 rifles, Ruger Mini-14, Steyr AUG, Heckler & Koch G3 and G41 rifles, and a wide variety of sniping equipment, including Finnish Tikka rifles and the new Accuracy International PM (now officially designated the L96A1). Infra-red, laser-assisted and image-intensifying sights have all been used to good effect, particularly after dusk when traditional open sights are useless. Submachine-guns, too, have found increasing favour for short-range work.

The use of submachine-guns is not without hazard. The massacre of Israeli Olympic athletes at the Munich Games of 1972, and the subsequent reaction by the West German authorities, highlighted the continual dichotomy between assault and dialogue. The terrorists initially seized eleven hostages, killing two; during the subsequent counter-attack, unfortunately, fifteen more died – all the surviving athletes, five terrorists and a policeman. The West German government was shocked into forming a specialist CTW unit under Ulrich Wegener, to prevent further occurrences on the Munich scale. Owing to an understandable reluctance to form an élite unit from the ranks of the army, GSG-9 was attached to the Bundesgrenzschutz, the Federal

▲39

border guard, and headquartered at Saint Augustin near Bonn.

One positive result was the anti-terrorist operation mounted at Mogadishu airport, in the Somali Republic, by Major Alastair Morrison and Sergeant Barry Davies of the SAS together with nearly thirty GSG-9 representatives led by Wegener himself. The aim was to free the crew and nearly eighty terrified passengers on a Lufthansa jet seized by four hijackers intent on bartering for the release of the notorious Baader-Meinhof gang. All hopes of a peaceful solution had vanished when the hijackers murdered the pilot.

On 17 October 1977, therefore, the main SAS/GSG-9 assault team hit the plane from both sides, entering through the emergency exits above each wing to the accompaniment of 'Flash-bang' concussion/ blinding grenades. Eight minutes later, it was all over: three of the four terrorists (two male, one female) lay dead and the surviving woman terrorist had no less than nine bullet wounds. None of the SAS/GSG-9 team had been seriously hurt, and the passengers had escaped virtually unscathed. But none could deny an element of good fortune. The seated passengers had been below the line of fire, the terrorists choosing to fight standing; neither of the two grenades had done anything other than damage

the substantially-constructed aircraft seats; and there had been no fire, despite the proximity of aviation fuel and a liberal sousing of duty-free alcohol.

After the event, much concern was voiced about the suitability of the S&W Model 36 revolvers, chambering the ineffectual .38 Special round. Hollow-point ammunition had not been used and the attackers had failed to stop the terrorists' leader throwing the grenades, despite hitting him at least four times. He had been finished off with a 9mm Parabellum-calibre HK54 (MP5) submachine-gun.

The concern was justifiable; lessons were plain for all to learn. However, not all future operations were to be so fortunate – not least being the assault by Egyptian Force 777 Commandos on a hijacked airliner at Valletta airport in September 1985, which cost the lives of nearly sixty people. Though many of the luckless hostages died from smoke inhalation, some had gunshot wounds and a few were even believed to have been shot after emerging from the aeroplane; clearly, the tactics were very poor.

Another bad mistake was made in September 1986, when a Pan-Am Boeing 747 was hijacked to Karachi airport. The Pakistani special services group elected to shoot the Palestinian terrorist leader, who

39. The rise of guerrilla warfare in the post-war era has provided the sniper with additional practice; here, in an attic in Andersontown, a district of Belfast, a particularly well equipped British marksman sights his Rifle L42A1 – a conversion of the Rifle No. 4 (itself a modernized SMLE) to handle 7.62×51mm NATO ammunition. Note the L9A1 pistol to his left, and an intensifier-sight equipped L1A1 rifle propped against the wall on the right. Courtesy of the Royal Marines Museum, Eastney.

40. Here, a police marksman from the élite 'Blue Berets', covering the approaches to the Libyan People's Bureau after the murder of WPC Yvonne Fletcher, demonstrates his telescope-sighted Heckler & Koch HK33 rifle. Combat shotguns were also used by the Metropolitan Police in this operation. London: 18 April 1984. Courtesy of Syndication International.

41. A typical modern sniper rifle: the bolt-action Parker-Hale M85, with its bipod and a Rank-Pullin SS80 intensifier sight. Courtesy of Parker-Hale Ltd.

had been observed spending much time in the cockpit, as a prelude to an all-out assault. Unfortunately, the chosen sniper, expert marksman though he may have been, was expected to hit a head-size target at a range of about 400 yards with a Finnish-made 7.62×51mm Tikka bolt-action rifle. However, no allowance was made for the strength or angle of the aircraft windshield – built to withstand the impact of large birds and tested, as Boeing subsequently confirmed, by hitting it with ten pounds of hamburgers travelling at 290mph. Two 7.62mm bullets struck the cockpit glass, but

failed to penetrate; and the sound of impact so unnerved the hijackers that they opened fire on the passengers, killing more than twenty.

Among the greatest successes in the history of counter-terrorist operations was the Israeli Operation 'Thunderball'. In June 1976, a combined PLO and Baader-Meinhof force had seized an Air France Tel Aviv-Paris flight and redirected it to Entebbe airport in Uganda. The resulting murder of one of the hostages persuaded the Israeli government to act decisively and members of the crack '269' Commando, drawn from Sayeret Golani and 35 Parachute Brigade, hit Entebbe on the night of 3/4 July 1976. The raid was a stunning success, 103 people being released for the loss of only the Israeli commander (Lieutenant-Colonel Netanyahu). One hostage had been murdered previously and two were killed during the raid, one having mistakenly attacked his rescuer, but the minimal cost in lives had justified the risk.

42. These members of the Italian Special Forces, the Nucleo Operativo Centrale di Sicurezza (NOCS), carry Beretta-made Mo.12 submachine-guns and Beretta Mo.92 SB pistols as part of their standard equipment. NOCS equipment includes H&K MP5SD1 silenced submachine-guns, HK33 and G3 rifles, Beretta Mo.70 and 70-90 rifles, and Beretta or Franchi combat shotguns. Courtesy of Pietro Beretta SpA.

43. SAS disembark from a Wessex helicopter of 848 Squadron, HMS *Albion*, during operations in Borneo in July 1966. Note that one man is carrying an M16 rifle rather than the L1A1. Courtesy of the Trustees of the Imperial War Museum.

▼42

43▲

Restrictions on the space available in the four C-130 Hercules transports dictated the choice of the Ingram submachine-gun, rather than the Uzi, and night-sighted Kalashnikov assault rifles in a search for an ideal combination of firepower in a small package. Identifying these 'Kalashnikovs' has proved difficult, some sources averring that they were Valmets supplied from Finland – as the Israeli Galil rifle (itself a modification of the basic Russian design) was still in its developmental phase. However, photographs of the Israelis' triumphant return show that some of the rifles, at least, once had folding bayonets under the muzzle; the mounting blocks are usually visible ahead of the auxiliary grip, added to facilitate holding the muzzle down in automatic fire. As only the Chinese Type 56 Kalashnikov variant has a folding bayonet, some (if not all) of the guns used at Entebbe must have been captured from the Egyptians or the PLO.

Operation 'Nimrod', the successful storming of the Iranian Embassy in Palace Gate, London, in May 1980, was another victory for the special forces in an urban environment. The British SAS Counter-Revolutionary Warfare (CRW) team was called in to rescue the 'survivors' of twenty hostages being held in the Embassy by seven terrorists, who had commenced an unacceptable series of executions by killing the Iranian press attaché and dumping his body on the steps. The operations was awkward and very risky, the hostages being kept in separate groups inside a building containing more than fifty rooms. The only way into the front of the Embassy was to abseil down the façade and blow out an armoured-glass plate, trusting to luck and the superior training of the SAS CRW squad. A simultaneous attack on the rear would, it was hoped, divide (and thereby conquer) the terrorists' efforts.

The Embassy assault was the first in which the SAS, wary of the inaccuracy of their Ingram submachine-guns, turned to the 'Hockler' (the Heckler & Koch HK54, now better known as the MP5) as a result of witnessing the events at Mogadishu in 1977.

Clothed in black, wearing CS gas-masks and flak vests, armed with Heckler & Koch submachine-guns and Browning GP pistols, they descended the ropes and began the attack confident in their 'Killing Room' training, which taught them to hit the target unerringly with a 'tap-tap' – two shots in the head or chest – even if they were tumbling, or if visibility was poor.

Unfortunately, a flailing boot broke one of the windows during the abseil down the back of the building and the element of surprise was gone. One man was trapped on the rope, preventing the forcible removal of the armoured glass with the explosive charge, and the glass was hacked and kicked-in to the accompaniment of 'Flash-bangs', the concussion grenades liberally laced with magnesium powder to give a brilliant blinding flash.

Inside the building, the terrorist leader, attempting to shoot the leading SAS man as he entered the back of the Embassy, was brought down by PC Trevor Lock, one of the hostages, and cut down by the SAS man's submachine-gun during the ensuing struggle. A hundred seconds after the first team had begun the descent, the second team blasted the armoured glass out of the front of the building and the 'front men' darted into the building under cover of concussion grenades (and a CS gas grenade calculated to disable the sixth terrorist hiding in an upstairs room).

The SAS man stuck on his rope, and in danger of burning every time he swung towards the offending window at the back of the building, was unceremoniously cut down. Running into the Embassy, he came face to face with a terrorist and instinctively shot him dead.

On the second floor, in Room Ten, the telex room, the SAS had taken no chances, shooting the three terrorists heedless of their attempts to hide among the hostages. One hostage lay dead, executed by the terrorists, and another had been seriously wounded. In Room Nine, the one terrorist guarding the five women hostages had surrendered, been uncompromisingly hurled down the stairs and dragged out into the street. Upstairs, the seventh man had also met his fate; eleven minutes had passed, six terrorists and two Iranian Embassy officials were dead. But the remaining hostages were free, and the CRW operations had been a great success.

COUNTER-TERRORIST WARFARE: PISTOL OR SUBMACHINE-GUN?

The submachine-gun is ideally suited to use in situations where the maximum rate of fire must be combined with an ability to place single shots with extreme accuracy at short range – not forgetting total reliability and lethality only sufficient to halt the intended target. The conventional high-power military rifle cartridge (even the intermediate 5.56mm M193 and 7.62mm M43) fires a jacketed bullet that will almost certainly pass through an animate target at short range, risking killing other, possibly innocent participants.

Though the same stricture was once applied to the traditional metal-jacketed 9mm Parabellum bullet, the development of many soft- and hollow-point rounds, together with ultra-high penetrating patterns, has invalidated such criticism. Among the most lethal of the new breed is the Glaser Safety Slug, a concoction of Teflon-encased shot inside a copper case specifically designed to penetrate and fragment. The Glaser Slug is especially effective.

'The Syrian major was at the right hand end. Becklin lunged for him, and smothered him in a flying tackle. I started to take care of the rest of the men along the sofa. The MP5 has a thirty-round magazine and I rippled it down the sofa, not in free fire but in controlled bursts, picking up three Druze and the remaining Syrian lieutenant. I fired from a crouch and the force of the bullets threw the men bodily against the sofa. When you're hit by a burst of 9mm Teflon-coated ammunition, you don't stay still. The impact seemed to be sending them climbing up the sofa . . .'[*]

Owing to the progress made with the projectiles, 9×19mm has made a comeback in special forces use. However, the use of the more arcane projectiles is often frowned upon by military and police authorities as being against the spirit of their operations and, more realistically, embarrassing to their political masters. The dilemma is not new; the use of Dum-Dum bullets was prevented by the Hague Convention of 1907 and, even during the First World War, the Germans switched from flat- to round-nose 9mm Parabellum bullets to prevent the Allies making capital out of atrocity stories; more recently, many individuals have discovered that a small coin or a piece of barbed wire embedded in the nose of a baton round increases its effectiveness appreciably, but also causes an appreciable nuisance politically.

There can be no justification for using 'doctored' rounds – plastic bullets or otherwise – for crowd control when other, less radical solutions can be sought. However, terrorists abide by no code other than their own and any attempt to impose 'political'

*Gayle Rivers, in *The Specialist* ('The Personal Story of an Elite Specialist in Covert Operations'), describing a raid in Beirut.

strictures on airport defence (for example) inevitably hamstrings the defenders.

Despite the outcry over the issue of 9mm Heckler & Koch MP5s to British police on airport patrol in 1985–6, the submachine-gun has tremendous advantages over large-calibre pistols; it is large enough to take the intensifier sight needed to repel night attacks, has a long enough sighting radius to promote accurate shooting, and an automatic-fire capability available in reserve.

Although the pistol is handier and can be got into action very quickly, it is appreciably

more difficult to shoot: recoil is greater owing to the low gun weight, inhibiting accurately placed follow-up shots, and the short sight radius magnifies aiming errors. The pistol is undoubtedly indispensable for rapid-fire at less than twenty yards, but not to repel a night attack from a co-ordinated force. Some armies rejected the pistol entirely in the 1960s, while others attempted to combine the functions of an infantry rifle and a submachine-gun in an assault rifle. Those who rejected the pistol soon found the bulk of the submachine-gun

awkward in circumstances where concealability was paramount, while the assault weapons were never as effective at long range as the large-calibre infantry rifles.

Special Forces have done much to re-establish the reputation of the submachine-gun in counter-terrorist operations, largely owing to a continual reassessment of the balance between firepower and handiness. The emergence of the current generation of submachine-guns is entirely coincidental, rather than a major contributory factor; although the Uzi, Beretta Mo.12S and

Ingram are undeniably very efficient, the publicity accorded them overlooks the fact that the world's best distributed design is the British Sterling – simple and reliable, but designed prior to 1945! The Heckler & Koch MP5 is not even a submachine-gun in the classic sense, but rather a diminutive automatic rifle.

44. A squad of the Belgian CTW group, 'Brigade Diane' of the Escadron Spécial d'Intervention (ESI), discuss a problem. Note the body armour, gas masks, and the FN-Browning GP pistol worn by the man on the left. Belgian official photograph.

▲45

The tactical use of the submachine-gun by CTW squads in the 1980s differs little, fundamentally, from the German Sturm-truppen of the First World War. The goal remains the same: maximum effect with the greatest possible surprise. Just as the early storm troops trained in mock trenches before mounting an assault, so the modern CTW specialist trains in 'Battle Houses' or 'Killing Rooms', where each corner may hide a pop-up terrorist. Some targets are partly obscured, many hold hostages, others need friend-or-foe identification before firing; the whole course is designed to simulate the conditions encountered in action, even to the extent of smoke, gas and concussion grenades, though the psychological strain of the real thing cannot be readily duplicated.

Modern training is geared to the totality of fighting in a modern urban environment, with the perfection of non-gun related techniques such as abseiling, unarmed combat and room-clearance. A greater premium is placed on marksmanship than previously, with one-shot or (particularly with the pistol or submachine-gun) a 'tap-tap' rapid two-shot kill being all but obligatory. In the confines of a small room, there's no second chance.

Combat shotguns and sniper-rifles were also to the fore in the embassy sieges and anti-hijack operations, and are a regular feature of combat teams. In each team of four or six men, at least one will have a

specialized firearm. Shotguns are useful to blow locks from doors (helping to minimize aiming errors) and are also a great deterrent; sniper rifles permit accurate placement of shots at long range.

The photograph reproduced here shows that optically sighted Heckler & Koch HK33 rifles were carried by some members of C13, Scotland Yard's anti-terrorist squad, and D11 (the élite Metropolitan Police marksmen) during the Libyan Embassy siege. Continued improvement in optical sights, together with the widespread distribution of passive infra-red and image-intensifying weapons sights, now enables the sniper to double as an intelligence-gatherer. A marksman may have to observe his target for hours before deciding whether to shoot or await a better chance. As a result, modern sniper rifles – particularly those used for counter-terrorist warfare – are often very much heavier than the army-inspired service patterns used during the Second World War and Korea, and even in Vietnam. This also explains the appearance of bipods, which to many seem anachronistic on a rifle; at least they allow the marksman to observe for long periods with a minimum of fatigue.

One of the very best recent examples of sniping occurred in Djibouti in 1976, when Somalian revolutionaries kidnapped a bus-load of French schoolchildren. The danger of the situation was such that only simultaneous elimination of the terrorists would

45. The demands of CTW warfare often require awesome, purely short-range firepower to minimize casualties among bystanders. Among the favoured firearms are Franchi combat shotguns, typified by the convertible pump-action/autoloading SPAS 12 shown here. The great advantage of these weapons, apart from their destructive capability, is the ease with which a wide range of live, smoke and baton rounds can be interchanged. Courtesy of Luigi Franchi SpA.

46. Typical of the fashionable 'bullpup' rifles—with the magazine behind the pistol grip—is the British L85A1, known during its developmental phase as the XL-70 and SA-80. This gun has a Rank Pullin SS80 sight. Courtesy of Rank Pullin Controls Ltd.

ensure the survival of the children. The task fell to the French national CTW unit, Groupement d'Intervention de la Gendarmerie Nationale (GIGN), led by Lieutenant Marcel Prouteau. His plan was to position his superbly trained snipers so that each man could be allocated to an individual target. A radio ring-link was established between the men and Prouteau so that firing could be ordered only when the snipers had a clear shot. When the command was given, five of the six terrorists were killed instantaneously with single shots from ranges up to 200m. Though one child was murdered before the GIGN squad could reach the bus to eliminate the sixth and final terrorist, the operation was adjudged a great success.*

*Interestingly, the marksmanship qualification necessary for consideration for the GIGN units is 75×100 with the service rifle at 200m; the minimum graduation achievement must be no less than 95×100.

State of the art

Since the first edition of *Guns of the Elite* was published, there has been no notable slackening in international tension. Though some of the major areas of conflict have stabilised—most notably, South Africa—countless new flashpoints have emerged to replace them.

Especially worrying in the short-term has been the fragmentation of what was once Yugoslavia into an ugly territorial war in which lines of demarcation are constantly being drawn and re-drawn. The situation is sometimes simplistically considered to be Catholic Croat against Russian Orthodox Serb against Bosnian Muslim, but the issues are far more complex. They can also be seen as a settlement of long-held grudges, and an expression of long suppressed desires for expansion.

Elsewhere, though the Iran-Iraq war has ceased (perhaps temporarily), the invasion of Kuwait by Iraq has caused a war in which leading Western powers became embroiled on a large scale. Trouble between Jew and Arab still rages in the Middle East; and though strides towards a lasting peace are undoubtedly being made, extremist factions on both sides are very reluctant to embrace them. The recent massacre of Palestinians by a supporter of the right-wing Israeli Meir Kahane, and the violence perpetrated on Jewish settlers in the Gaza Strip by the Fatah Hawks (extremists on the fringe of the PLO) underscore that problems will not be solved overnight.

Conflict between Christian Arabs and Muslim Arabs persists in the Lebanon, whilst sectarian violence in Northern Ireland remains a thorn in the side of the British Government even though—at the time of writing—the first hesitant steps may be being taken toward a lasting peace.

However, Hutu still kills Tutsi in Rwanda; Tamil kills Singhalese in Sri Lanka. The list is apparently endless.

On one day in July 1994—a quiet one—*The Times* reported the bombing of the Israeli Mutual Association in Buenos Aires, with the loss of nearly a hundred lives; the apparent victory of the Rwanda Popular Front in its bloody struggle against pro-government forces; clashes between resistance forces and Indonesian troops in East Timor; and all against the backcloth of the continuing struggle in Bosnia.

A particularly worrying long-term problem concerns the dismantling of the Soviet Union and its many satellites into disparate states of uncertain politics.

47. The Sterling submachine-gun, no longer in production in Britain (though a modified pattern is still being made in Chile), has been sold to more than a hundred agencies. Courtesy of Rank Pullin Controls Ltd.

Rejoicing has been apparent in the end of the Cold War, but the problems may only now be beginning. Though the political complexion of the Warsaw Pact was diametrically opposed to that of NATO, confrontation between two super-power blocs was essentially a stalemate. Each knew that the other possessed weapons of devastating capability, and that any pre-emptive strike would be followed by retaliation in kind before results could be achieved.

The bloody conflict between pro-Yeltsin and pro-Rutskoi forces in Russia in the autumn of 1993 ended in a violent attack on the White House—Moscow's parliamentary building—by units loyal to Yeltsin, supported by armoured vehicles, tanks and artillery. The cost is not known with certainty, though reports of as many as four hundred dead seem quite plausible. The democratisation of former Communist-led states has created its own share of uneasy alliances and flash points, whilst simultaneously heightening the internal tension that the Soviets had almost always managed to suppress.

There are undoubtedly some areas which will quickly regain stability: Poland, Hungary, the Baltic States, perhaps, plus the Czech Republic and Slovakia now that the artificial union has been dismembered. Almost all have a lengthy history, and a recent taste of independence. The same cannot be said of Azerbaizhan, Tazhikistan, Georgia and other former constituents of the USSR, in which newly-formed political groupings and rediscovered religious convictions jostle uneasily for supremacy.

Though many Western countries are using the so-called Peace Dividend to cut deeply into their armed forces, an obvious way of reducing financial burden, they may be doing so much too soon and much too greatly. Probably a decade or more will pass before the political squabbling in the formerly Communist areas dies down.

The need for weapons shows no signs of abating. Indeed, with the demise of the USSR, military-surplus guns are becoming available not only in great quantity but also at very low prices. This guarantees that, instead of demand contracting, Kalashnikov rifles will find their way onto the international market in rapidly increasing quantities. This will tend to force their price downward, and thus facilitate distribution in a way that was difficult (if not impossible) under the old

regimes. Russian mobsters are already armed with automatic weapons on such a grandiose scale that compared with 1992, according to *Izvestia*, the crime-rate in Moscow in 1993 had tripled and the murder rate had doubled. Large quantities of ex-Soviet equipment is said to be exported by way of the Baltic-state ports, particularly Tallinn in Estonia. In Kaliningrad, in the Spring of 1993, it was possible to buy an AK-74 for a mere $50.

The continuing need for policing duties, unabating terrorist activity, and the occasional small-scale war still assures continuing employment not only for the élite but also, by implication, for the guns of the élite.

THE WEAPONS

Special forces very rarely use unique weapons, preferring to use tried and well-tested designs that will guarantee good performance. These are often either the normal infantry weapons or minor variations of them. There is still appreciable diversity, however, and procurement for special forces is often undertaken with a latitude denied to regular units. This is particularly true of submachine-guns, sniper rifles and combat shotguns, but rather less so where pistols, rifles and machine-guns are concerned.

Great care should be taken when expressing opinions about weapons of the special forces too dogmatically. The truth may show far greater diversity than the base-camp quartermasters admit. Units operating in remote areas or behind enemy lines have often been armed with whatever was available.

In the Second World War, therefore, Carlson's Raiders (2nd Marine Raider Battalion) used many captured Japanese Type 96 and Type 99 light machine-guns, while one published picture of the US 28th Marine Regiment on Iwo Jima (1945) clearly shows a Japanese Type 92 heavy machine-gun pressed into service to provide extra covering fire. SBS personnel were to be seen with Schmeisser submachine-guns, German MG.15 and Italian Mo.30 ('Breda') machine-guns in addition to their Lee-Enfields, Brens and Sten Guns.

Many US M1 and M1A1 Carbines were carried by the French at Dien Bien Phu, during the first Indo-China War, and the

Israeli 202nd Parachute Brigade used some ex-German Kar.98k and MG.34 at the Mitla Pass in 1956.

Blurring of official issue continues today. Counter-insurgency operations in Southern Africa—by the Selous Scouts and PATU in Rhodesia/Zimbabwe, or by the SADF Pathfinders in South Africa—have often been undertaken with Kalashnikovs rather than FN FALs or the R4. Not only are Eastern-bloc guns common throughout the area, arming many (though not all) guerrillas, but carrying AKs also simplified the supply of ammunition on a lengthy incursion into hostile territory.

The British authorities purchased small quantities of M16/AR-15, M16A1 and CAR-15 rifles for Limited Theatre operations, commencing in Borneo but extending into and beyond the Falklands conflict; the US Army Rangers and the US Navy SEAL teams have used Heckler & Koch G3 and G3 SG/1 rifles since the 1970s. And, during the war in the South Atlantic (1982), British personnel became particularly fond of the folding-stock variant of the Argentine army's FN and FMAP-made semi-automatic rifles.

The equipment of the SAS has included such standard British weapons as the L9A1 pistol and L1A1 rifle, together with the L2A3 standard and L34A1 silenced Sterlings. In addition, use was made of the Ingram MAC-10 prior to the affair at Mogadishu in 1977 and a subsequent change to the Heckler & Koch HK54 (now known as the MP5). The L42A1 sniper rifle eventually gave way to bolt-action Finnish Tikkas, a few of which were purchased in .22-250, .243 and .308 Winchester (the .308 being dimensionally identical with 7.62mm NATO) as the situation demanded.

However, after the flirtation with the Tikka and the Steyr-Mannlicher SSG.69, the L96A1 rifle—winner of the British Army trials undertaken in the mid 1980s—is gaining widespread acceptance. The standard shotgun has been the Remington Model 870, with the Benelli and Franchi SPAS series steadily gaining favour.

The most recent trends are explored in the revised chapters of this book. The most far-reaching changes have been the development of more effectual handguns; a blurring of the distinctions between submachine-guns and assault rifles; and the sudden rise in interest in the long-range sniping rifle, often firing cartridges more readily associated with .50 machine-guns.

Handguns

In the original edition of *Guns of the Elite*, published in 1987, this chapter opened by observing that the 'role of the pistol has often been questioned, yet its use persists'. The situation in 1995 is no different.

Wars continue, and civil strife shows no real signs of lessening—merely changing the focus of attention periodically. The rise of a gangster sub-class in Russia, for example, has done nothing to remove the need for compact, easily concealable weapons; the Gulf War reaffirmed that the handgun still has an important military role, even if this is still to act as a back-up to more powerful weapons.

The adoption of the Beretta auto-loader by the US Army, together with the 9mm Parabellum cartridge, has led to a wholesale reassessment of police weaponry in the USA. Faced with the ever increasing use of large-calibre pistols, submachine-guns, auto-loading carbines, and even assault rifles by the criminal fraternities, the police have been forced to accept similar weapons. The .32 Smith & Wesson or Colt holster revolver so familiar to older generations of American policeman holds comparatively little threat for members of the drug-trafficking rings, who are as likely to be carrying an Uzi or a Kalashnikov as a handgun.

Consequently, the American police forces, long-time bastions of firearms conservatism, have been seduced by the lure of the auto-loading pistol. Many forces have patriotically bought the excellent Smith & Wessons; some have followed the military lead and taken the Beretta 92F; others have opted for the Glock. The advantages are clear to see. Not least of them are the prodigious cartridge capacities and the ease with which an empty box magazine can be replaced. In this context, despite its demonstrably greater reliability

48. This publicity photograph shows a CTW operative with gas mask, body armour, and a 9mm FN High-Power Sport Model pistol. Note the elongated slide/muzzle weight assembly. Courtesy of FN Herstal SA.

in adverse conditions, the five-or six-shot revolver is no longer as attractive a proposition as it was ten years ago. The pistols are also generally more powerful, often shoot more accurately, and are undeniably less tiring to shoot—though it should be remembered that most speed-shooting records have been set with revolvers.

Military pistols have undergone little real change, which is largely due to the long-term view with which official adoption is usually taken. Excepting the Special Forces, which are allowed appreciably more freedom of choice than the regulars, most armies retain conventional weapons—whether they are the Browning GP-35, perfected prior to the Second World War, or the post-war Beretta. Representatives of the 'hi-tech' genre, especially the Glock, have yet to convince the world's leading armies of their long-term utility. However, the US armed forces, perhaps acknowledging criticism of the Beretta M9, have recently begun another programme of tests.

It will be interesting to see how these resolve. After the JSSAP series, SIG and Smith & Wesson both alleged unfair treatment, whilst many commentators were prepared to champion the then-unproven Ruger P-85 as a better alternative to the M9. It may be fair to say that the Ruger, in spite of its good qualities, is still flattering to deceive. Smith & Wesson has even produced a synthetic-frame gun which has apparently persuaded the Glock designers to take a very close look at the small print in their patents.

Excepting the Glock, the only pistol to have achieved major market penetration in recent years is the CZ 75/CZ 85 pattern, which is actually a very traditional design in modern clothing. This gun has been copied in several countries—a sure sign of high quality—and regularly wins IPSC Practical Pistol competitions with a minimum of fine-tuning. It seems as though the CZ appeared in the wrong place and at the wrong time to gain significant military acceptance, though a contract to supply 50,000 to the Turkish state police was signed in 1993. But the CZ pistols remain a fitting inheritor of the traditions of a Czech firearms industry which, even during the period of Soviet domination, was always willing to pursue an independent line of thought.

Among significant recent developments in pistol design, apart from universal acceptance of large-capacity magazines, has been the insistence on ambidexterous magazine catches, safety levers and slide-release systems. The 'old guard' semi-automatics have gradually been replaced by adaptions meeting these criteria. Yet the basic actions are rarely new, and only a handful of the many pistol systems touted in the last twenty years have achieved service status.

The question must still be asked: exactly what should a combat handgun seek to achieve? It is one thing for a gun to win prizes on a Practical Pistol range in the hands of an Practical Pistoleer who has already sized his cartridges through the chamber, but quite another for the same gun to function effectually in desert sand in the hands of an inexperienced army conscript to whom ammunition of mixed parentage has been issued. During the Gulf War, Americans complained that dust jammed their Berettas, and British troops complained that sand jammed their Brownings.

History is littered with instances of men with marksman status on the firing-range freezing in the terror of combat, whilst mediocre shots with ice-cool nerves have often performed far beyond expectations. Assassinations have failed even though several hits from a weapon of 'the right type' were made on the intended target; others have succeeded when one shot from a theoretically ineffectual handgun has proved lethal. Once again, the arbiter has often been simply the nerve of the assassin.

Thus it could be argued that much of the protracted quest for the ideal handgun has been irrelevant, and that character and training are the vital factors. There are many psychologists who would agree. Virtually any handgun which meets basic criteria of calibre and lethality could be deemed acceptable. Questions of long-term maintenance, spare parts and availability of ammunition are obviously inseparable from the decision-making process when the armament of entire armies is concerned; for the average Special Forces member, however, it is often any gun in which an individual is happy to place his trust. That these are usually restricted to service calibres presents no particular problem, as 9mm Parabellum or .45 ACP cartridges are as good as any when loaded with the appropriate bullets.

Special-service guns are usually large-calibre locked-breech patterns, though small-calibre blowbacks have often been carried for covert use or personal defence. However, some modern 9mm Parabellum or .45 ACP pistols (such as the Detonics .45 MC-1 and the 9mm ASP) are small enough to compare with the blowbacks, whilst offering appreciably better hitting power.

Variations on the Browning Link action are virtually universal for military and paramilitary purposes, having proved their worth millions of times—e.g, in the Colt M1911A1, the FN-Browning GP-35, the SIG-Sauers, the Smith & Wessons and the Glocks. Of the current crop of full-bore military pistols, only the Walther P1/P5 series and the Beretta 92 group can offer something radically different.

In the Browning mechanism, recoil of the slide/barrel unit is used to drop the breech out of engagement with locking recesses, allowing the slide to recoil alone and return to strip a new round into the chamber. Towards the end of the return stroke, the slide picks up the barrel and locks it back into engagement—strong, simple and efficient. The original Colt-Browning, the US Pistol 0.45in M1911, used a special link; most of the newer guns, based on the 1923-5 patents leading to the GP Mle 35, use a cam-finger instead.

MODERN PISTOLS

There is little to choose between the best of these, competitions held during the last twenty years often proving contradictory. The German police trials of 1972–5 arose from the outrages perpetrated by the Baader-Meinhof Gang and the disaster of the 1972 Munich Olympic Games, when eleven Israeli athletes were murdered by terrorists from the Palestinian Black September Organization.

In addition to wholesale revision of German federal firearms laws, 9×19mm was standardized as the military/police cartridge to replace the motley collection of 7.65mm Short, 9mm Short, 9mm Police and 9mm Parabellum-chambered guns in service. Criteria were laid down for service pistols: maximum dimensions of 180×130×34mm, an unladen weight of 1kg, and magazines contaning at least eight rounds. Safe holstering with a live cartridge in the chamber was sought, yet the guns had to be ready for firing without any additional manipulation of safety catches or de-cocking levers. A high degree of ambidexterity was specified whilst service life was to be at least ten thousand rounds.

Four manufacturers accepted these stringent requirements and the Heckler & Koch PSP, Mauser HSP, SIG-Sauer P225 and Walther P5 duly appeared. After initial trials, the Mauser HSP was withdrawn, but—surprisingly—the remaining guns all passed with flying colours. As the German state police were allowed to choose what they liked, the diversity of subsequent issues merely reflected the inconclusiveness:

Pistole 5 (Walther P5): issued to the state police of Baden and the Palatinate.

Pistole 6 (SIG-Sauer P225): issued to the Bundesgrenzschutz (Federal border guard), Bereitschaftpolizei, the Bundeszolldienst (Federal customs service), and to police in Bremen, Hamburg, Hessen, Nordrhein-Westfalen and Schleswig-Holstein.

Pistole 7 (Heckler & Koch PSP): issued to the state police of Baden, Bayern and Niedersachsen, plus the anti-terrorist unit Grenzschutzgruppe 9 (GSG9).

Others: Saarland accepted the Heckler & Koch P9S whilst West Berlin, owing to long-standing agreements with the Soviet Union, retained the Walther P1.

THE US JSSAP TRIALS

The search for a new service pistol, undertaken in 1977–83, began under the aegis of the American Joint Services Small Arms Program (JSSAP), seeking a replacement for the venerable M1911A1 Colt-Browning pistol.

Among the new criteria were demands for a calibre of 9 × 19mm, double-action lockwork, ambidexterity and a magazine capacity greater than thirteen rounds. Leading European gunmakers participated, anxious to obtain a lucrative contract even though the terms of contract demanded the establishment of manufacturing facilities in the United States. Submissions included the German Heckler & Koch P9S and VP70; the Belgian FN GP, DA and FA pistols; the Spanish Echeverria Star Mo. 28 DA; the US Colt SSP and Smith & Wesson Model 459; and the Italian Beretta Mo. 92S. The .45 ACP Colt M1911A1 (US Army) and the .38-calibre Smith & Wesson Model 15 revolver (USAF) were included as control weapons.

The trials were spread over a number of years, during which many well-known handguns were conclusively rejected. Some individual results were shocking. However, cartridges supplied through the normal military channels were so unsuitable that commercial 9 × 19mm (9mm Parabellum) ammunition was substituted. That these did not suit some of the submissions is implicit in analysis of the failures.

The Beretta 92S was placed first, having passed the accuracy trials (fixed and freehand) and the environment test. There were fourteen failures in 28,000 rounds, which gave a 'Mean rounds between stoppage' figure (MRBS) of 2000. This comfortably bettered not only its rivals but also the 1500 rounds desired by the JSSAP. The stoppages had comprised three feed, two chambering, two ignition, six extraction and one 'other' failures: outstanding by any standards.

In contrast, at the bottom of the scale, the Star 28 DA had a disastrous time. After marginally passing the accuracy trials and failing the environment test, the pistol recorded 1142 failures in 5526 rounds—a MRBS of only 5. There had been 54 feed, 516 chambering, 430 firing, 137 extraction and five miscellaneous stoppages.

The Stars might have given a better account of themselves had better cartridges been available, though this did not appear to inhibit the Beretta, the Smith & Wesson M459 (MRBS 952) or the Colt M1911A1 (MRBS 748); unfortunately, fortunes have often been won or lost over a single trial series.

The JSSAP commission recommended the adoption of the Beretta 92S, but the army, mindful of developments made during the protracted trial period, demanded a second series with the Beretta 92SB, SIG-Sauer P226, Smith & Wesson 459A and Heckler & Koch P7M13. Despite a reduction of the desirable MRBS figure to 800, and the removal of the more stringent environmental requirements, the Beretta was still declared the winner.

The US Army formally adopted the Beretta 92SB-F in January 1992 as the 'Pistol, Semiautomatic, 9mm M9 (1005–01–118–2640)', much to the chagrin of Smith & Wesson. The first five-year contract was for nearly 316,000 guns.

Amid allegations that the decision to adopt the Beretta had been taken before the JSSAP trials had even begun, procurement of the M9 continued against a backcloth of

court cases questioning the conduct of the trials; there could yet be further twists in the story. Smith & Wesson remained convinced that its perfected pistol actually out-performed the Beretta, and, on the whole, has successfully persuaded many traditionally revolver-orientated American police forces to accept the auto-loader. The .45 ACP Model 645 has been especially favoured, though interest has now turned to guns chambering 10mm Auto or .40 S&W.

The current Joint Services Operation Requirement (JSOR) has demanded that handguns 'should be of .45 caliber'. Heckler & Koch, Colt and other manufacturers have responded, and the whole question of the US service handgun may be investigated once again.

HANDGUN UTILITY

Experience has shown that, when it matters most, a submachine-gun or riot shotgun is often a better weapon than a handgun in all but the most confined circumstances. Even the fashionable two-hand grip on a handgun will not better the shooting of guns such as the Heckler & Koch MP5, which have a longer sight radius and greater weight.

Although handguns are unsuitable for most infra-red sights and image intensifiers (many of which weigh several times as much as the gun), efforts have been made to develop pistols in conjunction with sights such as the IMT Mini-Laser Designator. This matches a battery-powered laser projector on the pistol with binocular-type night-vision goggles. The projector, aligned with the bore of the pistol, provides an aiming-point visible only with the goggles: the mark is simply superimposed on the intended target and the gun fired in the normal way, greatly increasing the chances of a hit under dusk or night conditions. Though the goggles restrict peripheral vision, leaving the user vulnerable to lateral counter-attack, systems of this type have great promise.

49. SIG-Sauer handguns are nominally products of Swiss-German co-operation, to avoid infringing Switzerland's ban on arms exports. From top to bottom: P230, P220, P226 (left), P225 (right) and P210 (foreground). Courtesy of SIG, Neuhausen.

P230

P226

P225

P220

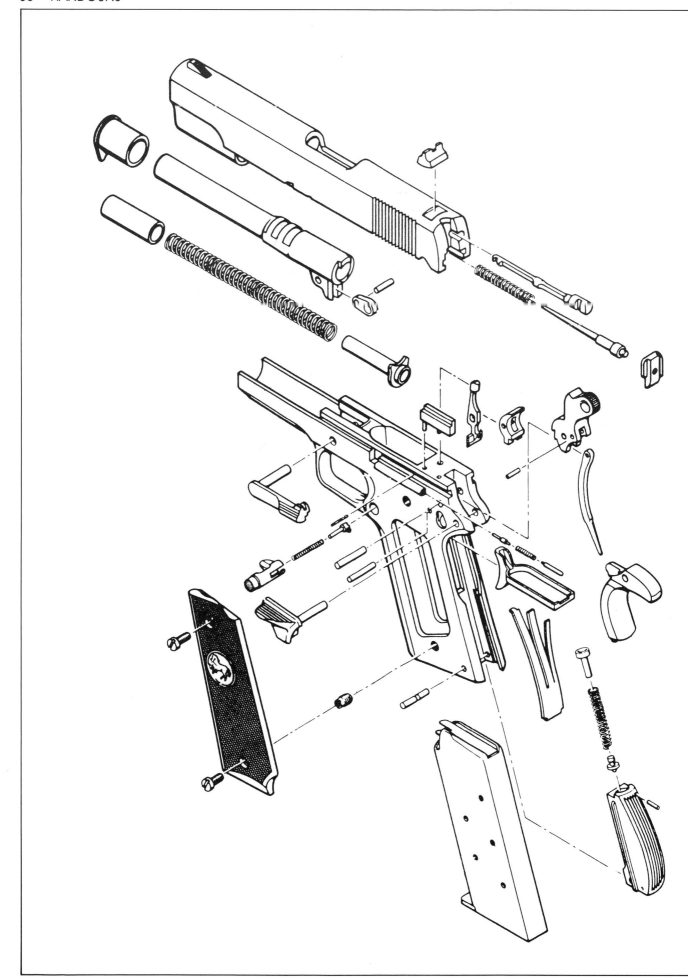

50. The classic man-stopper: the US .45 M1911A1 automatic pistol, which remained in service until replaced by the 9mm Pistol M9 (Beretta 92F) in 1985. Author's archives.

51

50

51. The 9mm Beretta Mo. 92-F Compact. Marked 'Berben Corporation, New York', this was one of the guns supplied from Italy whilst the Beretta factory in Accokeek, Maryland, was being constructed. Courtesy of Pietro Beretta SpA, Gardone.

Fig. 6. An exploded-view drawing of the .45 ACP M1911A1 Colt-Browning, a particularly rugged and consequently long-lived design. Note the locking ribs on the top surface of the barrel and the barrel-depressor link beneath the chamber.

COLT-BROWNINGS

The 1911-pattern Colt-Browning pistol, in its improved 1926-vintage M1911A1 form, is possibly the best-known auto-loading handgun of all time and steadfastly refuses to die a natural death—even though it was rejected by the US Army in 1982 in favour of the Beretta 92SB-F. Copies of the M1911A1 (some facsimiles, others radically altered) are still being made in the USA by a surprisingly wide variety of gunmakers.

The great advantages of the traditional .45 ACP M1911A1 are its ruggedness and proven stopping power. Its safety features are insufficient by today's standards, whilst it is difficult to shoot owing to appreciable recoil and a grip that may be a little too square to the axis of the bore.

But these arguments do not impress champions of the Colt-Browning, who see simplicity as a virtue and multiplicity of safety devices as evidence that the guns so equipped are designed more to protect inexperienced rookies than help a highly-trained man disable an opponent with the first shot.

Merit can probably be found in each argument, considered individually, and the lure of the big Colt-Browning has been dismissed as an irrelevant historical curiosity. However, Colt still gains a lucrative return from Government Model lookalikes, chambering the Delta Elite of 1987 for the fashionable 10mm Auto cartridge, and has even produced double-action Double Eagle pistols offering the same basic construction.

If the special-purpose role of the Government Model is questionable, there is little doubt that use has been made of compact derivatives—Colt-made Officer's Models, or those marketed by Detonics—in addition to high-power guns which can deliver a potent punch at long range.

Colt also promotes the All-American 2000, which presents a radical departure from the established Browning: a striker instead of a hammer, a double-action trigger, and even—horror of horrors—a rotating-barrel breech lock credited to Reed Knight and Eugene Stoner. The new gun promises to be accurate and dependable, but whether it will be able to challenge market leaders such as the Glock (q.v.) is another matter entirely.

52. This gate sentry at North Howard Street Mill, Belfast, displays an L9 (Browning GP) pistol, body armour and a visored helmet—all of which can be indispensable in counter-terrorist warfare. Courtesy of Headquarters, British Forces Northern Ireland.

THE FN-BROWNING GROUP

The GP Mle 35, designed by John Browning shortly before his sudden death in 1926, and subsequently perfected by Fabrique Nationale, has been accepted in more than sixty countries for army and paramilitary use. In view of its perceived obsolescence, however, FN developed the interesting, but complicated and ultimately unsuccessful GP Fast Action during the 1970s to overcome criticism of the conventional 'double-action' trigger system.

Although this has been popular in semi-automatics, permitting the first cartridge to be fired merely by pulling through on the trigger, the effort required for the first shot is appreciably greater than for the second and subsequent shots owing to the automatic cocking action.

The first shot fired from a double-action automatic almost always goes low, the greater trigger pull tending to pivot the muzzle down. The Fast Action eliminated the problem, but was insufficiently durable; rejected in the US JSSAP trials, it was replaced by the conventional double-action BDA, also known as the 'GP DA'.

The BDA was made in three guises: full-size (BDA9S, 200mm overall, with a fourteen-round magazine), medium (BDA9M, 178mm, fourteen rounds) and compact (BDA9C, 178mm, seven rounds). Each shared the conventional Browning cam-finger lock, the differences concerning dimensions and cartridge capacity.

As even the BDA was incapable of challenging guns such as the Glock, so Fabrique Nationale developed the BDM ('Browning Double Mode'), introduced in 1991. Though the BDM shares the basic GP mechanism, the trigger system has been altered to give the firer a choice, through a rotary selector, of conventional single-action 'pistol mode' or double-action-only 'revolver mode'.

If single action is selected, the hammer returns to the down position once the action has been cycled to load the chamber and the de-cocking lever has been pressed; when the gun fires, the slide returns to leave the hammer at full cock. In the double-

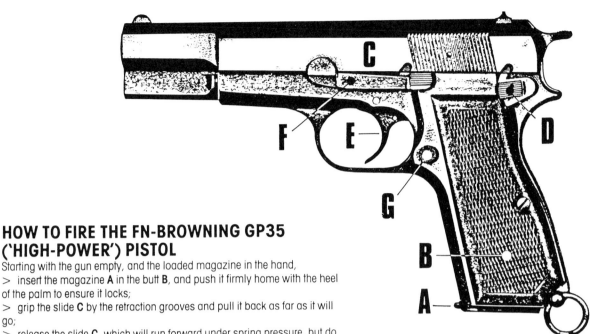

HOW TO FIRE THE FN-BROWNING GP35 ('HIGH-POWER') PISTOL

Starting with the gun empty, and the loaded magazine in the hand,
> insert the magazine **A** in the butt **B**, and push it firmly home with the heel of the palm to ensure it locks;
> grip the slide **C** by the retraction grooves and pull it back as far as it will go;
> release the slide **C**, which will run forward under spring pressure, but do not hold it during its travel;
> rotate the safety catch **D** upwards to SAFE;
> when ready to fire, push the safety catch **D** down to FIRE, take aim and squeeze the trigger **E**.

The gun will reload automatically and cock the hammer. When the magazine is empty, the slide stop **F** locks the slide open. When this happens:
> push the magazine-release catch **G** to release the empty magazine **A**;
> insert a new magazine;
> press the slide stop **F** down with the thumb.

This allows the slide to close, chamber a round, and the gun is cocked ready to fire. To clear the gun:
> press the magazine-release catch **G** and remove the magazine;
> retract the slide **C** to eject the chambered round;
> operate the slide again to make sure.
> set the safety to SAFE.

The magazine can then be emptied and replaced, the trigger being pulled to drop the hammer (preferably under control by hooking the thumb over the hammer to cushion its fall).

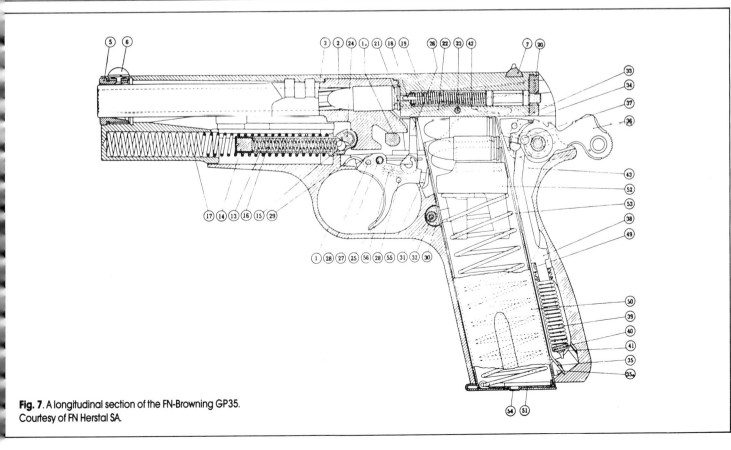

Fig. 7. A longitudinal section of the FN-Browning GP35.
Courtesy of FN Herstal SA.

53. The FN-Browning GP Mle 35 has seen remarkable success. Placed in production in 1935 after a thirteen-year gestation, the pistol had the unique distinction of being officially issued by *both* sides during the Second World War. It was as likely to be carried by German paratroops or tank-crews as by British commandos and special forces. The gun pictured above is a pre-1939 commercial example; most military-issue weapons had an optimistic tangent-leaf back sight. Author's archives.

54. The Beretta Mo.92 SB pistol has proved a favourite with the Italian CTW group, NOCS, one of whose members is seen here at practice. Courtesy of Pietro Beretta SpA, Gardone.

action mode, the hammer is dropped to an intermediate position by the de-cocking lever. When the gun fires, the slide returns to leave the hammer in the intermediate position, subsequent shots being fired by pressing through on the trigger.

The advantages of the revolver mode are partly a perceived improvement in safety but also a constant trigger pressure for all shots. In pistol mode, the single-action shots require far less pressure on the trigger lever than the initial double-action pull. Whether the complexity is worthwhile, however, must be in dispute.

THE BERETTA MODEL 92

This is an interesting gun with a lengthy pedigree, embodying a locking system derived from that of the Walther P38. The prototypes were made in 1951, but problems with the original alloy frame took some time to resolve; not until 1955 was the 'Brigadier', as it was named commercially, destined to achieve any real success. Since then, however, the Model 92 and its many derivations have gone on to great things.

55. The Beretta Mo.92 SB-C, generally chambered for the 9mm Parabellum round, is a short, small-frame variant of the standard Mo. 92. The abbreviated grip reduces magazine capacity to thirteen rounds instead of fifteen. Courtesy of Pietro Beretta SpA, Gardone.

56. Still in production after more than fifty years, the Walther P.38 (known officially as the P1 since 1963) has served the West German armed forces with distinction—in addition to inspiring the Beretta Mo. 92, which shares a similar locking mechanism. Courtesy of Carl Walther GmbH, Ulm.

57. Small-calibre automatic pistols have always been popular among European policemen and undercover agents, largely because they are much easier to conceal than a bulky service automatic. This Beretta Mo. 84, in 9mm ACP (9mm Short), is typical of modern designs. Note the staggered-row magazine, holding thirteen rounds but adding little to the bulk of the gun. Courtesy of Pietro Beretta SpA, Gardone.

Variants currently available range from the standard Model 92F to the Model 92F-M—a compact gun with an eight-round magazine—and two double-action only guns, 92D and 92DS. The Model 96 is a minor variant chambering the .40 S&W cartridge instead of 9mm Parabellum.

The most visible success has been the adoption of the Beretta 92F by the armed forces of the USA and France. Suspicion remains that the US trials were not entirely impartial, implying that the decision to adopt the Beretta was influenced by other factors—restrictiveness of the Swiss arms-exportation laws, the readiness of Beretta to build a factory in the USA, or the billions of dollars-worth of US military equipment that had been (and would continue to be) purchased by Italy.

The lock strength of the Beretta is generally reckoned to be less than the Walther, but the P5 did not appear in the US trials and no accurate comparison is available. Once the new M9 pistols were widely distributed in the US Army, reports of failures began to arise; most were due to frames cracking, necessitating the recall of many guns for inspection after firing only a thousand rounds. Whilst many potential long-term problems were discounted, minor changes were apparently made in the slide and suspicions linger that the M9 is suitable for use only with US M882 ammunition.

In addition to guns being made in Italy and the USA, Beretta-type pistols are being made in Brazil (by Forjas Taurus) and Chile (by FAMAE). The Beretta M8000 Condor pistol was exhibited at the 1984 IWA, Nürnberg, departing from the established '92' practice in the barrel-locking system, which relies on rotation instead of the Walther-type block. The implications of this design, offered in several chamberings and a choice of three safety systems, are not yet clear.

THE WALTHERS

Walther has traditionally relied on variants of the Polizei-Pistole and the Pistole 38 (PP and P.38), originally introduced in 1929 and 1940 respectively. By the standards of the 1970s, both were found wanting for special-purpose use. The Polizei-Pistole was too expensive, and had come to be regarded as not powerful enough to fulfil personal defence tasks effectually; the P.38, despite its double-action lockwork, was too bulky. After toying with half-measures—e.g., the PP Super and the P4—Walther progressed to the P5, an adaption of the P.38 which performed quite acceptably in the German police trials.

The P5 relied on the well-proven P.38-type locking system, but incorporated a new fail-safe trigger. When the action was at rest with the hammer down, the firing pin matches a hole bored into the hammer, which, resting on the face of the breech block, cannot move the pin. When the trigger is pulled, the hammer is rotated backwards and a cam lifts the firing pin. When the hammer is released, it flies forward to strike the pin-head and fire the chambered round. However, when the de-cocking lever releases a cocked hammer, the firing pin is still in its lowered position; thus, not even the rapidly descending hammer can drive it forward. As there is no safety in the traditional Walther manner, the gun can be fired simply by squeezing the trigger.

Though the P5 has been a moderate success, rival designs suggested that it clung too greatly to old technology. Though the guns generally shot very well, proving to be durable, the eight-round magazine and a lack of truly ambidexterous controls were criticised.

Consequently, Walther abandoned the proven Barthelmes locking system in favour of an adaption of the Browning cam-finger system pioneered in the FN-Browning GP-35. The result is the P88, offered in standard or compact forms. Unfortunately, the P88 is still recognisably the product of a long-established gunmaker clinging to traditional means of fabrication. And though this seems to work in former Soviet-bloc states such as the Czech Republic, it inevitably makes the product of a leading industrialized country such as Germany very expensive.

The P88 has been purchased in small quantities by individuals, but has not as yet attracted more widespread attention. It will probably continue to struggle against a legion of well-established competitors with so much more to offer.

THE SIG-SAUERS

Schweizerische Industrie-Gesellschaft (SIG) is another of the world's best-established gunmakers, with an unbroken pedigree stretching back to the 1850s. In 1949, the Swiss army adopted the 'Ordonnanzpistole 49 SIG', which was a military version of the SP 47/8 (or P-210) developed from the French Petter of the 1930s. The SIG pistol was beautifully made and soon attracted an enviable reputation for accuracy, which was widely ascribed to the length of the bearing surfaces between the slide and the frame—and to the care with which the tipping barrel was fitted in its muzzle bush. Quality came with a high price-tag.

In the 1960s, therefore, SIG modernised the P-210 in an attempt to win a share of

58. The Walther P5 shares the locking system of the P1 (P.38), though the shortened barrel is enclosed in a full-length slide. Several differing variants have been made, including a P5 Compact. Courtesy of Carl Walther GmbH, Ulm.

Courtesy of Carl Walther GmbH, Ulm.

59. Incorporating a Browning-type dropping-barrel lock, the Walther P88 is seen as a replacement for the venerable P1. The Walther is expensive, but has already sold in small numbers to specialist police units.

60. The 9mm P228, compact and effectual, is one of the latest in the successful SIG-Sauer series. It is basically a revision of the P225 with a thirteen-round staggered-column magazine. Courtesy of SIG, Neuhausen.

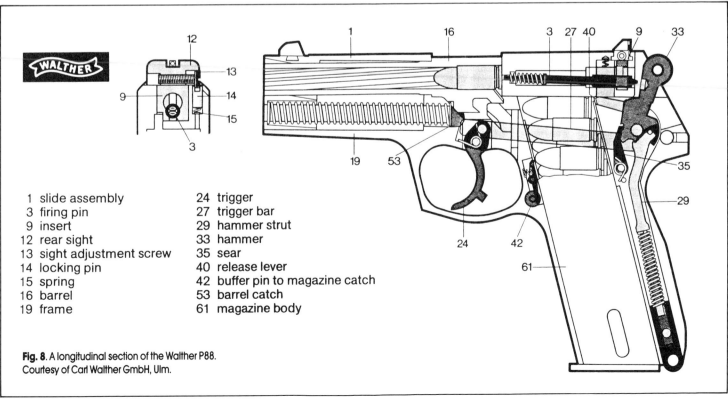

1 slide assembly	24 trigger
3 firing pin	27 trigger bar
9 insert	29 hammer strut
12 rear sight	33 hammer
13 sight adjustment screw	35 sear
14 locking pin	40 release lever
15 spring	42 buffer pin to magazine catch
16 barrel	53 barrel catch
19 frame	61 magazine body

Fig. 8. A longitudinal section of the Walther P88.
Courtesy of Carl Walther GmbH, Ulm.

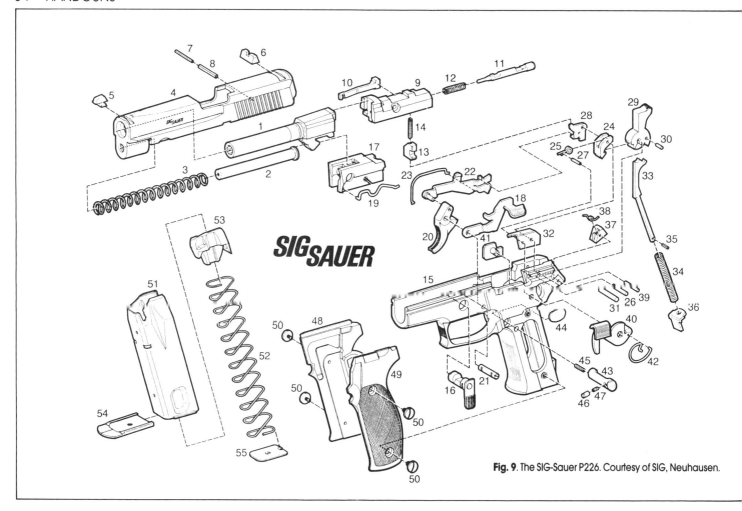

SIG SAUER

Fig. 9. The SIG-Sauer P226. Courtesy of SIG, Neuhausen.

the international mass-market. The major changes concerned a new double-action trigger system and simpler construction—e.g., the locking ribs were replaced by a large block that rose into the ejection port cutaway. The result was the P220, adopted in the mid-1970s as the Swiss army's 'Pistole 75'. SIG had already entered into agreement with J.P. Sauer & Sohn GmbH of Eckenförde, in West Germany, to circumvent restrictive Swiss arms-export laws.

To satisfy the German police, a compact variant of the P220 was produced: the P225 (later known in Germany as the P6). Its de-cocking system was essentially similar to that of the Walther P5, but locked the safety pin into the breech-block—strangely, practically identical with the system used on the Walther P1.

The P225 inspired an assortment of successors, including the P226 (9mm Parabellum, fifteen-round magazine), P228 (9mm Parabellum, thirteen rounds) and P229 (.40 S&W, twelve rounds). One version of these guns ran an extremely close second to the Beretta 92 in the US Army trials, apparently losing more on politico-economic grounds than performance.

HECKLER & KOCH

This West German gunmaking firm cut its teeth on the G3 rifle, before producing the first of its handguns in the early 1960s. This was a comparatively simple blowback general-purpose pistol designated 'HK4'—principally because it could be acquired with four differing barrels chambering .22 LR rimfire, 6.35mm Auto, 7.65mm Auto or 9mm Short. However, though the HK-4 was a well made and effectual product, it had only a minor impact on the market.

H&K followed with the P9, a large military/sporting pistol chambering the 9mm Parabellum cartridge. Renowned for widespread use of synthetic material, polygonal rifling and a roller-delayed breech system, the P9 was quickly upgraded to P9S standards by the addition of a double-action trigger system. The gun was good enough to attract the attention of police and military departments, and has seen small-scale use with Special Forces such as the Green Berets, the US Navy SEALs and GSG-9. But it was too

expensive and probably too radical to gain widespread adoption.

The PSP or Polizei-Selbstlade-Pistole (subsequently known officially as the P7) was a completely new design relying on a gas-bleed system to delay the opening of the breech until the pressure in the chamber had dropped to a safe level. Another radical departure from conventional practice was the cocking lever down the front of the grip. A pressure of about 7kg (15.5lb) on the lever cocks the gun—previously loaded by operating the slide—after which single-action fire can be continued as long as pressure of more than 500gm (1.25lb) is maintained on the cocking lever. When pressure is released, the firing pin is automatically lowered and the PSP can be carried safely with a live round in the chamber.

The P7, emerging from the German pistol trials with great credit, was an instantaneous success. It was followed by a selection of improved weapons, differing largely in detail or calibre. The P7M13 featured a large-capacity staggered column magazine, whereupon the original single-column gun was redesignated 'P7M8'. A variant was developed in .45 ACP.

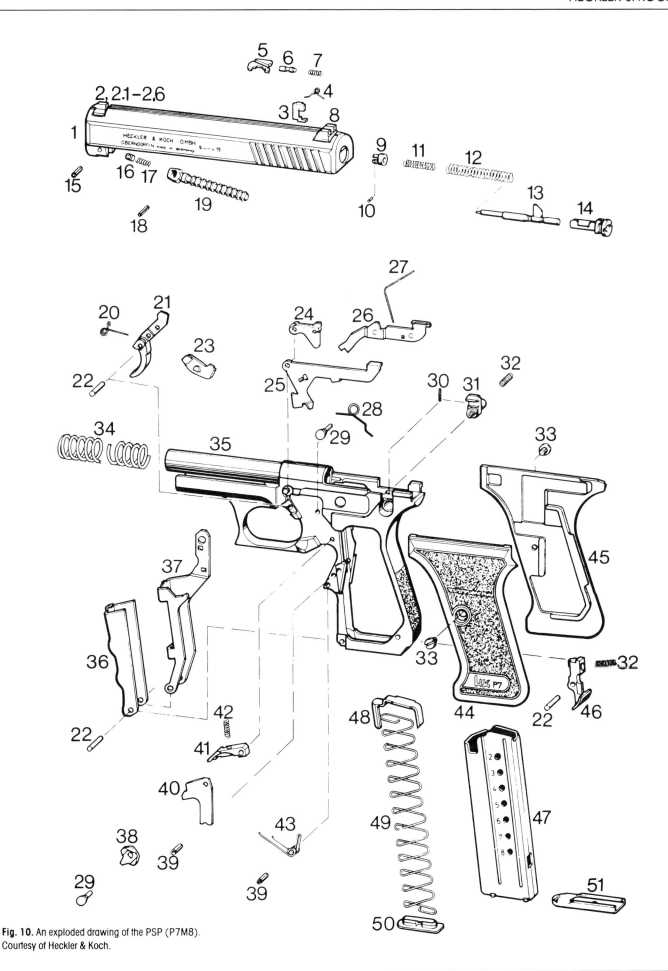

Fig. 10. An exploded drawing of the PSP (P7M8).
Courtesy of Heckler & Koch.

61

62

61. Mistakenly characterised as 'the gun that cannot be X-rayed', the 9mm Glock P-17 is nonetheless an innovative design. Adopted as the service pistol of the Austrian army in 1983, it has since been sold to military and police forces throughout the world. Courtesy of Glock GmbH, Deutsch-Wagram.

62. Regarded as a trend-setting design when it was introduced in the 1970s, the Heckler & Koch P7 (shown here in 'M13' guise) has recently lost ground to guns such as the Glock and the CZ 75. However, it remains a popular choice for CTW use. Courtesy of Heckler & Koch GmbH, Oberndorf.

Throughout the 1980s, therefore, the P7/PSP series was used extensively, particularly in Germany. However, its dominance has been challenged by the emergence of a new generation of guns and the P7 has never been able to duplicate the success of the Glock (q.v.) in North America. Heckler & Koch has now produced the Universal-Selbstlade-Pistole (USP)—in 9mm Parabellum and .40 S&W—based on experience gained in the US JSSAP and other trials. A modified gun has also been entered in the current SOCOM programme.

THE GLOCK

Developed in Austria, this unusual gun has provided one of the most unexpected successes of recent years. Glock GmbH of Deutsch-Wagram entered it in the Austrian trials of 1977–9, but few commentators expected it to compete effectually with

weapons submitted by gunmakers with far longer pedigree. Though the Steyr Pi-18 was generally reckoned as the favourite, Heckler & Koch, Walther, SIG-Sauer, Beretta, Smith & Wesson and others provided a real threat.

At the conclusion of the trials in 1983, to general amazement, the Glock was adopted as the 'Pistole 80'. Performance had been at least as good as the best of its rivals, so the scales had been tipped by the perennial political consideration: the gun was an Austrian design, made in Austria.

Once the surprise had receded, the Glock was inspected critically by interested parties. Excepting the unique trigger-within-a-trigger safety system, the design was not particularly innovative—but the way in which it was constructed, with a sizeable proportion of synthetic parts, was most unusual. It was so unusual, indeed, that the synthetic frame and grip inspired a campaign of scaremongering in newspapers and magazines throughout the world; the Glock was damned as the gun that could

not be detected by X-rays, and was thus certain to be misused.

The panic stories were soon followed by more realistic assessments, but it was the colourful untruth that entered popular mythology. Even today, more than a decade after adoption in Austria, the legend persists. Yet the Glock has a metal barrel, a metal slide, metal springs, metal pins, two metal strips set into the frame to accept the slide, and a magazine containing metal cartridges loaded with metal bullets; consequently, no successful evasion of an X-ray machine has ever been made.

Owing to good handling characteristics, simple-but-effectual safety features and an unusually large magazine capacity, the Glock 17 has been popular with Special Forces worldwide. By the early 1990s nearly four thousand police and protection agencies in the USA alone, together with the Special Forces of at least ten armies had acquired Glock pistols.

Gradually, the original 9mm gun has been joined by a series of modifications including one of the few selective-fire pistols available on today's market. The Glock 19 (9mm Parabellum, fifteen round magazine) is shorter than the standard version; the Glock 20 chambers 10mm Auto (fifteen rounds); the .45 ACP Glock 21 has a thirteen-round magazine; and the Glock 22 (fifteen rounds) or Glock 23 (thirteen rounds) chambers the .40 S&W round.

CZECH-INSPIRED DESIGNS

The Czech CZ 75 and its newer derivative, the CZ 85, have also attracted attention. The basic design borrows many features promoted originally by the SIG SP 47/8 (P-210), including a Browning-type locking system and an unusually lengthy slide-guide cut on the inner face of the frame. The CZ has an effectual double-action trigger and a high-capacity magazine. It handles well and, in its '85' form in particular, also offers easily mastered safety/magazine controls.

Like the Beretta M92, but totally unlike the Glock, the CZ pistols are conventional designs made in largely traditional fashion. They have also been amazingly successful; they may have become even more popular had not Soviet-bloc origins attracted hostile propaganda. A better indicator of potential is that they have been extensively copied in the West.

The first guns, if not those of current production, were actually made from parts made in Italy by Tanfoglio.

The former Industrial Technology & Machines AG of Solothurn (now part of Sphinx Industries) introduced the AT-84 in the mid 1980s, whilst Tanfoglio Armi of Gardone Val Trompia has made a variety of near facsimiles. Even the IMI 941 Jericho pistol is little more than a cosmetically altered CZ 85 with a polygonally rifled Israeli-made barrel.*

It has been suggested that guns such as the CZ 75/CZ 85 series succeed because traditional-looking construction impresses those who take the final procurement decisions—high-ranking officers, leading politicians—much more greatly than the guns that are made at the forefront of technology from synthetic parts. Whatever the reason, the Czech design is currently acknowledged as one of the world leaders.

SOVIET GUNS

Since the demise of the Tokarev (even though production of modified versions continues in China and Serbia), the Pistolet Makarova ('PM') has been the principal handgun of the Soviet bloc. Made in Russia and many lesser states, it is a simple blowback chambered for a special 9 × 18mm cartridge generating power midway between that of the 9mm Short (.380 ACP) and 9mm Parabellum. In spite of

Soviet attempts to claim credit for the design, the Makarov is little more than an adaption of the Walther Polizei-Pistole. This makes it an effectual personal-defence weapon, but not really powerful enough for special-purpose use.

The improved PSM was designed around a cartridge perfected in 1979. Credited to Lashnev, Simarin and Kulikov (though still retaining Walther-inspired elements), the pistol attracted considerable attention in Western military circles. This was partly because it was unusually flat, had alloy grips, and fired a necked cartridge with the unusually small calibre of 5.45mm.

This was initially assumed to be a production expedient, as it allowed barrels for 5.45mm pistols, assault rifles and light machine-guns to be made on the same basic machinery. When examples of the PSM eventually reached the West, the standard Soviet cartridge, firing a light bullet at marginally sub-sonic velocity, proved capable of piercing multiple layers of vaunted Kevlar body armour in a way no Western military handgun cartridge could match.

Thoughts began to turn toward more sinister motives; was the PSM designed for the KGB, perhaps as an assassination weapon? Did its flatness mean that it was designed primarily for covert operations? At the time of writing, the reasons for its development are by no means clear.

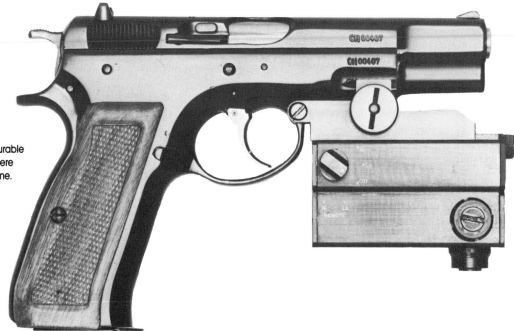

3. Copied from the Czech CZ 75, the solid and durable 9mm ITM AT-84 is an excellent design. It is shown here with an ITM Mini-Laser designator beneath the frame. Courtesy of Sphinx Industries, Solothurn.

However, shortly before his death in 1991, Anatoliy Simarin told the Russian authority David Bolotin* that the design specification included requirements for light weight, low bulk and good combat characteristics.

Clearly, therefore, the PSM was neither developed for second-line forces nor as an officers' sidearm. The gun has had no effect on the design of Western combat handguns, in which the discernible trends are currently towards larger cartridges (e.g., 10mm Auto, .40 S&W) which fill the gap between 9mm Parabellum and .45 ACP.

* Author of *Sovetskoe Strelkovoe Oruzhiye*, the standard Russian-language text book on the development of Soviet small arms.

SPECIAL-PURPOSE PISTOLS

The small size and relatively low power of the service handguns generally prevent them being used in conjunction with special equipment. However, special silenced High-

Standard Model B pistols were issued to the OSS during the Second World War and used by US Special Forces until comparatively recently. The Hand Firing Device Mk 1 ('Welrod') and the Sleeve Gun were typical of the unique pistols developed for SOE during the Second World War.

Silencers are usually bulky, but some of the special pistols produced in the Chinese bloc have the silencer integral with the barrel/receiver group. The Type 64 'assassination pistol' can operate as a conventional semi-automatic or fire single shots, as the slide can be locked shut to reduce the amount of mechanical noise generated in the normal auto-loading action. The gun fires a 7.65 × 17mm cartridge similar to the 7.65mm Browning, and has a large-diameter barrel casing containing a perforated baffle-type silencer. The Type 67 is similar, but has an improved tubular silencer extending from the muzzle.

The North Koreans have also made a silenced pistol, a variant of the standard Type 64 (a copy of the 1900-model Browning blowback!), but this is a much more conventional weapon capable only of semi-automatic fire.

Impressed by the performance of Chinese Type 64 and 67 pistols captured during the Vietnam war, the US Special Forces demanded silenced weapons of their own, the navy promoting development of a silenced Smith & Wesson 9mm automatic pistol for SEAL teams. The gun was intended to silence watch-dogs—hence its nickname, 'Hush Puppy'—but was equally useful to assassins.

Known during development as the WOX-13A, the gun was initially based on the S&W Model 39 and then on the improved Model 59. After initial problems had been overcome, it became the Pistol, Mark 3 Model 0. Caps, plugs and special accessories allowed the assembly to be carried safely under water.

For maximum efficiency, the Hush Puppy was issued with special green-tipped 9mm Parabellum cartridges, firing heavyweight 158-grain bullets to reduce the muzzle velocity well below the speed of sound. Life of the silencer insert was thirty of these Mark 144 Model 0 cartridges, or a mere six standard supersonic ones. The accessory kit issued with the pistol contained 24 special cartridges and a replacement silencer insert. The unladen weight of the entire assembly was only 34oz, overall length being 12.8in.

Very few purpose-built silenced pistols have been built in the West in recent years, reliance being placed instead on minor modifications of standard designs. This has not been true of the Soviet Union, where silenced versions of the Stechkin and Makarov have been made in small numbers.

The APB was a comparatively minor adaption of the standard selective-fire Stechkin pistol (APS), which has been adjudged a failure in its intended role of sub-submachine-gun. The mechanism relied on an annular chamber around the barrel, into which gas was released through bleed-ports; when the bullet had passed out of the barrel, the gas flowed back into the bore and out through the silencer attached to the muzzle. The frame was extended to support the breech of the silencer and a skeletal shoulder-stock could be attached when needed.

The PB, or silenced Makarov, was a different proposition. Apparently designed in the Tula factory, its slide contained a shroud filled with fine steel mesh. Propellant gas was allowed to leak through bleed holes in the bore into the mesh, and then out through the silencer attached to the muzzle. Owing to the position of the shroud around the barrel, the return spring was moved into the grip behind the magazine well.

The Soviet designers have also produced a compact silenced auto-loading pistol

64. The elegant Swiss-made 9mm ITM AT-84, derived from the CZ 75. Courtesy of Sphinx Industries, Solothurn.

65. A typical Soviet-made 9mm Makarov pistol, a double-action design adapted from the Walther PP. Courtesy of Ian Hogg.

66. Among the most interesting of recent designs are the Chinese silenced pistols, this being a Type 67 made in 1968. It differs from the earlier Type 64 principally in the design of the silencer. Courtesy of Ian Hogg.

known as the PSS. This 7.62mm gun relies on a special piston-cartridge to achieve noise suppression. When the gun fires, the piston thrusts the projectile forward whilst simultaneously sealing residual propellant gas inside the special thick-wall cartridge case. The ammunition presumably has a short effective range, but performance details are lacking.

Soviet designer Vladimir Simonov succeeded in developing the 4.5mm SPP-1, a silenced underwater pistol introduced in the early 1970s. Its features include a tipping block of four barrels and a sequential firing mechanism. Performance is said to include an effective range of twenty metres at depths of up to 40 metres.

The comparative ineffectiveness of silencers when used with supersonic ammunition—though 'noise suppressors' have appeared on guns such as the M16A1, they are not always especially successful—has forced most special forces to turn to silenced submachine-guns (q.v), where the penalties of weight and size are not as severe as they can be with a pistol.

REVOLVERS

Revolvers are generally much simpler than pistols, and less susceptible to jamming caused by bad ammunition. Mechanical actuation means that a chamber containing a defective round can simply be swung away and the next one fired instead. Revolvers are also less vulnerable to structural failure, though this advantage has been eroded somewhat by the inclusion of transfer bars, mechanical safeties and otherwise desirable features in the trigger system. However, revolvers are usually bulkier than the pistols, particularly across the cylinder (restricting cartridge capacity in some small guns), more difficult to load, and incapable of such a high volume of fire in the hands of anyone other than an expert.

Prior to the appearance of the 0.357 Magnum, most police revolvers were cursed with the poor ballistics of the standard 0.32in and 0.38in Colt and Smith & Wesson cartridges, none of which are anywhere near as effectual as the 9mm Parabellum. Closing the gap between the cylinder and the barrel has also presented insuperable problems, solved only by the now obsolete 'gas-seal' revolvers that cammed the cylinder forward at the instant of firing. However, the best of the revolvers made by Colt, Smith &

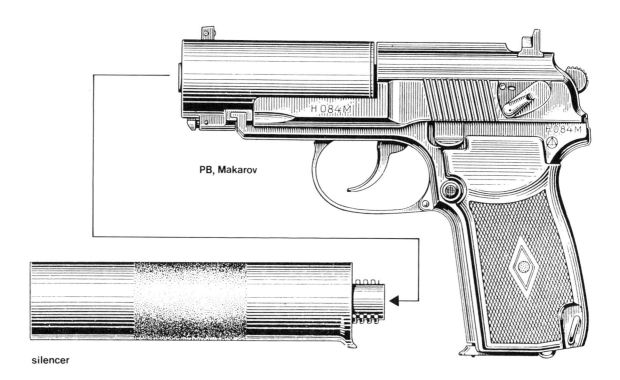

Figs. 12 and 13. Typical Soviet silenced pistol. Drawings by Aleksandr Zhuk.

PB, Makarov

silencer

67. The .38 Llama Piccolo is typical of the compact revolvers favoured by individual members of the special forces and CTW squads. Automatics may offer larger magazine capacities, but revolvers often have the edge in reliability. Courtesy of Llama-Gabilondo y Cia, Vittoria.

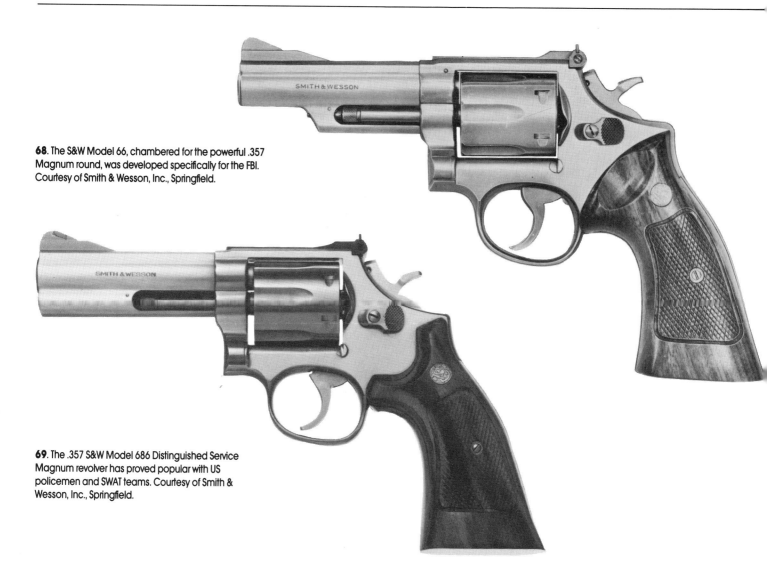

68. The S&W Model 66, chambered for the powerful .357 Magnum round, was developed specifically for the FBI. Courtesy of Smith & Wesson, Inc., Springfield.

69. The .357 S&W Model 686 Distinguished Service Magnum revolver has proved popular with US policemen and SWAT teams. Courtesy of Smith & Wesson, Inc., Springfield.

Wesson and Ruger, joined by the FN Barracuda and other European products, are widely favoured by police, SWAT teams and individual members of Special Forces throughout the world.

The most widely distributed Smith & Wesson revolver has been the 0.38in Model 10 Military & Police, nominally the service weapon even of the Metropolitan Police and the RCMP—though its efficacy is being increasingly questioned in counter-terrorist activities.

The 0.357 Magnum designs are much better man-stoppers, but many police agencies have chosen the small-framed 'magnum' revolvers that cannot handle the continuous battering of full-power ammunition. Instead, practice is supposed to be undertaken with 0.38 Special, the switch to the Magnum cartridges being made only when on duty. As the recoil of the two cartridges differs appreciably, this not only complicates changing from one to the other, but also minimizes the value of the training.

For many years, the Smith & Wesson Model 15 revolver was the weapon of USAF aircrew, whilst the FBI specifically requested development of the S&W Model 66 in 0.357 Magnum to improve stopping power. The French 'Presidential Hunting Service', the police CTW team, was still carrying the Manurhin MR-73 and MR-FI guns in the early 1990s.

Many attempts have been made to smooth the contours of service revolvers to prevent snagging on clothing or in the holster, and a selection of proprietary grips and sights has undoubtedly promoted better snap-shooting over the last two decades. At the time of writing, however, the Special Forces revolver is fighting a desperate rearguard action against the encroaching automatics.

The US Federal Bureau of Investigation has traditionally been armed with S&W 0.357 Magnum revolvers, though the FBI SWAT teams of the 1980s carried 9mm S&W Model 59 auto-loaders and the FBI Hostage Rescue Teams had specially

adapted examples of the FN-Browning GP-35. Then came the infamous 'Miami Massacre', when eight agents attempted to capture two armed criminals in 1986.

The FBI men had revolvers, a basic pump-action shotgun or two, and at least one 9mm S&W auto-loading pistol. Their opponents had handguns and a .223 Ruger Mini-14 carbine. Ill-considered tactics left one criminal dead and another dying of wounds, but not before they had killed two of the FBI agents, permanently disabled three, and seriously injured two of the remainder. Only one of ten men involved escaped injury.

The bullet that fatally injured the man with the Mini-14, a 9mm jacketed hollow-point, penetrated about a foot into the body tissue. However, as it had passed through several layers of clothing and an arm, the shot was not instantaneously disabling; before he died, the gunman had been able to kill the two agents.

The outcome was an immediate call within the FBI for a handgun that offered better hitting power. This would clearly have to fire a larger-diameter bullet at a greater velocity. That 9mm JHP bullets would probably have performed acceptably had the Miami gunman been struck from the front, and the possibility that plugs of cloth prevented proper bullet expansion, were apparently overlooked in the hysteria.

A reversion to .45 ACP was rejected on the dubious grounds that the ballistics of the cartridge could not be improved, and so the new 10mm Auto was selected instead. The S&W Model 1076NS pistol was subsequently selected to replace the assortment of revolvers and smaller-calibre auto-loaders.

The Smith & Wessons have been a qualified success since their adoption in 1991, though the 10mm Auto cartridge promotes a hefty recoil and a sharp muzzle blast. Unexpectedly, after reports of the firing mechanism jamming, the guns were all suddenly withdrawn in 1992; SIG-Sauers were issued as temporary replacements. The problem was eventually traced to a most unexpected source.

The components of all guns have specific dimensional tolerances within which they are deemed acceptable. But it took field service to reveal that a tiny proportion of the M1076 FBI pistols incorporated a series of parts whose dimensions—though acceptable when judged individually—were sufficiently critical to lock the firing system when acting in concert. The replacement of only a single component usually unlocked the 'tolerance jam' and returned the gun to perfect order. Minor changes to the manufacturing specifications have ensured that the problem has never recurred.

70. The .38 Barracuda revolver is shown with an optional cylinder chambered for rimless 9mm Parabellum rounds, which require the cartridge-retaining clip to function effectually. Courtesy of FN Herstal SA.

71. Revolvers made by Sturm, Ruger & Company have presented Colt and Smith & Wesson with healthy competition. This is a Ruger .38 Speed Six, now superseded by the GP-100 series. Courtesy of Sturm, Ruger & Co., Inc., Southport.

Submachine-guns

The increased popularity of the assault rifle, particularly after the introduction of the US 5.56mm cartridge, has brought an appreciable decline in the fortunes of the sub-machine-gun. The US Army has effectively ceased to use it, even though stocks of the .45 ACP M3A1 are held in reserve, and many others have questioned its utility. Consequently, the esteem in which guns such as the Thompson and the Sten Gun were held by the special forces of the

72. The range of Sterling submachine-guns, machine carbines and machine-pistols. *Clockwise, from top left*: the Para-Pistol Mk 7 A4; the Mk 7 A8 with the auxiliary handgrip; the Mk 7 police carbine; the Mk 7 A8; and the Mk 7 A4 with the handgrip. Courtesy of Ian Hogg.

73. Classic in its simplicity, the British Sterling is used by the British special forces (including the SAS) alongside the Heckler & Koch MP5. Shown here is the standard Mk 4 Sterling, similar to the British Army's L2A3, with a Rank Pullin SS82 Pocketscope weapons sight. Courtesy of Ian Hogg and Rank Pullin Controls Ltd.

◄72

Second World War – or the Shpagin-designed PPSh by Russian Tankoviy Desant (tank-borne infantry) forces – is no longer relevant.

THE STERLING

Almost alone among the major powers, Britain clings to a traditional submachine-gun – the Sterling, developed from the 1944-vintage Patchett prototype to replace the crude, cheap but surprisingly efficient Sten Gun. The Sterling was adopted by the British Army in 1956 and has now been in service for thirty years; its design is unremarkable by later standards, with a conventional in-line barrel/bolt layout, but it is very simple, reliable, easy to make and shoots well. Among the differing models are the standard Mk 4 (British Army designation L2A3), the silenced Mk 5 (L34A1), a long-

barrelled semi-automatic Mk 6, several variants of the Mk 7 Para Pistol, and a special semi-automatic Mk 8.

The silenced Sterling is a much underrated gun, capable of firing fully automatically without unduly damaging the silencer system, while the Mk 7 Police Carbine was specifically developed at the request of Metropolitan Police D11 marksmen to provide a handy carbine with an adjustable butt and optical sights. The Mk 8, developed specially for the British security forces to provide greater accuracy, fires from a closed bolt. Owing to its adoption in the British Army, Canada and elsewhere, the Sterling is believed to have been made in greater quantities than any post-war submachine-gun. It even attained a measure of notoriety as the weapon used to kill WPC Yvonne Fletcher outside the Libyan People's Bureau in St James's Square, London, in 1984.

73 ▼

HOW TO FIRE THE STERLING Mk 4/L2A3 SUBMACHINE-GUN

Starting with the gun empty, the selector **A**, (inset in the left side of the pistol grip) in its rearmost position at 'S' ('Safe') and the loaded magazine in the hand:

> insert the magazine **B** in the housing **C**, ensuring that the magazine is pushed firmly home until the magazine-release catch **D** locks;
> retract the charging handle **E** as far as it will go;
> push the selector to either front ('A', automatic) or middle ('R', single-shot) positions;
> take aim and squeeze the trigger **F**.

The gun will reload automatically. When the magazine is empty, the action closes on an empty chamber. When this happens:

> push the magazine-release catch **D** to release the empty magazine **B**;

> insert a new magazine, remembering to push it home until it locks;
> retract the charging handle **E**.

The gun is now cocked ready to fire. To clear the gun:

> press the magazine-release catch **D** and remove the magazine;
> retract the charging handle **E** to eject any chambered round;
> set the safety to 'R' and pull the trigger to close the breech, holding the charging handle to minimize the impact;
> reset the safety to 'S'.

The magazine can then be emptied and replaced.

Note: the selector levers of semi-automatic Sterling 'police carbines' have only 'S' and 'R' positions.

HOW TO FIRE THE IMI UZI SUBMACHINE-GUN

Starting with the gun empty, the selector **A** in its rearmost position at 'S' ('Safe') and the loaded magazine in the hand,

> insert the magazine **B** in the grip **C**, ensuring that the magazine is pushed firmly home until the magazine catch **D** locks;
> holding the Uzi by the pistol grip, pull the charging handle **E** back as far as it will go;
> push the selector to either front ('A', automatic) or middle ('R', single-shot) positions;
> take aim and squeeze the trigger **F**.

The gun will reload automatically. When the magazine is empty, the action closes on an empty chamber. When this happens:

> push the magazine-release catch **D** to release the empty magazine **B**;
> insert a new magazine, remembering to push it home until it locks;
> retract the charging handle **E**.

The gun is now cocked ready to fire. To clear the gun:

> press the magazine-release catch **D** and remove the magazine;
> retract the charging handle **E** to ensure that there is no chambered round;

> set the safety to 'S', locking the trigger, or
> set the safety to 'R' and pull the trigger to close the breech.

The magazine can then be emptied and replaced.

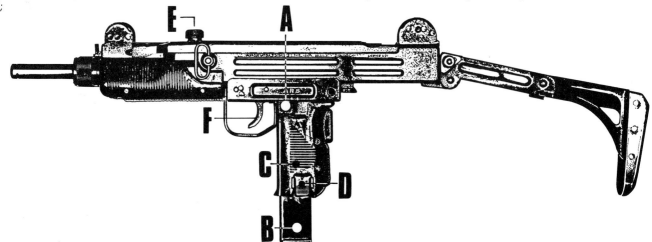

THE UZI

During the early 1950s, the Israeli Uziel ('Uzi') Gal perfected a submachine-gun by taking many ideas from Czech prototypes and adding ideas of his own. The Uzi submachine-gun uses an overhung bolt, running forward above the barrel to restrict overall length, while the magazine runs up through the grip. With the stock folded, the gun measures only 470mm – appreciably shorter than the majority of its contemporaries – and has performed efficiently under virtually all conditions. It was adopted by the Israeli forces, being made by Israeli Metal Industries (IMI) in Tel Aviv, and was subsequently licensed to Fabrique Nationale. The participation of such a well-known manufacturer in the Uzi programme brought greatly increased success and the Uzi has prospered, being widely adopted for police, paramilitary and special-purpose use.

The current variant, available in 9×19mm or .45 ACP, is a particularly 'safe' submachine-gun: in addition to the manual safety on the left side of the receiver above the grip, there is a grip safety and an additional ratchet to prevent the bolt flying shut if the firer's hand slips during cocking. A shortened variant known as the Mini-Uzi, just 360mm long, will also be encountered, together with semi-automatic 'civilian' carbine derivatives, and even a genuine fully-automatic pistol derivation known as the Micro-Uzi. Without its folding stock, the Micro-Uzi measures just 250mm overall and weighs 1.95kg with an empty magazine.

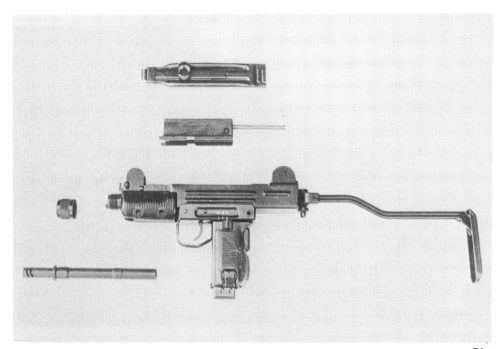

74. The Mini-Uzi in 9mm Parabellum. Courtesy of Israeli Metal Industries.

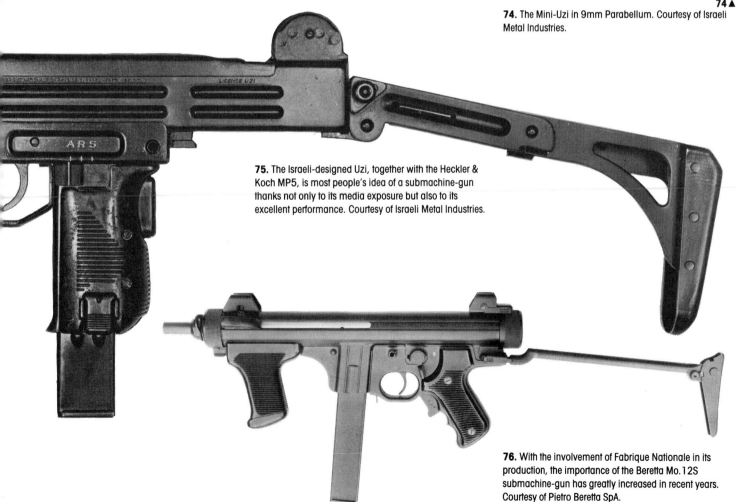

75. The Israeli-designed Uzi, together with the Heckler & Koch MP5, is most people's idea of a submachine-gun thanks not only to its media exposure but also to its excellent performance. Courtesy of Israeli Metal Industries.

76. With the involvement of Fabrique Nationale in its production, the importance of the Beretta Mo.12S submachine-gun has greatly increased in recent years. Courtesy of Pietro Beretta SpA.

Fig. 14. A general arrangement drawing of the Beretta
PM12S. Courtesy of Pietro Beretta SpA.

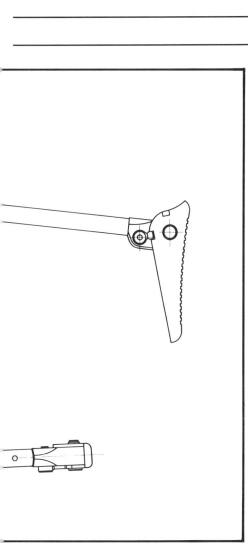

THE BERETTA Mo.12S

When Fabrique Nationale acquired a substantial interest in Beretta, production of the Belgian-made Uzi ceased in favour of the Italian Modelo 12, developed by Domenico Salza into a comfortable, well-made and reliable tool. But the spectacular success of the Uzi (and the limited market for sub-machine-guns) has restricted the FN-Beretta Modelo 12S to a few small armies, a handful of police forces, and special units such as the Italian Nucleo Operativo Centrale di Sicurezza (NOCS). Like the Uzi, the Mo.12S makes use of an overhung bolt, which greatly reduces its overall length; unlike the Uzi, at the time of writing, no attempts have been made to produce micro-light derivatives.

77. The Beretta Mo.12S has proved popular with special forces throughout the world. Here it is being carried by members of the élite Italian GIS (Carabinieri) CTW team. Note the distinctive fore-grip on the nearest gun, containing an aiming projector. Courtesy of Pietro Beretta SpA.

78. Beretta submachine-guns carried by the Italian NOCS counter-terrorist group. Courtesy of Pietro Beretta SpA.

THE HECKLER & KOCH MP5

The most popular of the current sub-machine-guns is the Heckler & Koch HK54, a 9mm gun adopted by the Bundeswehr as the Maschinenpistole 5 (MP5, the name by which it is best known). The MP5 has largely replaced the Walther MPK and MPL used by West German police during the counter-attack after the 1972 Munich Olympic Games tragedy. The MP5 may be seen in the hands of special forces from Britain – the SAS used them for the first time during the Iranian Embassy siege in 1980, and they are issued to police guarding important terrorist targets such as airports. They are also popular in Germany (with GSG-9), Italy (NOCS) and the USA.

79, 80. The Walther MP-L (**79**) and MP-K (**80**) were favoured by the German special forces and CTW units prior to the perfection of the rival Heckler & Koch HK54. The Walthers were in evidence during the 1972 counter-attack on the Black September faction after the Munich Olympic Games atrocity. Courtesy of Carl Walther GmbH.

81, 82. A standard MP5A4 (**81**) and a partially dismantled model (**82**). Courtesy of Heckler & Koch GmbH.

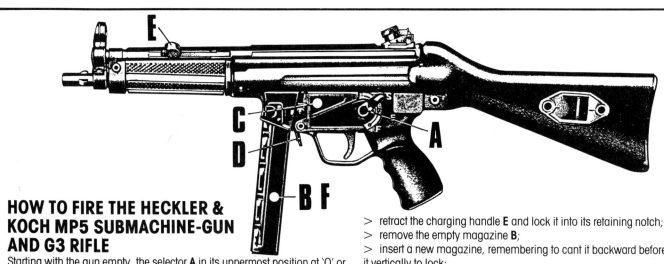

HOW TO FIRE THE HECKLER & KOCH MP5 SUBMACHINE-GUN AND G3 RIFLE

Starting with the gun empty, the selector **A** in its uppermost position at 'O' or 'S' ('Safe') and the loaded magazine in the hand,

> holding the rifle by the pistol grip, pull the charging handle **E** (above the barrel) back as far as it will go and lock it into its retaining notch;
> insert the magazine **B** in the receiver **C** ahead of the trigger guard, ensuring that the magazine is canted slightly forward. Swing the magazine back and up into its housing, pushing it firmly home until the magazine-release catch **D** locks;
> release the charging handle **E**, and the breechblock will run forward under spring pressure;
> rotate the selector down to its mid position ('1' or 'E', single shot) or the lowest position ('20' or 'F', automatic) positions, take aim and squeeze the trigger **F**.

The gun will reload automatically. When the magazine is empty, there being no hold-open:

> retract the charging handle **E** and lock it into its retaining notch;
> remove the empty magazine **B**;
> insert a new magazine, remembering to cant it backward before turning it vertically to lock;
> release the charging handle **E**.

This allows the breech to close, chambering a round, and the gun is cocked ready to fire. To clear the gun:

> set the safety catch to its upper (safe) position;
> retract the charging handle **E** and lock it in its retaining notch;
> remove the magazine **B**;
> release the charging handle **E**.

The magazine can then be emptied and replaced.
Note: the G41 is similar to the G3, but has an auxiliary or 'silent' bolt closure device on the right side of the receiver. Many of the latest MP5 submachine-guns and G41 rifles have modified selectors marked with a selection of bullets. The catch-lever is rotated so that a white line on its base aligns with a white bullet (safe), a single red bullet (single-shot), three red bullets (burst-fire) or seven red bullets (automatic fire).

81▲   82▼

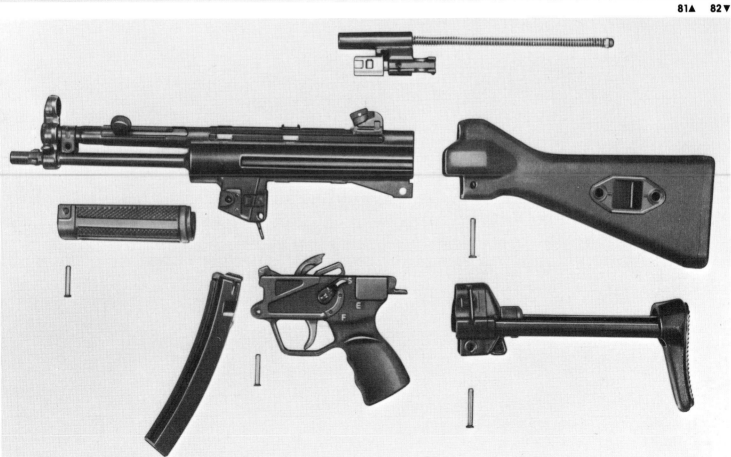

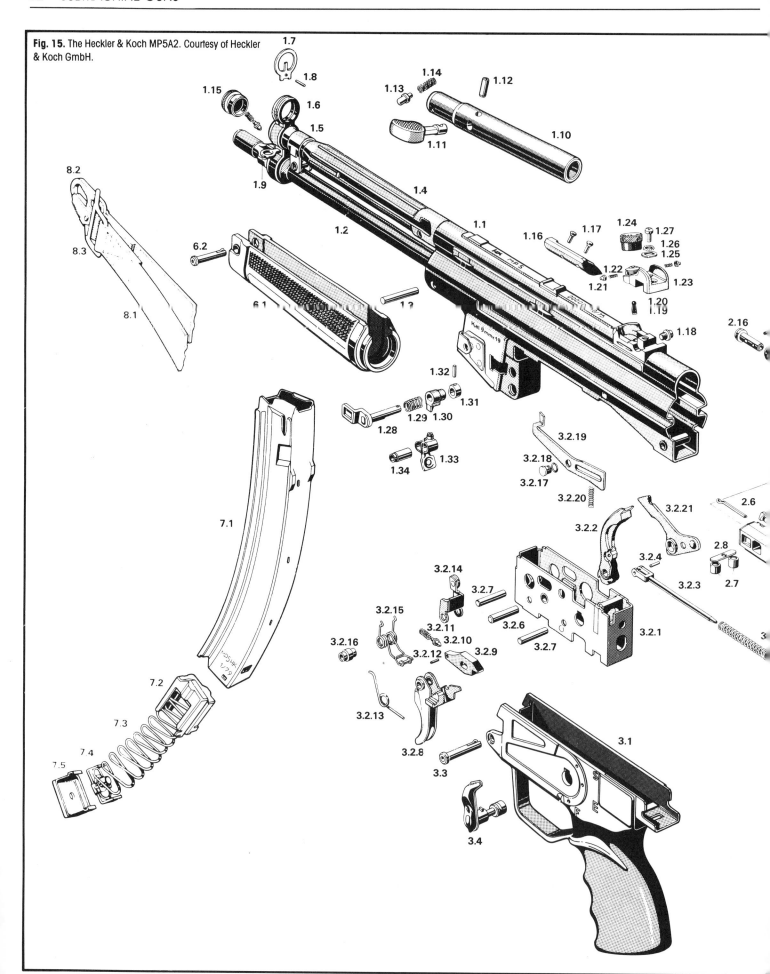

Fig. 15. The Heckler & Koch MP5A2. Courtesy of Heckler & Koch GmbH.

Assembly Group 1 Receiver with barrel

1.1 Receiver
1.2 Barrel
1.3 Dowel pin
1.4 Cocking lever housing
1.5 Retaining clip with bush
1.6 Front sight holder
1.7 Front sight
1.8 Clamping sleeve
1.9 Eyebolt
1.10 Cocking lever support with collar
1.11 Cocking lever
1.12 Axle for cocking lever
1.13 Catch bolt
1.14 Spring for catch bolt
1.15 Cap
1.16 Cartridge case deflector
1.17 Rivet for cartridge case deflector
1.18 Adjusting screw
1.19 Compression spring
1.20 Ball

1.21 Catch bolt
1.22 Spring for catch bolt
1.23 Rear sight support
1.24 Rear sight cylinder
1.25 Washer
1.26 Toothed lock washer
1.27 Clamping screw
1.28 Magazine catch
1.29 Spring for magazine catch
1.30 Contact piece
1.31 Push button
1.32 Clamping sleeve
1.33 Magazine release lever
1.34 Bush for magazine release lever

Assembly Group 2 Bolt

2.1 Bolt head carrier
2.2 Stop pin
2.3 Clamping sleeve
2.4 Bolt head
2.5 Extractor
2.6 Extractor spring
2.7 Locking rollers
2.8 Holder for locking rollers
2.9 Clamping sleeve
2.10 Locking piece
2.11 Firing pin spring
2.12 Firing pin
2.13 Recoil spring
2.14 Recoil spring guide rod
2.15 Guide ring for recoil spring
2.16 Stop pin for recoil spring
2.17 Riveting pin

Assembly Group 3 Pistol Grip with Trigger/Safety Mechanism

3.1 Pistol grip
3.2 Trigger housing, assembled (without illustration)
3.3 Locking pin for pistol grip
3.4 Selector lever

Assembly Group 3.2 Trigger Housing

3.2.1. Trigger housing
3.2.2. Hammer
3.2.3. Pressure shank for hammer
3.2.4. Riveting pin for pressure shank
3.2.5. Compression spring for hammer
3.2.6. Axle for hammer
3.2.7. Axle for trigger and catch
3.2.8. Trigger
3.2.9. Sear
3.2.10 Trigger bolt
3.2.11 Spring for trigger bolt
3.2.12 Clamping sleeve
3.2.13 Elbow spring for trigger
3.2.14 Catch
3.2.15 Elbow spring with roller for catch
3.2.16 Distance sleeve
3.2.17 Axle for ejector
3.2.18 Spring ring
3.2.19 Ejector
3.2.20 Ejector spring
3.2.21 Release lever

Assembly Group 4 Fixed Butt stock

4.1 Butt stock
4.2 Back plate
4.3 Locking pin for butt stock

Assembly Group 6 Handguard

6.1 Handguard
6.2 Locking pin for handguard

Assembly Group 7 Magazine

7.1 Magazine housing
7.2 Follower
7.3 Follower spring
7.4 Spring floor plate
7.5 Magazine floor plate

Assembly Group 8 Multi-purpose carrying sling

8.1 Carrying sling
8.2 Carbine hook
8.3 Double eye
8.4 Buckle
8.5 Spring hook

▲83

▲84

▲85

86▲

83–8. The incredible versatility of the H&K MP5: a short MP5A3 (**83**); a miniature MP5KA4 (**84**); a silenced MP5 SD5 (**85**); a commercial HK53 fitted with an aiming projector (**86**); an MP5 with an optical sight (**87**) and a Zeiss Orion 80 image-intensifier (**88**). Courtesy of Heckler & Koch GmbH.

◄ 87

88 ▲

▲89

Unlike most submachine-guns, which fire from an open breech (scarcely conducive to accuracy), the Heckler & Koch features a scaled-down roller-lock delay system adapted from the G3 rifle. This supports the cartridge case until the bullet has all but left the barrel, and accuracy is greatly enhanced as a result of firing from a closed bolt. The MP5 is reasonably heavy, too, and has a reputation for excellent single-shot performance. In addition, the MP5 has far better open sights than most submachine-guns in which crudity is almost obligatory. This facilitates accurate shooting in a way that is all but impossible with a pistol, minimizing hits on wrong targets – with potentially damaging political connotations in the event of urban terrorism. Experiments with various kinds of 9mm projectile have improved lethality, too. Teflon-coated man-stoppers and even special SFM-made 'Très Haute Vélocité' (THV, extra-high velocity) bullets are available when required.

The MP5 can also be fitted with optical sights, image intensifiers, infra-red sights and aiming projectors in pursuit of operational flexibility. The success of the design has permitted a constant updating programme, the latest products of which include improved construction, burst-firing capabilities and better handling characteristics. Three highly effective silenced variants can be obtained, together with ultra-short guns which can be carried in a holster.

THE INGRAM

The success of the MP5 has rather eclipsed the Ingram Model 10, which, for much of the early 1970s, looked as though it would achieve universal approval. Developed by Gordon B. Ingram, the short-barrel 9mm Parabellum gun measures a mere 269mm overall with the stock retracted and weighs

only 3.46kg with its loaded 32-round magazine. Unfortunately, the Military Armament Corporation (MAC), the original promoter, was liquidated in 1976 and interest in the Ingram lapsed until SWD Inc. of Atlanta, Georgia, became involved. Now known as the 'Cobray', the Model 10 has proved popular in South America, and also among American police SWAT teams. Ingrams were carried by the Israeli 259 Commandos on Operation 'Thunderball', the raid on Entebbe airport in 1976, where their compact design – smaller even than the Uzi – was beneficial in the cramped confines of the raiders' aircraft. Small quantities were even bought by the British in the 1970s, principally for the SAS, but were too inaccurate to protect bystanders – vitally important in raids such as that undertaken by GSG-9, with SAS advisers, on the Lufthansa jet hijacked to Mogadishu in 1977. By 1980, the SAS had replaced the Ingram with the Heckler & Koch MP5.

SILENCED SUBMACHINE-GUNS

Silenced submachine-guns have been popular since the Second world War, when they were used by Commandos, SAS, OSS and SOE. In 1942, the OSS ordered 1,000 .45 ACP M3 submachine-guns from High-Standard, fitted with Bell Laboratories silencers. Surviving guns were issued to selected American airborne personnel on D-Day in June 1944. Ironically, a copy of the OSS silenced M3 in 9mm Parabellum (the Chinese Type 37) was used by North Vietnamese regular troops in night raids, intent on silencing US and ARVN guards before attacks began.

The OSS silenced M3 was not particularly popular, the men preferring the British Sten Mk 2S which had been proven on commando and special forces missions. The silenced Sten gun was replaced by the silenced Sterling, which is still in British

89, 90. Whispering Death: two silenced submachine-guns. A thousand silenced .45 ACP M3 submachine-guns were made for the Office of Strategic Services (OSS) by High-Standard in 1942, some serving until the modified Swedish m/45B 'Carl Custav' (**90**) was issued to the CIA in the late 1960s. The Ingram Model 10 (**89**) is currently available. The minuscule proportions of the Ingram can be visualized by subtracting the silencer and retracting the stock. Courtesy of Ian Hogg.

service. However, the L34A1 is appreciably longer than the silenced MP5 and is generally restricted to regular personnel. The CIA reputedly used a silenced version of the Swedish-made Carl Gustav (KP m/45B) in the 1960s, when efficient silenced submachine-guns were in comparatively short supply. This, too, was a conventional and comparatively clumsy gun. The design of the Heckler & Koch MP5 SD1, however, benefits from the compact bolt system and also from the integral fore-end/silencer casing. The Ingram Model 10 may also be encountered with a 'noise suppresser' attached to the muzzle, but this adds about 545 grams to the laden weight as well as almost doubling overall length.

It has been estimated that a silencer suppresses about three-quarters of operational noise, and that the firing report is

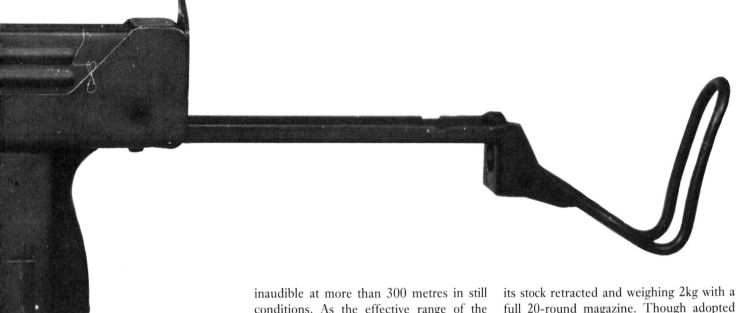

inaudible at more than 300 metres in still conditions. As the effective range of the 9mm Parabellum or .45 ACP cartridges is appreciably less than this, however, the value of silenced submachine-guns has been widely questioned.

MACHINE PISTOLS

In addition to conventional submachine-guns, there have been a number of true 'machine pistols'. The best known is the Czech vz/61 Skorpion, basically little more than an enlarged blowback pistol firing the 7.65mm Browning cartridge, with a retractable skeletal shoulder stock and a lengthened box magazine. The vz/61 is very small indeed, measuring just 269mm overall with

its stock retracted and weighing 2kg with a full 20-round magazine. Though adopted by the Czech army and internal security forces – and evident during the Prague riots in August 1969 – the ineffectual 7.65mm cartridge restricts its utility. Consequently, variants have been made for the 9mm Short, the 9mm Makarov and the 9mm Parabellum (vz/63, vz/64 and vz/68 respectively). It has also been made under licence in Yugoslavia.

The Polish wz/63 shares a similar concept. Though comparatively uncommon in the West, the efficient little wz/63 offers a good combination of firepower with the size of a large pistol and is being encountered in increasing numbers in aircraft hijacking. One was even used to gun down Shlomo Argov, the Israeli Ambassador in London, in 1982. The most distinctive feature of the

90▼

wz/63 is the long compensator at the muzzle and the folding forward handgrip.

The success of the vz/61 Scorpion and the Ingram Model 10, particularly, encouraged other manufacturers to reduce their submachine-guns to the dimensions of a large pistol. The Micro-Uzi is a 'one-hand' version of the popular Israeli submachine-gun, whilst the Sterling Mk 7 Para-Pistol was a much shortened version of the standard Mk 4 (L2A3) with barrels of 3in or 8in and a shortened receiver. Though the Mk 7 was abandoned with the demise of Sterling, the remains of which were sold to Royal Ordnance in 1988, a similar gun is now being made by FAMAE in Chile.

A plausible alternative to the minimal submachine-gun is the truly automatic pistol, very few of which have ever been successful despite pedigree stretching back by way of the Mauser-Schnellfeuerpistole and its Spanish copies to a Borchardt of 1893. The problem has simply been that cyclic rates as high as a thousand rounds per minute are valueless in light pistols,

which climb too quickly. Though designers have added shoulder stocks, supplementary hand grips, and burst-limiters (generally restricted to three rounds), few have been able to solve the inherent instability.

Among the best of the contenders is the Beretta 93R, which has been purchased in small quantities by the Italian NOCS and Carabineri. It is only marginally larger than the standard Model 92SB pistol, about 240mm overall and weighing merely 1,170gm with an empty 20-round magazine. The 93R has a multi-port muzzle-brake and a selector above the left grip, marked ● for single shots and ❀ for three-shot bursts. An auxiliary hand-grip pivots downward ahead of the enlarged trigger guard, whilst an extending shoulder stock can be supplied to order.

The pistol is just about light enough for effectual one-handed use, but its special features are only beneficial during burst fire; ideally, the fore-grip is folded down and grasped with the fingers of the non-firing hand, the thumb of which can

then be hooked around the front of the elongated trigger guard. Thus the muzzle can be held down during firing, to counteract the tendency to climb.

The future of classical submachine-guns remains uncertain. Though phenomenal numbers of the Heckler & Koch MP5 have been sold around the world, to military and police forces alike, there has been a perceptible move towards compact versions of assault rifles such as the AK and AKM. This has been most evident in Soviet-bloc and similarly aligned countries. These guns, however, unlike the MP5 or the 9mm AUG,

91. A need to master the other side's weapons is often paramount. Here, men of the US Special Forces, training in Puerto Rico, display Type 43 submachine-guns taken from the Communist Chinese and K-50M patterns captured from the Viet Cong. Courtesy of the Department of the Army, Washington DC.

92. Made under licence by Zavodi Crvena Zastava in Kragujevač, the M61J is a variant of the Czech vz.61 Skorpion machine pistol. Chambered for the 7.65mm Short cartridge (.32 ACP), the gun is under-powered but easily controlled. Courtesy of Ian Hogg.

still offer virtually the same power as an assault rifle (q.v.).

A few ultra-compact patterns are still available, though the once-popular Ingram has lost much of its reputation to the MP5; this has not been helped by a chequered production history. Currently entrusted to the SWD Corporation and renamed the 'Cobray', the Ingram may be chambered for 9mm Short ammunition (as the 'Model 11') or 9mm Parabellum (Model 11/9).

Particularly interesting in this class is the Steyr Tactical Machine Pistol of 1988, which owes something to the abortive Pi-18, the Steyr-Hahn pistol of 1911, and the AUG. The TMP, made largely of synthetic material, has the appearance of a large pistol—excepting that the magazine protrudes beneath the butt and a folding hand-grip will be found under the fore-end.

The Spectre M-4, developed in Italy by Sites SpA, was introduced publicly in 1984 and has since attracted the attention of many security agencies. The most unusual feature is a double-action trigger system, which allows the gun to be carried with the chamber loaded and the hammer dropped against its stop by a de-cocking system. The Spectre can then be fired simply by pulling through on the trigger. A unique 50-round quadruple-column magazine has also attracted favourable attention.

An alternative approach to the problem of providing suitable intermediate weapons has been made by FN with the 5.7mm P-90. This interesting selective-fire design fires a cartridge generating power about mid-way between 9mm Parabellum and 5.56 × 45mm, allowing a blowback action to be used in safety.

The P-90 is also remarkable for its novel, futuristic appearance. Though created to arm soldiers serving well away from the combat line, the P-90 is being hailed by some authorities as a means to fulfil additional special-purpose tasks.

93. The Beretta Mo. 93R, issued to the Italian Carabinieri and 'internal security' (CTW) units, is one of the few pistols to successfully embody a burst-firing capability. The enlarged trigger-guard and folding fore-grip, together with muzzle brake, enhance controllability. The selector, marked ● and ⁞●, lies on the left side of the frame directly above the grip. Courtesy of Pietro Beretta SpA, Gardone.

94. A different approach to machine-pistol design: the 9mm submachine-gun derivative of the Steyr AUG features an ultra-short barrel, with a diagonally-slotted compensator, but is otherwise the same as the AUG rifle. This capitalizes on user-familiarity. The most obvious feature is the narrow magazine in its auxiliary housing. Courtesy of Steyr-Daimler-Puch AG, Steyr.

Rifles

The supersession of the bolt-action infantry rifle by the 'assault rifle', pioneered by the Germans towards the end of the Second World War and then developed in the USSR in the late 1940s, has allowed a handful of manufacturers to monopolise production.

This has also ensured that only a handful of designs have achieved significant distribution. These are not always the best, but sometimes simply those made by manufacturers with sufficient power to influence the decision-taking process. And, whilst accepting that this is not inevitably malign, there are occasional rumours of favours being bought at the highest level.

There have been many examples in the history of firearms where weapons have been adopted more because they were indigenous products than because they were especially effectual. Prior to 1945, virtually no self-respecting military power would have adopted foreign-made infantry weapons; to do so was often seen as a blow to national pride. Consequently, the French adopted a series of sub-standard weapons prior to the Second World War—some of the machine-guns, in particular, were very poor—whilst Italian and Japanese small arms were often equally deficient.

The British SMLE rifle was castigated on its adoption in 1903 by those who favoured Mauser-type actions; protracted combat experience in the First World War eventually rehabilitated the short Lee-Enfield, but only after a decade of abuse. The US Garand rifle was also the subject of hostile propaganda. The British, for example, were soon claiming that it would not have passed their mud and dust tests.

These traits are still evident; the French have adopted the 5.56mm FA MAS, which some commentators have claimed to

95. A Polish soldier, equipped with a gas-mask and a folding-butt AKMS, clears an obstacle during a Warsaw Pact training exercise. Courtesy of the Polish State Photographic Agency, Warsaw.

operate only just within the margins of safety, whilst the British have spent large sums of money in developing the 5.56mm L85A1 rifle that is still by no means universally accepted as a success . . . even after twenty years of development.

By far the most successful of all the assault rifles, judged by distribution, has been the Kalashnikov. Like many Soviet-designed small arms, the AK and its derivatives are essentially simple. They are effectual enough to have persuaded many countries outside the former Soviet bloc—e.g., Finland, India, Israel and South Africa—to modify the Kalashnikov action in detail before beginning production of their own.

The Kalashnikov rifle has been the traditional weapon of the freedom fighter for many years, particularly men whose leftward-leaning political views had been nurtured by the USSR or China. Hopes have now waned that fragmentation of the Soviet bloc and the redrawn political map would influence control on the distribution not only of Kalashnikovs but also much more effectual weaponry. Reductions in the military establishments of Eastern Europe have created a vast pool of surplus weapons that can be bought for hard currency at ridiculously low rates.

Recently, the Russians unveiled a new assault rifle designated ASM, formerly known as the 'Abakan' after the bureau in which it had been developed. Said to have been designed by Gennadiy Nikonov, and to have won a protracted competition extending over two years, the ASM embodies a currently unidentified form of delayed blowback (the Russians have referred to it as 'shifted pulse operation'). It chambers the standard 5.45 × 39mm M74 cartridge, measures 945mm overall and weighs about 3.85kg, apparently without the thirty-round magazine.

One major difference between the ASM and the AK-74 is the positioning of the selector lever on the left side of the breech, where it can be operated with the thumb of the firing hand. Options include single-shot fire, two-round 'doubles', or fully automatic operation. When set to function continuously, the ASM fires two rounds at about 1,800rpm and the remainder at 600. But whether it will ultimately replace the AK series is still an open question.

THE KALASHNIKOV

Many Western observers have damned this rifle as clumsy, obsolescent, and firing a poor-performance cartridge. From the purely technical standpoint, the criticism has some validity: the 7.62 × 39mm M43 bullet loses velocity quickly, and its high, looping trajectory magnifies range-gauging errors in a way that contrasts poorly with the comparatively flat-shooting 5.56mm round preferred by NATO.

However, the Kalashnikov is simple, solid, very reliable and, particularly when fitted with the latest muzzle brake, quite effective when firing automatically. Though it undoubtedly benefited from issue throughout the Soviet bloc, to the exclusion of native designs other than the Czech vz/58, the AK has operated effectually in arctic cold, desert heat, constant drought and tropical rain forest alike. In addition, it is as accurate as the standard M16 in the hands of average shots, though marksmen invariably extract better results from the latter at longer ranges.

The rifle was designed by Mikhail Kalashnikov in 1944–5 to handle the intermediate cartridge credited to Elizarov and Semin, but apparently influenced by captured examples of the German 7.9mm Kurz. The competition to design the 'Avtomat', or assault rifle, produced two viable projects—Kalashnikov's, and the Simonov competitor that was to become the SKS of 1949.

The Kalashnikov offered the best long-term prospect, but it is believed that the Simonov rifle, a comparatively conventional diminution of the existing PTRS anti-tank rifle, was ordered into immediate production as a safeguard against failure of the more radical concept. Though the SKS carbine only equipped the Soviet Army for a short period, it provided the basis for many guns produced in later years in China and Yugoslavia.

The AK was introduced in 1949. Its layout clearly owed something to the MP.43, but appreciably less use was made of stampings.

Propellant gas is tapped at the mid-point of the bore to strike a piston attached to the bolt carrier, driving the piston/bolt carrier backward and rotating the bolt out of engagement. The assembly retreats behind the magazine well, riding over and cocking the hammer, and then returns under the influence of the spring to strip a new round into the chamber. The AK is easy to strip for cleaning or inspection—unlike many rival designs—and has been made in many Soviet bloc countries.

The original AK, chambering the 7.62 × 39mm M43 intermediate round, measures 869mm (34.2in) overall, has a barrel of 414mm (16.3in), and weighs about 11.3lb (5.12kg) with a loaded 30-round magazine. Bore diameter varies between 0.298in and 0.301in (7.57–7.65mm), the groove diameter measures 0.311–0.314in (7.90–7.98mm), and the bullet has a diameter of 0.310in (7.87in). The rifling is four-groove right-hand twist, making one turn in about 260mm (10.2in). Muzzle velocity is 710mps (2,330fps), giving a maximum effective range of 350–400 metres. The cyclic rate of the AK, when firing fully automatically, is about 800rpm.

The AKM was introduced in 1959, once lessons had been learned from construction

96. The semi-automatic SKS carbine was developed concurrently with the Kalashnikov, its conventional design providing a safeguard against failure of the AK. The SKS served the Soviet army for some years, and is still often carried on ceremonial duties. It proved to be particularly popular in the People's Republic of China, where many million 'Type 56' and '56-1' rifles were made. Courtesy of Ian Hogg.

of the original gun and Soviet industry had mastered new production techniques. The most obvious difference concerns the receiver. The U-shape pressing permitted a considerable reduction in weight compared with the earlier machined forging, though the lightened gun is more difficult to control when firing automatically. A rate-reducer in the trigger mechanism holds back the hammer after the bolt-carrier has depressed the safety sear, relying on the inertia of the hammer to slow fire. But whether it has any real effect or simply adds complexity to an otherwise unusually simple design seems questionable. Some experts consider it to be no more than an additional mechanical safety.

Though much the same length as its predecessor, judicious use of stampings, pressing and welding reduces the weight of the AKM to 8.93lb (4.05kg) unladen compared with 9.48lb (4.30kg) for the AK. Amongst the major constructional changes are the additional rate-reducer, a stamped receiver with riveted-in bolt-lock recesses, and a stamped receiver cover with prominent lateral ribs. In addition, the gas-piston tube of the AKM has semi-circular vents behind the gas-port assembly instead of the eight circular holes (four on each side) found on the AK; the bolt carrier is parkerized instead of bright- or chromed steel; and the butt and fore-end are generally laminated wood. Pistol grips are usually made of wood on the AK, but are injection-moulded plastic on the AKM.

Soon after the first AKMs had been introduced, a short compensator was added to the muzzle to prevent the gun climbing to the right when firing automatically. Bayonet fittings are also present on AKM rifles, but only on some AKs.

HOW TO FIRE THE AVTOMAT KALASHNIKOVA

Starting with the gun empty, the selector **A** pushed up as far as it will go, and a loaded magazine in the hand,

> insert the magazine **B** in the receiver **C** ahead of the trigger guard, ensuring that the magazine is canted slightly forward. Swing the magazine back and up into its housing, pushing it firmly home until the magazine-release catch **D** locks; **rotate A down to the fire position.**

> holding the rifle by the pistol grip, pull the charging handle **E** back as far as it will go;

> release the charging handle **E** and the bolt and bolt carrier will run forward under spring pressure, but do not hold the handle during its travel;

> rotate the selector to either its mid (automatic) or lowest (single-shot) positions;

> take cim and squeeze the trigger **F**.

The gun will reload automatically. When the magazine is empty, the action closes on an empty chamber. When this happens:

> push the magazine-release catch **D** to release the empty magazine **B**;

> insert a new magazine, remembering to cant it backward before turning it vertically to lock;

> retract and release the charging handle **E**.

This allows the breech to close, chambering a round, and the gun is cocked ready to fire. To clear the gun:

> press the magazine-release catch **D** and remove the magazine;

> retract the charging handle **E** to eject the chambered round;

> replace the selector lever in its uppermost (safe) position.

The magazine can then be emptied and replaced.

Note: there are many variants of the Kalashnikov, and their selector markings differ greatly. The most common are the Russian guns, marked 'AB' for automatic fire and 'ОД' for single shot. Most of the Kalashnikovs made in Yugoslavia have hold-open systems to retain the bolt-carrier after the last round has been fired and extracted. The similar Israeli Galil and its derivatives, which are based on the Kalashnikov, have an entirely different selector lever on the left side of the receiver above the pistol grip. Somewhat unnaturally, this moves forward to the safe position.

97. This group of Soviet marines displays a selection of guards badges, parachutists insignia, and AKMS rifles. Courtesy of Ian Hogg.

The 7.62mm AK and AKM, and their folding-stock 'paratroop' derivatives (AKS and AKMS), were supplemented by the AK-74 in the mid 1970s. Mechanically, this rifle is identical with the AKM, but fires a 5.45mm cartridge and has a cylindrical muzzle-brake/compensator precluding use of the standard bayonet. The origins of the AK-74 appear to lie in the success of the M16/5.56mm M193 cartridge combination, many of which were captured in Vietnam and extensively tested in the USSR. The Russian 5.45mm cartridge is virtually a reduced-calibre derivative of the 7.62mm pattern, but has an odd two-piece bullet with a hollow tip within the jacket—presumably, an attempt to improve lethality by allowing the tip to deform when striking the target. The compromise is still less effectual than the M193.

The AK-74—chambered for the rimless 5.45 × 39mm M74 cartridge—has a 400mm (15.7in) barrel, but the large muzzle-brake/compensator gives the gun an overall length of 928mm (36.5in). Weight remains much the same as the AKM, though the magazines are slightly lighter. Longitudinal grooves are cut into both sides of the butt to identify the calibre in the dark. The AK-74 is occasionally seen with 40-round plastic-body magazines, shared with the RPK-74 light machine-gun.

The AK-74M was approved in the 1980s to overcome some of the weaknesses of the AK series in comparison with Western equipment. First among these was the lack of an optical-sight mounting rail; though some AKM and AK-74 rifles had been converted for special purposes, the Soviet military authorities demanded that all new guns should be suitably fitted. In addition to a rail on the left side of the receiver, therefore, the AK-74M has an improved muzzle brake, a new design of plastic furniture, and a better knife bayonet. The butt hinges to the left.

The Soviet authorities have also developed shortened versions of the AK series, reducing the dimensions to those of a large submachine-gun. The AKS-74U, introduced in 1979, has a folding stock and a 200mm barrel. This reduces its overall length to 420mm with the stock folded, or 675mm with it extended. The standard tangent-leaf back sight has been replaced with a two-position rocking sight contained in a special housing on the receiver cover above the ejection port, and the muzzle

brake has been refined. The SU variant has been used by internal security forces, marine commandos, Spetsnaz, armoured vehicle crews and similar units to which compact dimensions are useful. A 7.62mm 'U' version of the AKMS has also been seen, but it is assumed that production was comparatively small—possibly an expedient whilst the AKS-74U was being perfected.

Though the Kalashnikov rifle has been widely used by Soviet-bloc special forces, it is insufficiently powerful for snipers' use and the SVD (Dragunov) was developed instead. As far as Western special forces are concerned, the AK and AKM are still the rifles most commonly encountered in the hands of terrorists, guerrillas and freedom fighters.

The ready availability of captured Soviet bloc weapons in the West has even enabled exercises such as 'Fortress Gale' (USA, 1979) or Operation 'Brave Defender' (Britain, 1985) to be undertaken with genuine equipment to familiarize Allied forces with guns that may be needed in an emergency.

SOVIET-BLOC KALASHNIKOVS

Something exceeding sixty million guns have been made in the last forty years, many differing models emanating from the USSR, the People's Republic of China, Poland, Romania, Hungary, the German Democratic Republic, Yugoslavia and other Soviet bloc countries.

Bulgarian AK rifles appear to have been supplied by Poland before indigenous production began. Standard, apart from the omission of the bayonet lug and the cleaning rod, they have selectors marked 'E' and 'AB' (early) or 'O' and 'J' (late) for single-shot and automatic fire respectively.

The People's Republic of China has made several minor variants of the AK and AKM rifles under the designation Type 56 (fixed butt) and Type 56-1 (folding butt). Though the Kalashnikov was once believed to have been superseded by the indigenous Type 68 rifle and its variants, the latter is

98. A typical Soviet 5.45mm AK-74, the Warsaw Pact's equivalent of the M16. Courtesy of Ian Hogg.

99. Easily identified by the stippled finish to the synthetic butt and pistol grip, this 7.62mm MPiKM was made in the German Democratic Republic. Pattern Room Collection, Royal Ordnance plc, Nottingham.

100. Soviet marines carrying 5.45mm AK-74 rifles march past the podium during the annual celebration of the Russian Revolution; Red Square, Moscow, November 1979. Courtesy of Ian Hogg.

now known to have been developed specifically for the People's Militia; the AKM remains the Chinese service rifle.

The original AK-type Chinese Type 56 rifles have very distinctive all-metal bayonets, permanently attached to the muzzle, pivoting back under the barrel when not in use. The front sight hood is a short cylinder pierced by a hole on the top surface, and the folding stock, of the Type 56-1 has two large rivets on each strut. The selector is marked 單 and 连 (early) or 'L' and 'D' (late/'export') for single shot and automatic fire. The Type 56-2 is a copy of the AKM, distinguished by a laterally folding stock with a red plastic cheek piece. Chinese 'Model 22' Kalashnikovs are still being made for export in 7.62 × 39mm, 5.45 × 39mm or 5.56 × 45mm.

In the Czech Republic, a modified AK-74 awaits a decision on its future. Developed by Jiri Kleček and a design team in the Uherský Brod factory, the LADA series includes a submachine-gun, an assault rifle and a light support weapon based around a common group of components. The guns were originally developed for the Soviet 5.45 × 39mm cartridge, but have now been re-engineered for 5.56 × 45mm. Their future is currently uncertain, though the attraction of export orders could change the situation appreciably.

Prior to recent reunification with West Germany, the German Democratic Republic made the AK as the 'Maschinenpistole Kalashnikow' (MPiK). The gun has a wooden butt, fore-end and handguard, but lacks the cleaning rod and butt-trap for cleaning equipment. The MPiKS is similar, but has a folding butt with plain struts. All German Kalashnikov rifles have selectors displaying 'E' (for Einzelfeuer, 'single-shot fire') and 'D' (Dauerfeuer, 'continuous fire').

The MPiKM, the East German variant of the AKM, was originally made with wood stocks; however, newer guns have a plastic handguard, a wood fore-end and a blue-grey plastic butt with a distinctively stippled finish. The MPiKM-72 has an odd skeletal folding stock, whilst a 5.6mm rimfire AK-type trainer is also encountered.

Egypt makes a variant of the AKM, called the 'Misr', in a factory built with Russian aid whilst the two countries had strong diplomatic ties. The Egyptian AKM has a laminated wood butt and fore-end, together with a chequered plastic pistol grip. Its selector markings are in Arabic, though export versions may be marked 'A' and 'R' for automatic and single-shot fire respectively.

Hungarian troops have used indigenous Géppisztoly-K, similar to the Russian AK excepting for selectors marked '1' and '∞' (for single shot and automatic fire respectively). The guns have cleaning rods, but lack the bayonet lug. Derived from the Russian AKM, the Géppisztoly-KM 63 has a unique metal fore-end, formed integrally with the receiver, and an additional fore pistol-grip. The butt was originally wood, but the pistol grips (and replacement/late issue butts) are greyish or dark-green polypropylene. A short version of the KM 63, the MD 65, has a simple tubular stock which folds to the right, a short barrel and a distinctive double-port muzzle-brake/compensator. Selectors are marked '1' and '∞'. Some guns have been converted for

101. The Hungarian 7.62mm AMD-65 was a radical remodelling of the basic Kalashnikov, with a modified fore-end, an additional fore-grip, and a tubular steel butt. Courtesy of Ian Hogg.

grenade-firing, with a muzzle-mounted launcher, a special optical sight carried high above the receiver on a mounting-plate, and a shock-absorber in the tubular butt.

The Hungarians have also made a version of the AK-74 chambered for the 5.56 × 45mm cartridge in the hope of obtaining export orders. Production of this weapon, known as the Géppisztoly-NGM, stopped about 1989 and does not seem to have recommenced.

The North Korean Kalashnikov copies include the Type 58, a standard AK, and a variant of the AKM (called the Type 68)

without the rate reducer. A folding-stock variant of the Type 68 has a slotted stock-strut and a laminated wood pistol grip. The fore-end is smooth instead of the beavertail Russian AKM type. Korean guns display ᄄᄂ (single shot) and ᄍ (automatic) on their selectors.

Usually known as the Pistolet Masynowy Kalasznikow or — alternatively — as the Karabinek Awtomata Kalasznikow (PMK or Kbk-AK), the original Polish-made assault rifle was practically a standard AK with 'C' and 'P' on the fire-selector. A folding-stock variant is also known.

The PMK-DGN or Kbk.g wz./1960 grenade-launching rifle fires the F1/N60 anti-personnel or the PGN-60 anti-tank grenades from LON-1 launchers, using a distinctive leaf sight and a ten-round magazine. A special gas-cylinder cut-off valve permits grenade-firing. The PMK was replaced by the Karabinek awtomatyczny wz./88, a copy of the AK-74S with a GDR-style folding butt and an additional three-round burst-firing facility. The fire selector lies on the left side of the receiver.

Together with a fixed-butt version designated wz./89, the wz./88 was

Pattern Room Collection, Royal Ordnance plc, Nottingham.

102. Essentially similar to the standard 7.62mm AKM, the Romanian-made AIM variant has a distinctive fore-grip ahead of the magazine.

103. Made in Kraguyevač, the 7.62mm M70B1 was mechanically identical with the standard Kalashnikov. Note the grenade-launching sight folded back on top of the gas-port and piston housing, and the distinctive shape of the pistol grip. Courtesy of Ian Hogg.

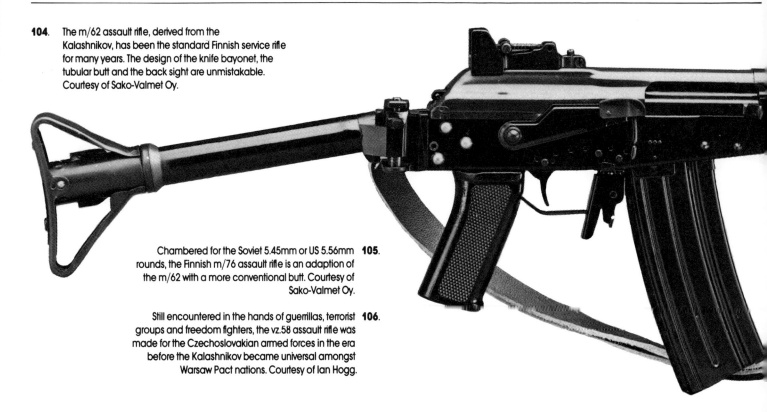

104. The m/62 assault rifle, derived from the Kalashnikov, has been the standard Finnish service rifle for many years. The design of the knife bayonet, the tubular butt and the back sight are unmistakable. Courtesy of Sako-Valmet Oy.

Chambered for the Soviet 5.45mm or US 5.56mm **105.** rounds, the Finnish m/76 assault rifle is an adaption of the m/62 with a more conventional butt. Courtesy of Sako-Valmet Oy.

Still encountered in the hands of guerrillas, terrorist **106.** groups and freedom fighters, the vz.58 assault rifle was made for the Czechoslovakian armed forces in the era before the Kalashnikov became universal amongst Warsaw Pact nations. Courtesy of Ian Hogg.

developed by a team led by Bogdan Szpaderski and made by Zaklady Metalowe Lucznik in Radom (though it is believed that production has ceased pending a reassessment of armament policy). M74 40 × 46mm grenade launchers (kbk.g. wz./74) may be fitted to these guns when required.

Romanian troops have been issued with a copy of the standard AK, then with an indigenous variant of the AKM with a plastic pistol grip, a laminated butt, and a laminated fore-end with an integral forehand pistol-grip. The selectors are marked 'S', 'FA' and 'FF' for safety, automatic operation and single-shot fire respectively. Known collectively as the 'AIM' series, these guns have been accompanied by a sniper-rifle derivative of the Soviet RPK light machine-gun known as the 'FPK'. This chambers the old 7.62mm rimmed round rather than the M43 intermediate pattern.

The Yugoslavs have made some of the most striking variants of the Kalashnikov, starting with the M64. This introduced several non-standard features, such as a wooden pistol grip with finger grooves, an integral grenade-launching sight (the launcher replaces the compensator/muzzle-brake when required) and a mechanical hold-open. Variants known as the M64A and M64B had short barrels—375mm instead of 414mm—and the 64B also had a folding stock. The M70 and M70A

were manufacturing variants, generally encountered with ribbed plastic pistol grips and a flat-muzzle compensator, while the current M70B1 and M70AB2 feature Russian-style spatulate compensators. The selector lever and receiver designs have also been modified, the former displaying 'U', 'R' and 'J' (safe, automatic, single-shot) like all Yugoslav Kalashnikov derivatives.

The Crvena Zastava factory even offers versions of the M70B1 chambered for the 5.56 × 45mm or 7.62 × 51mm NATO rounds. The former are designated M78B1 (fixed stock) and M78AB2 (folding stock), while the latter is the M77B1. A special long-barrel sniper rifle, the M76, chambers the 7.9 × 57mm Mauser round.

The armed forces adopted the 5.56 × 45mm round in 1990 to replace the Soviet 5.45 × 39mm pattern, but the changes had not been implemented when the Yugoslavian state fragmented. The principal manufacturing facility—Zavodi Crvena Zastava ('Red Banner Factory'), Kragujevač—is now in Serbia.

WESTERN KALASHNIKOVS

Finland has produced several versions of the Kalashnikov for military use, and a number of semi-commercial derivations. The army guns are the Rynnäkkökiväärit ('assault rifles') m/60, m/62, m/71 and

m/76. The unsuccessful m/60 had a plastic fore-end, a tubular steel butt, the back sight on the receiver-cover and an Arctic trigger without a guard. It was replaced by the more conventional m/62, with a different handgrip and a conventionally guarded trigger. A commercial variant known as the m/71, reverting to the standard butt style, encountered limited success and has now been superseded by the m/76. This is essentially similar to the m/62, but is of less radical appearance. Used by the Finnish army in 7.62 × 39mm M43, it may also be obtained in 5.56 × 45mm and 7.62mm NATO from Valmet Oy (now Sako-Valmet), currently the sole manufacturer though Sako apparently made some guns during the late 1960s.

Minor variants include the m/76F, m/76P, m/76T and m/76W—with folding, plastic, fixed tubular and wood butts respectively. There is an m/83S sniper rifle and a semi-experimental m/82 bullpup. A semi-automatic commercial sporting rifle known as the Petra, can also be obtained. The selectors of Finnish service rifles display ● and ●●●, for single-shot and automatic fire respectively.

The Indian armed forces adopted the 5.56 × 45mm INSAS ('Indian Small Arms System') in 1990, development in ARDE[W], Poona, beginning in 1988. The assault rifle is basically an adaption of the Kalashnikov with additional features such as transparent-body magazines, chromed

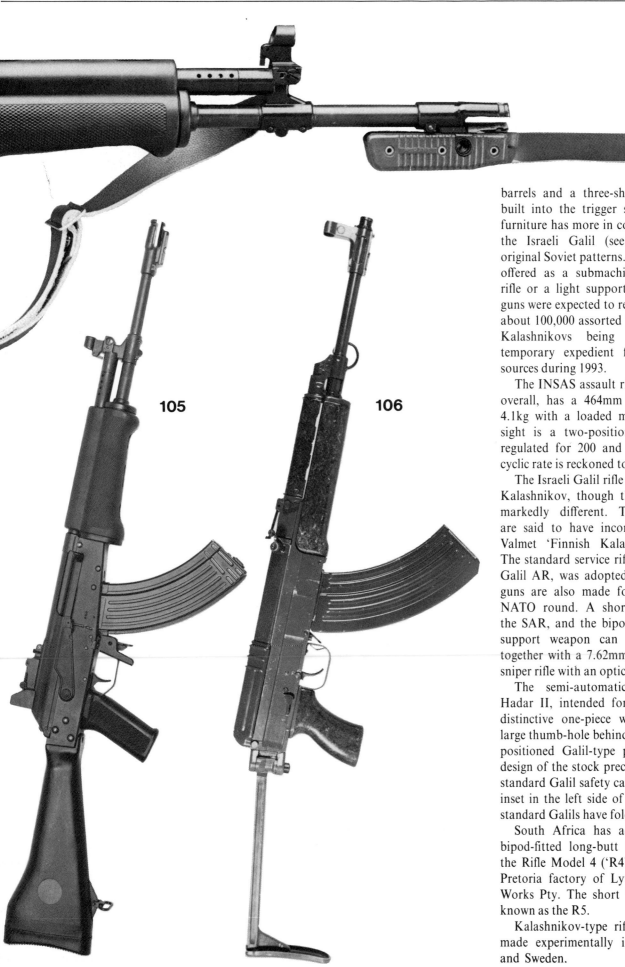

105

106

barrels and a three-shot burst capability built into the trigger system. The plastic furniture has more in common with that of the Israeli Galil (see below) than the original Soviet patterns. The INSAS is to be offered as a submachine-gun, an assault rifle or a light support weapon. The first guns were expected to reach service in 1994, about 100,000 assorted 7.62mm AKM-type Kalashnikovs being purchased as a temporary expedient from a variety of sources during 1993.

The INSAS assault rifle is about 965mm overall, has a 464mm barrel and weighs 4.1kg with a loaded magazine. The back sight is a two-position rocking pattern, regulated for 200 and 400 metres, whilst cyclic rate is reckoned to be about 650rpm.

The Israeli Galil rifle is also based on the Kalashnikov, though the safety system is markedly different. The first examples are said to have incorporated unmarked Valmet 'Finnish Kalashnikov' receivers. The standard service rifle, the 5.56×45mm Galil AR, was adopted in 1972: however, guns are also made for the 7.62×51mm NATO round. A short-barrelled variant, the SAR, and the bipod-fitted ARM light support weapon can also be obtained, together with a 7.62mm NATO wood-butt sniper rifle with an optical sight.

The semi-automatic 7.62mm NATO Hadar II, intended for police use, has a distinctive one-piece wood stock with a large thumb-hole behind the conventionally positioned Galil-type pistol grip. As the design of the stock precludes the use of the standard Galil safety catch, a radial lever is inset in the left side of the pistol grip. All standard Galils have folding metal butts.

South Africa has adopted a modified bipod-fitted long-butt Galil derivative as the Rifle Model 4 ('R4'), making it in the Pretoria factory of Lyttleton Engineering Works Pty. The short 'carbine' version is known as the R5.

Kalashnikov-type rifles have also been made experimentally in the Netherlands and Sweden.

HOW TO FIRE THE FN FAL RIFLE

Starting with the gun empty, the selector **A** in its uppermost position at 'S' ('Safe') and the loaded magazine in the hand,
> insert the magazine **B** in the receiver **C** ahead of the trigger guard, ensuring that the magazine is canted slightly forward. Swing the magazine back and up into its housing, pushing it firmly home until the magazine-release catch **D** locks;
> holding the rifle by the pistol grip, pull the charging handle **E** back as far as it will go;
> release the charging handle **E**, and the breechblock will run forward under spring pressure, but do not hold the handle during its travel;
> rotate the selector to either front ('A', automatic) or rear ('R', single-shot) positions;
> take aim and squeeze the trigger **F**.
The gun will reload automatically. When the magazine is empty, the slide stop **G** locks the slide open. When this happens:
> push the magazine-release catch **D** to release the empty magazine **B**;
> insert a new magazine, remembering to cant it backward before turning it vertically to lock;
> press the slide stop **G** forward with the thumb.
This allows the breech to close, chambering a round, and the gun is cocked ready to fire. To clear the gun:
> press the magazine-release catch **D** and remove the magazine;
> retract the charging handle **E** to reject the chambered round;
> reset the safety to 'S'.
The magazine can then be emptied and replaced.
Note: many guns are restricted to semi-automatic fire, and have two-position selectors giving a choice of 'S' (upward) or 'R' (backward).

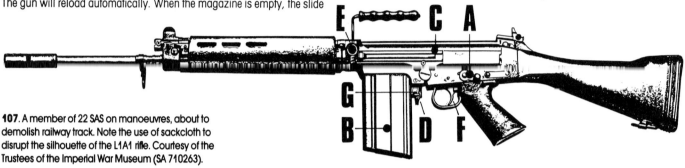

107. A member of 22 SAS on manoeuvres, about to demolish railway track. Note the use of sackcloth to disrupt the silhouette of the L1A1 rifle. Courtesy of the Trustees of the Imperial War Museum (SA 710263).

108▲

109▼

THE FUSIL AUTOMATIQUE LEGER (FAL)

If the Kalashnikov assault rifle can be said to represent the first, highly successful efforts of the Soviet bloc design-school, the Fusil Automatique Léger (FAL) developed by Dieudonné Saive of Fabrique Nationale is its Western equivalent. Though the inspiration of the FAL was the Garand and the SVT rather than the MP.43, its world-wide success from 1953 into the 1970s is a tribute to its efficiency.

FN's pre-war experiments with a tilting-block locked rifle were interrupted by the German invasion of Belgium in 1940. However, Saive and many other FN technicians escaped the clutches of the Wehrmacht, fleeing to Britain where work continued at

108–10. The FN FAL (known in English as the LAR) has been exported to more than fifty countries, and, though heavy and somewhat unwieldy, is widely regarded as the best full-power 7.62mm automatic rifle ever made. The standard infantry rifle (**108**) has a fixed butt, but a folding butt 'Para' pattern is also made (the subject of the exploded drawing). Picture **109** shows the standard British Rifle L1A1 in the hands of a Royal Marine Commando in Norway. Note how the surprisingly efficient camouflaging breaks up the lines of the weapon: a pre-requisite of stealth and covert operations. A heavy barrel derivative, the FALO or LAR HB (**110**), is widely sold as a light squad automatic. However, some of these HB guns — for reasons that have never been satisfactorily explained — have a tendency to 'second round jamming' when firing fully automatically. This has inhibited their widespread distribution; in Britain, for example, the Bren Gun has been retained instead. Courtesy of Fabrique Nationale and the Royal Marines Museum, Eastney.

110▼

111. An L1A1 rifle.
Courtesy of Headquarters,
British Forces Northern Ireland.

the Royal Small Arms Factory at Enfield. The experimental SLEM automatic rifle became the post-war SAFN, ABL or Mle 1949, adopted by the Belgian army and sold to Egypt and some South American countries. The success of the ABL bought time necessary to perfect the prototype FAL.

NATO's FIRST ATTEMPTS TO STANDARDIZE

Immediately after the end of the Second World War, the newly-formed NATO alliance sought to standardize equipment in its constituent armies. The three principal entries in the rifle trials were the US T44 (a modified Garand), the British EM-2 and the Belgian FAL. By 1947, the US representatives had rejected the British 0.280in cartridge; ironically, not only did this embody many of the ideal characteristics of the later 7.62mm NATO and 5.56mm rounds, but it also bore an appreciable resemblance to the 0.276in pattern 'adopted' by the US Army in the 1930s. The Americans were not impressed by the revolutionary EM-2 rifle either, and the project foundered in 1953. Piqued, the British then backed the FAL against the US

T44. A strange compromise was finally reached: the American-backed 0.30in T65E3 became the 7.62×51mm NATO round, but both rifles were accepted. In June 1957, the US Army accepted the perfected T44 as the Rifle M14, while most major European armies other than the French adopted the FAL.

The FAL is a conventional, sturdy semi- or fully-automatic rifle, made in a variety of guises for export to the armed forces and paramilitary organizations in more than fifty countries. Locking is achieved by a tilting block, displaced downward into the receiver immediately behind the magazine well. When the gun is fired, gas bled from the barrel impinges on the head of the piston rod. The rod strikes the bolt carrier, which, as it moves backwards, lifts the locking block out of its recess; the bolt and bolt-carrier recoil together, clearing the magazine well and cocking the hammer, and then return to strip a new round into the breech. The FAL, therefore, is a lightened and improved ABL with a much-modified trigger mechanism and appreciably lighter construction. It is, however, large, heavy and cumbersome by the standards of the M16 and even the AKM. In recent years, this had militated against it, even though it is sufficiently accurate at short range to be used for sniping by many regular armies. And during the Falklands War between Britain and Argentina (1982), the FAL was successfully employed by both sides, alongside the FN-designed GP Mle 35 pistol and the MAG.

The tremendous export success of the FAL hindered the development of semi-automatic rifles for several years, particularly as the US Army was satisfied with the M14. For much of the period prior to American embroilment in Vietnam, which effectively began in 1961, the NATO

powers were firmly wedded to the concept of full-power/long-range performance, intermediate weapon needs being satisfied by submachine-guns – or, in the case of the British, Australian and New Zealand SAS units, shotguns or the US M1 Carbine.

THE CETME AND G3 RIFLES

The dispersal of German smallarms technology at the end of the Second World War allowed Fabrique Nationale to create a monopoly which lasted for a decade. The FAL was even adopted by the armies of Federal Germany (as the Gewehr 1) and Austria (StG.58). During this period, however, wartime expertise was kept alive by German technicians working in the Iberian Peninsula – where an ex-Mauser engineer named Ludwig Vorgrimmler continued development of the Mauser Gerät 06, the most promising entrant in the abortive StG.45 competition. Mauser's roller-lock system had been developed from the MG.42 by Ernst Altenburger and Herbert Illenberger, and was potentially very efficient. It had even been appropriated for the abortive British Thorpe Rifle (EM-1). During the 1950s, however, the system was refined at the Centro de Estudios Tecnicós de Materiales Especiales – CETME – in Madrid, under the direction of Dipl.-Ing. Heynen and General José Cantero.

The first CETME rifles fired a distinctive intermediate cartridge with an extra-long unusually light bullet, the 7.9×40mm, to combine good long-range performance with recoil low enough to facilitate accurate burst fire. The rifle was perfected by about 1955, and a licensing arrangement was concluded with NWM – though NWM-marked rifles were actually supplied from Spain. Ultimately, a successful demonstration for

112. The Heckler & Koch G3, the service rifle of the Bundeswehr (and the GSG-9 CTW units), is another successful design occasionally seen in the hands of the SAS and US special forces. The roller-locking system was adapted from the MG.42 machine-gun in 1944–5 and perfected in Spain (as the CETME) after the end of the war. Many G3 variants have been made, including the G3A4 (current pattern illustrated). Courtesy of Heckler & Koch GmbH.

112▼

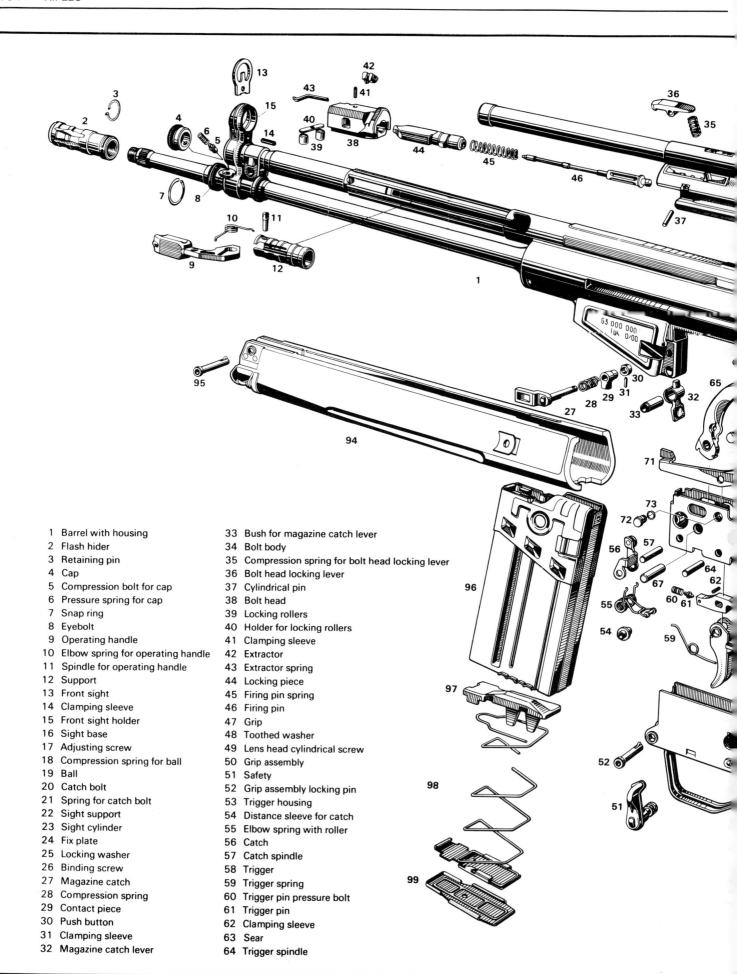

1	Barrel with housing
2	Flash hider
3	Retaining pin
4	Cap
5	Compression bolt for cap
6	Pressure spring for cap
7	Snap ring
8	Eyebolt
9	Operating handle
10	Elbow spring for operating handle
11	Spindle for operating handle
12	Support
13	Front sight
14	Clamping sleeve
15	Front sight holder
16	Sight base
17	Adjusting screw
18	Compression spring for ball
19	Ball
20	Catch bolt
21	Spring for catch bolt
22	Sight support
23	Sight cylinder
24	Fix plate
25	Locking washer
26	Binding screw
27	Magazine catch
28	Compression spring
29	Contact piece
30	Push button
31	Clamping sleeve
32	Magazine catch lever

33	Bush for magazine catch lever
34	Bolt body
35	Compression spring for bolt head locking lever
36	Bolt head locking lever
37	Cylindrical pin
38	Bolt head
39	Locking rollers
40	Holder for locking rollers
41	Clamping sleeve
42	Extractor
43	Extractor spring
44	Locking piece
45	Firing pin spring
46	Firing pin
47	Grip
48	Toothed washer
49	Lens head cylindrical screw
50	Grip assembly
51	Safety
52	Grip assembly locking pin
53	Trigger housing
54	Distance sleeve for catch
55	Elbow spring with roller
56	Catch
57	Catch spindle
58	Trigger
59	Trigger spring
60	Trigger pin pressure bolt
61	Trigger pin
62	Clamping sleeve
63	Sear
64	Trigger spindle

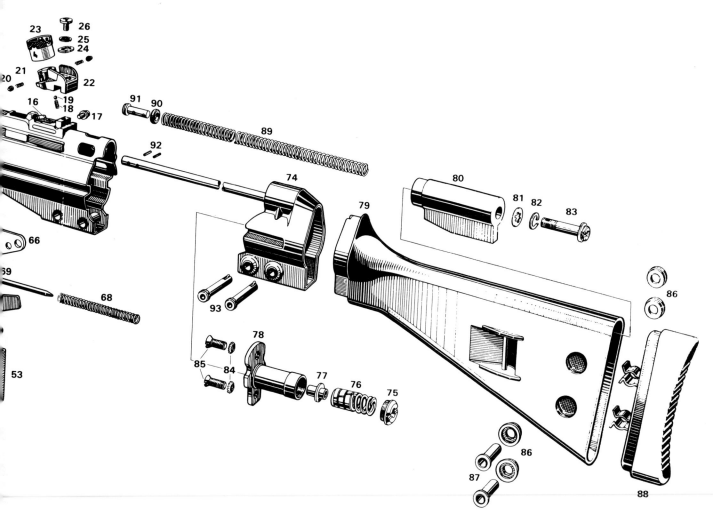

Fig. 17. The Gewehr 3, service rifle of the Bundeswehr. The G3 is another highly successful design, being made in many countries — including Greece and Portugal. Small numbers have even been made in the United Kingdom. Courtesy of Heckler & Koch.

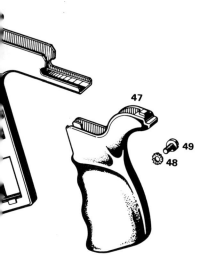

65	Hammer	85	Countersunk screws
66	Release lever	86	Bush for tubular rivet
67	Hammer spindle	87	Tubular rivet
68	Pressure spring	88	Butt plate
69	Pressure shank	89	Recoil spring
70	Ejector pressure spring	90	Guide ring
71	Ejector	91	Stop pin
72	Ejector spindle	92	Rivet
73	Snap ring	93	Butt stock locking pins
74	Back plate	94	Handguard
75	Buffer closure	95	Handguard locking pin
76	Buffer with brake rings	96	Magazine housing
77	Buffer pin	97	Follower
78	Buffer housing	98	Follower spring with safety plate
79	Butt stock	99	Magazine floor plate
80	Support for buffer housing		
81	Internal teeth type lock washer		
82	Spring ring		
83	Buffer screw		
84	Toothed washers		

▲113

▲113

the Bundesgrenzschutz (BGS), the Federal German border guard, attracted the attention of a Bundeswehr far from enamoured with the G1 (FAL). After a false start with a 7.62×40mm cartridge, the Germans requested redevelopment for 7.62×51mm NATO, though the resulting wholesale changes lost many of the advantages of the original lightweight CETME. Once agreement from the remainder of NATO had been forthcoming, the Bundeswehr retrieved the licence from NWM to enable production to begin in Germany.

After successfully negotiating stringent trials, the new rifle was adopted as the Gewehr 3 (G3). Initially made by Heckler & Koch and Rheinmetall, the weapon has been a great success, and the subsequent exploits of H&K – who have produced everything from minimal submachine-guns to belt-fed sustained-fire machine-guns on the basic action – have now completely overshadowed CETME's contribution.

All CETME and H&K guns incorporate a delayed blowback system in which two rollers, between the bolt-head and the bolt carrier, lock into the barrel extension. When the gun fires, part of the backward pressure on the cartridge case attempts to force the rollers into the breechblock. The bolt-carrier and firing-pin assembly move backward to make sufficient room. However, this is opposed by the remainder of the recoil force acting outwards into the receiver body. A brief period of delay ensues, allowing the chamber pressure to drop to a safe level before the rollers re-enter the bolt and the whole unit begins to move backwards against the recoil spring. Once the bolt and its carrier have cleared the magazine well, and cocked the hammer, the recoil spring reasserts itself, returns the bolt and strips a new round into the chamber. When the bolt-head stops against the chamber, the cam-shoulders on the separate locking piece in the bolt carrier (which is

113. The G3 series is robust, reliable, possesses a particularly good rotary backsight and can be fitted with a number of accessories (the example illustrated is fitted with a noise suppressor). Courtesy of Heckler & Koch GmbH.

still moving) push the rollers out into their recesses. This halts the mechanism and firing can take place again. The roller system lacks something of the solidity of the genuine locked-breech designs, but the G3 and its derivatives have a reputation for reliability under adverse conditions or with a wide variety of cartridge-loadings. They have been adopted in Norway, Portugal and elsewhere, and have been used by US Army Rangers, US Navy SEALS, the SAS and other special forces from Aden to the Arctic.

114. A typical full-power military rifle of the late 1950s: the Swiss Stgw.57, a surprisingly complicated – but beautifully made – roller-lock design. The straight-line configuration is reminiscent of the wartime German FG.42 paratroop rifle. Courtesy of SIG.

▼114

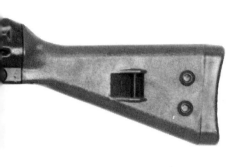

EARLY ARMALITES

During the period in which the CETME/G3 was being developed, a new full-power rifle was being developed in the USA. In October 1954, the Fairchild Engine and Airplane Company had created an Armalite Division in which to develop modern lightweight smallarms. Development of the AR-10 began in 1954, based on a rifle Eugene Stoner had devised before being appointed as Armalite's chief engineer. The gas-operated rotating-bolt design featured an integral carrying handle and a straight-line layout intended to minimize climb in the automatic mode. By 1956, it had gained a titanium-lined aluminium barrel, a fibreglass stock and a synthetic magazine in an attempt to combine lightness with strength.

However, Fairchild had neither the production expertise nor the facilities to contemplate mass production, and the AR-10 was licensed to NWM in the Netherlands in 1957. Changes were made, including the elimination of the original flash suppressor and the removal of the gas-tube to a better position above the barrel. However, though belt-fed derivatives appeared, the project was unsuccessful and sales were very poor.

Nicaragua, Sudan and Burma are known to have taken some AR-10s, but a large order for Portugal defaulted after just 1,200 had been delivered. The Portuguese took the G3 instead, and production of the NWM-Armalite ceased.

THE AR-15 AND M16

In 1957, the Commanding Officer of the US Army's Continental Army Command (CONARC) had issued a specification for an infantry rifle weighing no more than 6lb, with selective-fire capabilities, accuracy comparable with the Rifle M1 (Garand) and lethality bettering the 0.30 M1 Carbine cartridge at distances up to 500 yards. Though no calibre was specified, and the weight requirement seemed completely unattainable, Winchester and Armalite showed interest. Stoner began development of a small-diameter cartridge by loading 55-grain commercial Sierra bullets into 0.222 Remington cases, which developed into the longer-case 0.222 Remington Special (later renamed 0.223 Remington) to compete against Winchester's 0.224E1 and 0.224E2. The first ten 0.222 Special AR-15 trials rifles were delivered to the US Army Infantry Board at the end of March 1958. At only 6.12lb complete with a loaded 25-round magazine, they all but met the CONARC specifications. Initial reports were enthusiastic, and much interest was shown in the AR-15.

Despite the standardization of the T44E4 experimental rifle as the M14 in June 1957, both lightweight high-velocity rifles (LWHVR) were tested at Fort Benning, Aberdeen Proving Ground and Fort Greely throughout 1959. Results were generally encouraging, but doubts were expressed about the lethality of such small-diameter bullets.

During 1958, therefore, a group of General Officers—the Powell Board—was convened to consider the small-calibre rifles, but rejected 0.223 and 0.224 in favour of an optimal '0.258'. CONARC then requested that a final series of trials should be undertaken by the US Army Combat Development Experimentation Center (or ACDEC) at Fort Ord, California, to determine the future of the LWHVR project. The trials began on 1 December 1958, but, before they could be finished, the Army Chief of Staff rejected the LWHVR in favour of the 7.62mm Rifle M14 'on the basis of all available facts'. The high-ranking factions that opposed the 0.223 cartridge on personal grounds—believing that a military weapon should be 'man-size' rather than a 'toy'—had covertly disrupted the LWHVR project.

At the end of May 1959, ACDEC reported that the 0.224 Winchester rifle had proved more accurate but appreciably less reliable than the 0.223 AR-15. By this time, however, the US army had lost interest, cancelled the programme, and turned to the 6mm SPIW instead.

All seemed lost until, in May 1961, the USAF agreed to purchase AR-15 rifles in quantity and classified the 5.56mm Rifle AR-15 (later XM16, then M16) as standard in January 1962. An airforce contract for 8,500 guns and 8.5 million cartridges was passed to Colt on 23 May 1962.

While the USAF was finalising its first purchase, the AR-15 had been extensively demonstrated in the Far East and had attracted special attention in Vietnam. In December 1961, the Secretary of Defense authorized the supply of 1,000 AR-15 rifles for the ARVN, the first guns being shipped in January 1962. By the summer, trials had been completed; it was clear that the AR-15 was a great success, being hailed as a suitable replacement for most of the guns in ARVN service—including the M1 and M14 rifles, the M1 Carbine, the BAR and the M3 submachine-guns. No parts-breakages were reported in a trial allegedly lasting 80,000 rounds!

General Haskins, Commander of the US Military Advisory Command in Vietnam, was so impressed that he unsuccessfully attempted to order 'substantial' quantities of AR-15 rifles for front-line ARVN troops. Owing to the lack of progress on the 6mm SPIW, army interest in the AR-15 grew once more: 338 XM16 rifles were acquired in October 1962 so that tests could be undertaken against the M14 and the AK-47. In January 1963, a 'final' report recommended continued acquisition of the M14 during the period in which the SPIW was being perfected.

However, the AR-15/M16 still had its champions; indeed, the Army Materiel Command had actually recommended it for universal issue. As an investigation by the Inspector General of the Armed Forces revealed that trials had been strongly biased in favour of the M14—guns used had been specially selected, fired match ammunition, and were often shot by experienced marksmen—the Armalite design was given another chance. Finally, in 1963, 85,000 guns were ordered for airborne, assault and special forces units to whom the light weight was advantageous.

As the US Army had been made sole purchasing agency, 104,000 rifles were to be ordered in fiscal year 1964: 19,000 M16 rifles for the USAF and 85,000 XM16 for the US army. By this time, there had been a severe difference of opinion among the services, and the government had toyed with the idea of ordering guns from several

115. An M16 in use in the Falklands campaign, 1982. Note the absence of the bolt-closure device. The closed ejection port indicates that firing has not yet commenced. Courtesy of the Royal Marines Museum, Eastney.

contractors simultaneously. The army then refused to take the XM16 unless some changes were made, the most important being the incorporation of a bolt-assist on the rear right side of the action. This was intended to close the bolt in the event of problems, though neither the USAF nor the US Marine Corps considered it necessary.

Airforce representatives pointed to the phenomenal reliability of the test rifles in ARVN hands, and that normal procedure in the event of a misfire or bolt problem was to retract the cocking handle and try again; they considered the army's addition to be an unnecessary complication, and even to compromise safety. In addition, a reduction of the twist-pitch from one turn in fourteen inches to one in only twelve—necessary to extend the operating range of the XM16 so that it became −65° to +125°F—seriously compromised the lethality of the M193 bullet.

The new army rifle was labelled the 5.56mm Rifle XM16E1, and was not reclassified M16A1 until 1967. Until the end of 1965, when purchasing was finally rationalized, the M16 (USAF, USMC) was made concurrently with the XM16E1 (US Army). The addition of the bolt-assist mechanism is not a consequence of later troubles in Vietnam.

During this period, the Government's preference for single-source procurement was increasingly questioned, particularly as Colt was not only reluctant to license production to other manufacturers until more than 500,000 assorted M16 and M16A1 rifles had been ordered, but was also making more than permissible from the fixed-profit government contracts. Finally, a licence was concluded between Colt and the US Department of Defense on 30 July 1967. The rights had cost the US Treasury no less than $4.5 million, plus a 5.5 per cent royalty on each gun made by companies other than Colt—who, at the time, also held orders for 632,500 guns extending in 1970.

Harrington & Richardson of Worcester, Massachusetts, and the Hydra-Matic Division of General Motors subsequently made M16A1 rifles. Guns have also been made in the Philippines, by Elisco, and by Chartered Industries Ltd (CIS) of Singapore.

The service début of the XM-16 (as the AR-15 had become) was eagerly awaited, but initial enthusiasm soon waned. Jamming soon presented a serious problem, as the weapons quickly became unusable. It was due to poor maintenance—the gun had been optimistically touted as 'self cleaning'—and an unappreciated change in ammunition.

During 1966, so many reports of severe problems with the XM16E1 filtered back from the US forces in Vietnam that representatives of the Army Weapons Command and Colt were immediately dispatched to the Far East. There they found many of the guns in a dreadful state. Their report stated that:

'. . . with the exception of the 1st Brigade of the 101st Airborne Division, the 173rd Airborne Brigade and the 5th Special Services Group, the weapons were in unbelievable condition of rust, filth, and lack of repair. The filthy condition ranged from actual dirt, grit and mud on various components of the weapon and ammunition to a heavy deposit on various components. The most significant trouble spots were the chamber,

HOW TO FIRE THE M16A1 AND COLT AR-15 RIFLES

Starting with the gun empty, the safety catch **A** at SAFE and the loaded magazine in the hand,
> simultaneously press in the bottom of the bolt latch **B** and pull the charging handle **C** back as far as it will go;
> return the charging handle **C** until it locks, and then remove pressure from the bolt latch;
> insert the magazine **D** in the receiver **E** ahead of the trigger guard, ensuring that the magazine catch **F** locks it in place;
> press in the top of the bolt latch **B**, allowing the bolt and bolt-carrier to come forward and chamber a round;
> rotate the safety catch to FIRE;
> take aim and squeeze the trigger **G**.
The gun will reload automatically. When the magazine is empty, the bolt will remain open:
> remove the empty magazine **D** by pressing the magazine-release **F**;

> insert a new magazine;
> press the top part of the bolt latch **B**.
This allows the breech to close, chambering a round, and the gun is cocked ready to fire. To clear the gun:
> set the safety catch to SAFE;
> retract the charging handle **C**, while pushing in on the bottom of the bolt latch **B**, and leave the charging handle open;
> remove the magazine **D**;
> release the charging handle **C**, together with the bolt and bolt-carrier, by pushing in the top portion of the bolt latch.
The magazine can them be emptied and replaced.

Note: if the bolt fails to close properly, which usually indicates that the action needs cleaning, the bolt-assist **H**, absent from early AR15 and M16 rifles, can be used to force the bolt-head into its locking recesses.

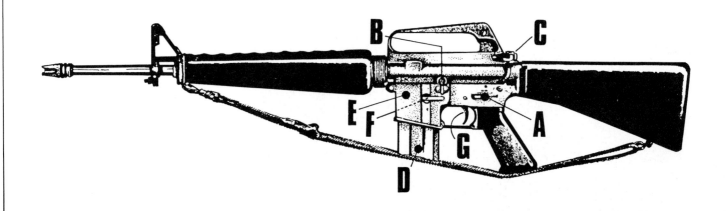

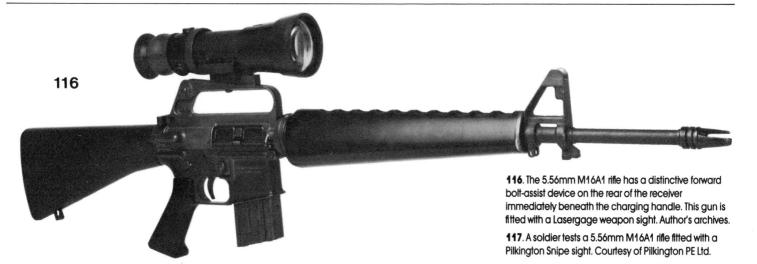

116. The 5.56mm M16A1 rifle has a distinctive forward bolt-assist device on the rear of the receiver immediately beneath the charging handle. This gun is fitted with a Lasergage weapon sight. Author's archives.

117. A soldier tests a 5.56mm M16A1 rifle fitted with a Pilkington Snipe sight. Courtesy of Pilkington PE Ltd.

the outside of the gas tube extension in the upper receiver, and the inside of the carrier key . . .

Approximately 5% of the ammunition was found to be unserviceable due to corrosion and an additional 10% would have given trouble due to being dirty. From 30 to 50% of the magazines appeared unserviceable due to bent or spread lips.'

The problems were soon isolated: poor training, appalling maintenance and poor lubrication were easily cured by better instruction and development of better equipment, a trap being added in the butt; excess copper deposits in the bore arose from firing too much tracer; chroming the chamber (also, subsequently, the bore) minimized carbon deposition, corrosion and extraction problems; alterations were made to the gas system; and a new buffer, designed by F.E. Sturtevant, slowed the cyclic rate.

The major problem proved to be the ammunition. Cartridges fired in the early AR-15/XM16 trials had been loaded with the Du Pont IMR (Improved Military Rifle) propellant customarily used by the US armed forces. However, IMR had generated operating pressures with such low margins of safety that the first nineteen million cartridges supplied by Remington to the USAF contained Olin Mathieson WC-846 ball powder. This, together with IMR (CR) 8136, was a permissible substitute. During the fiscal year 1964, therefore, a million cartridges had been loaded with IMR 4475, fifty million with IMR (CR) 8136, and the remaining 81 million with WC-846.

Though USAF endurance trials in March 1964 had given a mere 55 stoppages whilst firing 162,000 cartridges loaded with IMR 4475, the WC-846 batches not only gave appreciably more fouling but also raised the cyclic rate above the acceptable maximum. Though a minimum fouling requirement had already been added to the ammunition specifications, this applied only to the pre-production deliveries: in theory, a manufacturer could supply a few thousand cartridges to pass the fouling test, and then make millions which did not.

Tests undertaken in Frankford Arsenal in December 1965 showed that ammunition containing WC-846 was more than five times as liable to stoppages as IMR loads.

IMR 8208M powder was adopted in May 1966—but even as late as August 1967, no USMC unit in Vietnam had received anything other than WC-846 loads. Thus propellant fouling in XM16E1/M16A1 rifles continued unabated until the end of the year, though its effect was minimized by greater attention to maintenance.

In sum, the M16 has been developed into an unusually battleworthy weapon, but only after a decade of hard work and the traumatic experience in Vietnam. The story also illustrates the considerable problems of developing a soldier-proof weapon for general service, even though the M16 and M16A1 are much appreciated by the SAS and other special forces to whom good preventive maintenance is second nature.

In addition to the AR-15, XM16, M16, XM16E1 and M16A1—and the latest M16A2, with revisions to the gas system and a new back sight—several variants of the basic design have been made for military and commercial sale. Apart from the heavy-barrel guns submitted to the SAWS project as a light machine-gun, there is also a shortened version known as the Commando, XM177, XM177E1 or XM177E2.

The XM177 was an M16 with a 10in barrel and a long flash-hider; the XM177E1 was the army derivative of the XM177, with a bolt assist; and the XM177E2 was an XM177E1 with a grenade launching muzzle attachment. In May 1993, the US Army placed an order for 18,597 XM4 5.56mm carbines, intending to buy 52,000 by 1997. These will supplement about five thousand guns acquired for trials and Special Forces use in 1988–93. The XM4 is the perfected version of the XM177 series.

The success of the AR-15, M16 and M16A1 throughout the world—the British Army acquired several thousand for Limited Theatre and SAS use in Borneo—led to a radical revision of tactical doctrines, and the development of similar small-calibre rifles in many other countries.

OTHER 5.56MM GUNS

Despite undoubted efficacy, the AR-15/M16 series requires specialized machine tools and metal-fabricating techniques for effective mass-production, the requisite capital investment being repayable only by lengthy production runs. Most small countries simply could not afford to make M16s, though several Far Eastern countries were interested and small numbers were made by Elisco Tool Corporation in the Philippines.

Guns are also being made by Diemaco of Kitchener, Ontario, as the C7/C7A1 and C8. Diemaco has successfully tendered to provide the Royal Netherlands Army with M16-type guns (C7 and C7A1 rifles, and C8 carbines), paying Colt a suitable royalty. The latest US Army contract for M16A2 rifles, indeed, has been placed with Fabrique Nationale Manufacturing, Inc., of Columbia, South Carolina.

The first generations of M16 rivals were simply scaled-down variants of existing guns, the FN CAL/FNC being derived from the FAL and the HK33/G41 from the G3. Though sales were soon made in many non-aligned countries, it was some years before major powers adopted weapons of this type. In this period of uncertainty, lesser guns such as the Armalite AR-18 simply disappeared.

There are many competitive designs on today's scene, ranging from the best of the guns made in Europe to some interesting South American products—e.g., the Brazilian LAPA or the Argentine FARA 83. Potentially excellent weapons have been made in the Far East, notably by CIS in Singapore, whilst a derivative of the M16 has been made in some quantity in Taiwan. The addition of oddities such as a modified version of the Czech vz.58, introduced in Thailand some time in the early 1980s, has led to the extraordinary selection of equipment being carried by some subversive and anti-government units. The rifles recovered in Ethiopia or Somalia, for example, provide testimony to this incredible diversity.*

* See Edward C. Ezell, *Small Arms Today*, second edition, 1988, pp. 142–6; and 'Fact Sheet: Somalia, December 1992' in *Small Arms World Report*, vol. 3 no. 4/vol. 4 no. 1, December 1992.

118. The ill-fated Stoner M63A1, tested by the US Army as the XM22, was never granted the indulgence given to the AR-15/M16 series. It was judged to be too heavy and insufficiently reliable. This gun lacks the detachable box magazine. Author's archives.

119. Ruger's Mini-14/5F is an interesting amalgam of the full-power M14 rifle with the short-stroke gas piston system of the M1 Carbine. Guns of the Mini-14 series—including the Mini-14/20GB and AC-556—have been purchased by US government agencies. In addition, they are popular with police SWAT, special-purpose and CTW groups throughout the world. Courtesy of Sturm, Ruger & Co., Inc., Southport.

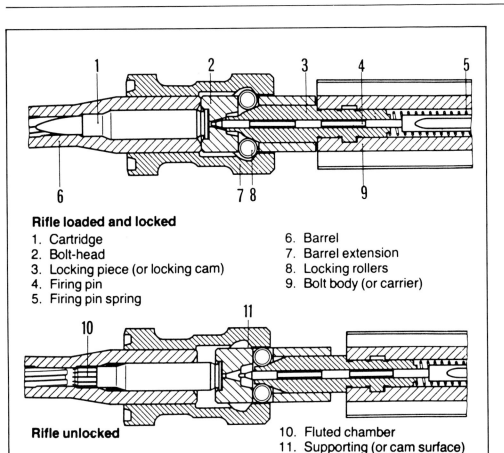

Rifle loaded and locked

1. Cartridge
2. Bolt-head
3. Locking piece (or locking cam)
4. Firing pin
5. Firing pin spring
6. Barrel
7. Barrel extension
8. Locking rollers
9. Bolt body (or carrier)

Rifle unlocked

10. Fluted chamber
11. Supporting (or cam surface)

The FN CAL was a lightened version of the FAL, introduced in 1966, but was complicated, expensive and insufficiently durable. Its replacement, the FNC-80, has advanced through several developmental models since 1975. A 'Para' model may be obtained with a folding butt.

When the first edition of *Guns of the Elite* was published, several European countries were considering the FNC for adoption. However, apart from Belgium, only Sweden has translated this interest into large-scale purchase. Known as the Ak-5, the Swedish rifle was adopted in 1984 to replace the Ak-4 (7.62mm Heckler & Koch G3). Tooling began in the Eskilstuna factory of FFV in 1986, the first guns being delivered a year later.

Heckler & Koch has been championing the 5.56mm G41, a diminution of the standard G3. Simultaneously, however, the company actively promoted the caseless cartridge G11—a remarkable project whose story has yet to be wholly told. The West German government apparently cancelled the G11 to save money after reunification, and it has been alleged that Heckler & Koch destroyed most of the documentation before being purchased by Royal Ordnance in 1991. The G41 is, therefore, in limbo.

The Italians announced the original competition to replace the venerable BM-59 (Garand) rifle as long ago as 1984. However, though substantial numbers of Beretta AR-70 and SC-70 rifles were acquired for the Special Forces (GIS, NOCS) and the Italian airforce, not until 1990 was the improved AR-70/90 deemed acceptable. Re-equipment is only now getting underway.

The CETME Models L (rifle) and LC (carbine) are 5.56mm diminutions of the 7.62mm Spanish CETME, made by Empresa Nacional 'Santa Barbara'. Like most of its rivals, the small-calibre CETME has undergone searching trials during development. During this period, the original drum sight was replaced by a simple two-position pattern and the burst firing mechanism—in the opinion of many commentators, a needless complication—was finally abandoned. The original twenty-round magazine was replaced by a standard NATO thirty-round pattern shortly before the Model L was adopted by the Spanish

Fig. 18. The Heckler & Koch roller-locking system.

120. The back sight of the FN FNC-80 is typical of modern designs in which a premium is placed on simplicity and sturdiness. Courtesy of FN Herstal SA.

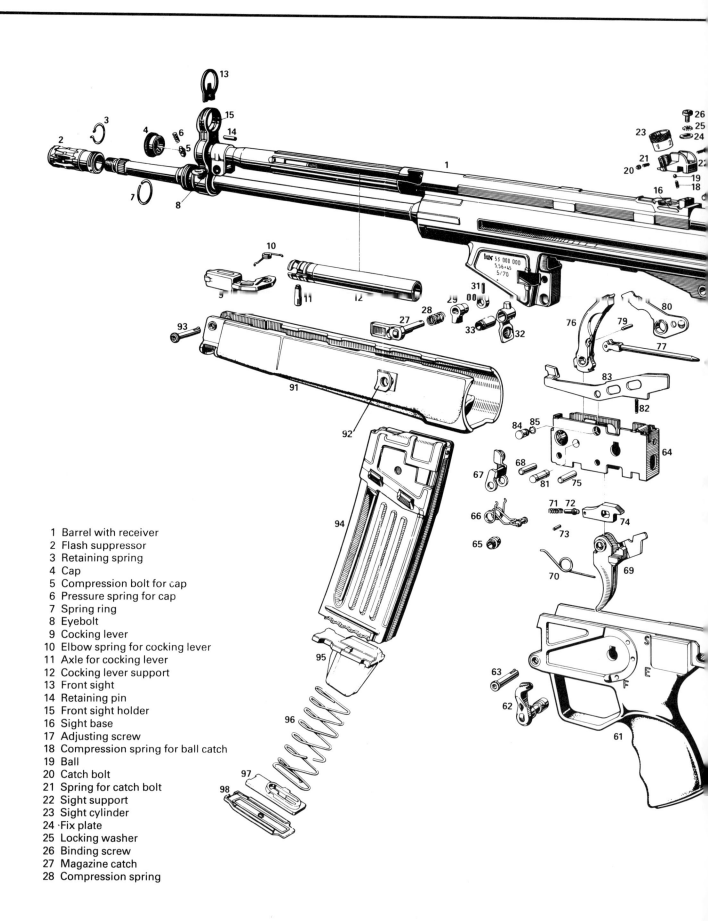

1   Barrel with receiver
2   Flash suppressor
3   Retaining spring
4   Cap
5   Compression bolt for cap
6   Pressure spring for cap
7   Spring ring
8   Eyebolt
9   Cocking lever
10 Elbow spring for cocking lever
11 Axle for cocking lever
12 Cocking lever support
13 Front sight
14 Retaining pin
15 Front sight holder
16 Sight base
17 Adjusting screw
18 Compression spring for ball catch
19 Ball
20 Catch bolt
21 Spring for catch bolt
22 Sight support
23 Sight cylinder
24 ·Fix plate
25 Locking washer
26 Binding screw
27 Magazine catch
28 Compression spring

Fig. 19. The Heckler & Koch HK33E is a small-calibre version of the G3. Courtesy of Heckler & Koch.

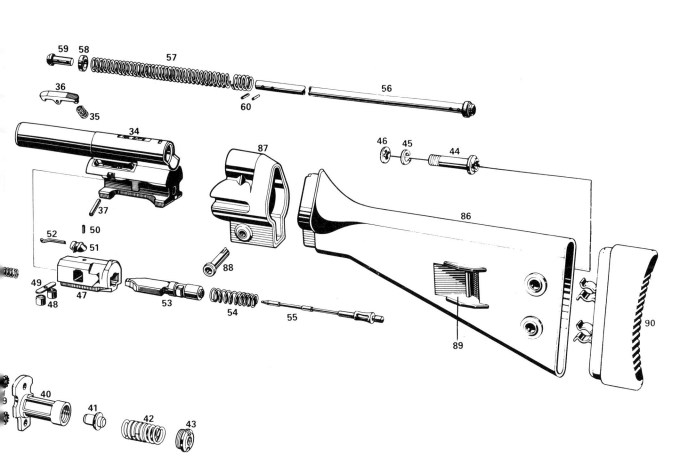

Fig. 19. The Heckler & Koch HK33E is a small-calibre version of the G3. Courtesy of Heckler & Koch.

29 Contact piece	52 Extractor spring	75 Axle for trigger
30 Push button	53 Locking piece	76 Hammer
31 Retaining pin	54 Firing pin spring	77 Pressure shank
32 Magazine release lever	55 Firing pin	78 Pressure spring
33 Bush for magazine release lever	56 Recoil spring guide rod	79 Rivet
34 Bolt head carrier	57 Recoil spring	80 Release lever
35 Compression spring for bolt head locking lever	58 Recoil spring guide ring	81 Axle for hammer
36 Bolt head locking lever	59 Stop pin	82 Ejector pressure spring
37 Cylindrical pin	60 Rivet	83 Ejector
38 Countersunk screws	61 Grip	84 Axle for ejector
39 Toothed washers	62 Safety	85 Spring ring
40 Buffer housing	63 Grip locking pin	86 Butt stock
41 Buffer pin	64 Trigger housing	87 Back plate
42 Buffer with brake rings	65 Distance sleeve for catch	88 Butt stock locking pin
43 Buffer closure	66 Elbow spring with roller	89 Carrying sling support
44 Buffer screw	67 Catch	90 Butt plate
45 Spring ring	68 Axle for catch	91 Handguard
46 Internal teeth type lock washer	69 Trigger	92 Hook
47 Bolt head	70 Trigger spring	93 Handguard locking pin
48 Locking rollers	71 Compression spring for trigger pin	94 Magazine housing
49 Holder for locking rollers	72 Trigger pin	95 Follower
50 Retaining pin	73 Clamping sleeve	96 Follower spring
51 Extractor	74 Sear	97 Spring floor plate
		98 Magazine floor plate

121△

122

121–3. Embodying the well-known Heckler & Koch delayed-blowback locking system, relying on rollers on the bolt head engaging seats in the receiver wall, these rifles are the 5.56mm HK33E (**121**); a telescope-sighted 5.56mm G41 (**122**); and a G41 dismantled into its principal component groups (**123**). Courtesy of Heckler & Koch GmbH, Oberndorf.

▽**123**

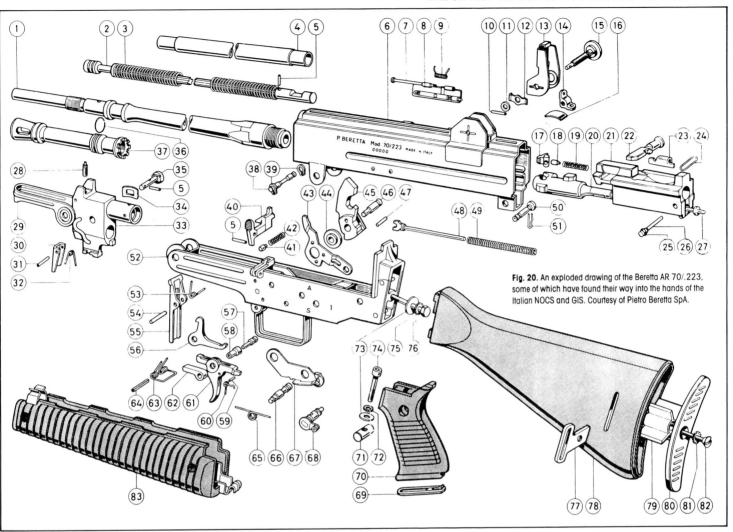

Fig. 20. An exploded drawing of the Beretta AR 70/.223, some of which have found their way into the hands of the Italian NOCS and GIS. Courtesy of Pietro Beretta SpA.

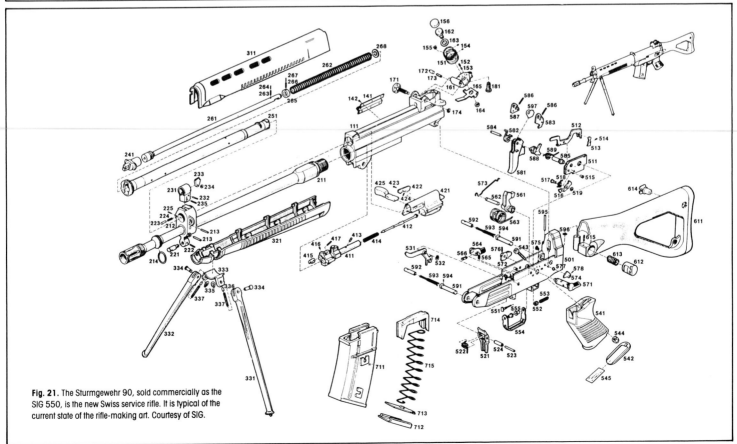

Fig. 21. The Sturmgewehr 90, sold commercially as the SIG 550, is the new Swiss service rifle. It is typical of the current state of the rifle-making art. Courtesy of SIG.

124. The FNC Type 2000 (or FNC-80) replaced the comparatively unsuccessful 5.56mm CAL. The perfected rifle has been adopted in Belgium and, in a modified form, by Sweden. Courtesy of FN Herstal SA.

125. A minor adaption of the Belgian-designed FNC, the 5.56mm Ak-5 was made by FN until production started in the FFV factory in Sweden. Courtesy of FN Herstal SA.

126. This example of Beretta's folding-butt 5.56mm SC-70/223 rifle dates from 1983. Small quantities were supplied to the Italian armed forces and CTW groups. Courtesy of Pietro Beretta SpA, Gardone.

Courtesy of Pietro Beretta SpA, Gardone.

127. This Beretta AR-70/90 of the 1992 series is the perfected version of the AR70/223, being readily identifiable by a folding carrying handle above the receiver.

128. A short or 'Paracudisti' version of the 5.56mm Beretta assault rifle, known as the SCP-70/90. Note the optional flash-hider/grenade launcher unit. Courtesy of Pietro Beretta SpA, Gardone.

129. The SG 530, the first of SIG's 5.56mm-calibre rifles, was comparatively unsuccessful. Small quantities were sold—often for specialist use—but the design was superseded by the SG 540. Courtesy of SIG, Nehausen.

130. The 5.56mm SG 540 was a perfected form of SIG's SG 530, with a rotating-bolt lock instead of rollers. Courtesy of SIG, Neuhausen.

131. This SG 540 has a distinctive laterally-folding tubular butt. The SG 543 is similar, but has a much shorter barrel. Courtesy of SIG, Neuhausen.

132. The 5.56mm SG 550, offered in several guises, is the commercial version of the perfected SIG small-calibre automatic rifle. Courtesy of SIG, Neuhausen.

133. Intended for those for whom a full-length assault rifle is unnecessary, this short-barrelled StG.90 (otherwise known as the SIG SG 551) serves with the Swiss armed forces. Courtesy of SIG, Neuhausen.

army in 1988. It had previously seen service in small numbers with the Special Forces.

The Swiss SIG rifles were originally based on the StGw.57, which itself owed something to the wartime German FG.42 and MG.42. The StGw.57 was replaced in the mid 1960s by the SIG 510 series. These rifles proved to be too expensive for most of the armies of the time, though a large quantity went to Chile; once 5.56mm became popular, therefore, SIG produced the unsuccessful SG530-1 before proceeding to SG540 and SG541 (5.56mm) and the SG542 (7.62mm). All of these were designed with an eye to simplifying production. During the mid 1970s, the SG540 series was licensed to Manurhin, which made substantial numbers of 5.56mm rifles for the French army whilst the FA MAS was being perfected.

The SG541 was upgraded to SG550 standards in the early 1980s, and accepted by the Swiss army as the StGw.90.

THE BULLPUPS

In addition to the conventional 5.56mm rifles, three of more idiosyncratic 'bullpup' layout have been adopted. The Fusil Automatique F3 MAS (better known as the FA MAS) was developed at Saint-Etienne and introduced to the French army in 1973, though development problems prevented adoption for six years. Nicknamed 'le Clairon' (the bugle), owing to the curious combined carrying handle/sight base, it displays some very unusual features; for example, it is readily convertible for left- or right-hand ejection.

Light and comfortable to fire on the credit side, the adequacy of the delayed blowback action for the high-pressure cartridge has often been questioned. It remains in service, though the French have also acquired substantial quantities of the Manurhin-made (but SIG-designed) 5.56mm SG540 rifle.

The British entry into the 5.56mm field is the L85A1, adopted in 1985 after protracted development (latterly as the SA-80) lasting a decade. The rifle bears an external affinity to the old EM-2, but looks more conventional than the FA MAS. It is seen as part of a system including a light machine-gun, and perpetuates the post-war British belief that infantry weapons should have optical sights. The L85A1 is fitted with

134

a compact 4× SUSAT optical unit, though emergency open sights are contained in the pistol grip.

In spite of tortuous development, the L85A1 has not been a success. So many problems arose during the Gulf War that British newspapers were full of scare stories. The *Observer*, claiming to quote from a Ministry of Defence report, suggested that:

The Individual Weapon [L85A1] and the Light Support Weapon [L86A1] did not cope with the sand. Infantrymen faced the enemy in combat unsure whether their weapons would fire or stop. Tactical drills were affected, in that provision had to be made to cover a man with a stoppage. Some section and platoon commanders considered that casualties would have been suffered because of weapons shortages . . . had the enemy put up more resistance in close combat.'

It was suggested that the problems arose from very poor standards of manufacture; that the gun and its accessories had effectively been 'designed down to a price' by financial constraints applied by the Treasury; or that the project—having been many years in creation*—was rushed through to sweeten the sale by the government of Royal Ordnance. One senior military commander complained that the L85A1 was basically 'a poor rifle with good sights', and this is a reputation it has yet to shake off. In virtually every competitive trial, the British gun has been trounced by the Steyr AUG.

The SA-80, the prototype of the L85A1, was announced as 'The British Army's New Rifle" as long ago as 1976.

134, 135. The extraordinary French FAMAS 5.56mm rifle—colloquially named 'Le Clairon' ('the bugle')—is a very compact design. Courtesy of Ian Hogg.
136. Now known as the Rifle L85A1, the British SA-80 was adopted to replace the L1A1 (FN FAL) after trials lasting for ten years. The authorities are so convinced of the value of sophisticated sights that the L85 is issued with the 4× SUSAT or the Pilkington Kite image-intensifier (seen here on an XL70E3 rebuilt to SA-80 standards). Courtesy of Royal Ordnance plc, Nottingham.

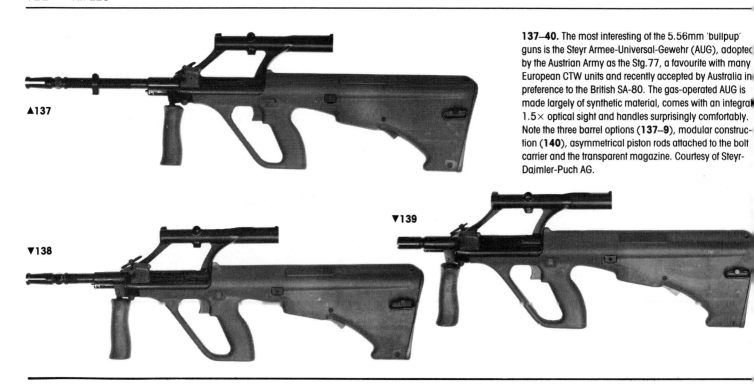

▲137

▼138

▼139

137–40. The most interesting of the 5.56mm 'bullpup' guns is the Steyr Armee-Universal-Gewehr (AUG), adopted by the Austrian Army as the Stg.77, a favourite with many European CTW units and recently accepted by Australia in preference to the British SA-80. The gas-operated AUG is made largely of synthetic material, comes with an integral 1.5× optical sight and handles surprisingly comfortably. Note the three barrel options (**137–9**), modular construction (**140**), asymmetrical piston rods attached to the bolt carrier and the transparent magazine. Courtesy of Steyr-Daimler-Puch AG.

WHAT CAN I HIT?

Very few non-shooters, brought up on a diet of fiction wherein the hero never misses the vital shot, can visualize what can be expected of a modern submachine-gun or assault rifle. For the purposes of *Guns of the Elite*, therefore, shooting results were obtained from a number of guns. Interestingly, these indicated that there is actually little to choose between most modern military weapons.

The results, so graphically presented here, indicate that most modern rifles will place approximately half the shots inside a two-inch diameter circle at 100 yards; at 200 yards, the average is nearer six inches; and, at 500, somewhere between twelve and twenty inches. Though these sound quite impressive, it must be remembered that many shots lie outside the mean diameter – in a few cases, some distance away. This means that, at 500 yards, a few stray individual shots may lie *four feet* away from the group-centre.

The inherent inaccuracy of the gun/ cartridge combination is also affected by the efficiency of the sights which, on most military rifles, are sturdy rather than sophisticated. Many modern rifles have fixed aperture-type battle sights in which the aperture has to be large enough to accommodate a variety of eyesight. This, however, may allow the eye to wander and the aim to vary. Generally, few concessions are made to range apart from providing a rocking-L with two or more settings. The

		Mean radii (in)				
Gun	Calibre	100yd	200yd	300yd	400yd	500yd
M16A1	5.56mm	1.0	3.0	3.8	6.3	7.0
XM22	5.56mm	1.1	3.0	4.7	6.2	8.5
AR18	5.56mm	1.0	2.7	4.1	6.2	8.2
AKM	7.62mm	1.2	3.2	5.0	7.4	9.0
vz/58	7.62mm	1.0	2.8	4.2	6.5	7.6
L1A1	7.62mm	1.2	2.6	5.1	6.0	6.8

Averages of five 5-shot groups per gun at each distance, from a sandbag rest; open sights.

open tangent-leaf AK and AKM back sights are notably coarse, particularly compared with the adjustable rotary pattern on the Heckler & Koch rifles or the adjustable aperture of the new M16A2. Thus, it is easier to shoot well with the H&K G41, for example, than with the AKM even though there would be little to choose between the rifles were they to be fired from a fixed rest.

Although the 5.56mm rifles – the M16A1, AR18 and the Stoner XM22 – do not appear to show much advantage over the 7.62×39mm Warsaw Pact rivals as far as accuracy is concerned, the looping trajectory associated with the AKM and the vz/58 hinder range-gauging. At 400 yards, with the sights set for 250, the 5.56mm M193 bullet strikes about 18 inches below the aim-point, the muzzle velocity of 3,100fps having declined to 1,550fps. For the standard M43 Russian cartridge, the figures are about 36in, 2,325fps and 1,050fps respectively. The full-power 7.62mm NATO cartridge returns about 20in, 2,820fps and 2,035fps, showing no real trajectory advan-

tage over the lightweight faster-moving 5.56mm bullet, but retaining much more striking energy (980 ft lb compared with about 145 ft lb at 600 yards).

The sniper rifles, of course, shoot appreciably better than assault rifles: the Finnish Valmet M86, for example, will put all its shots within a 15cm-diameter circle at 500 metres.

To illustrate the performance of the modern semi-automatic rifle in greater detail, Heckler & Koch very kindly supplied three series of 3×10 shots fired with a 5.56mm G41, a 7.62mm G3 and a PSG/1 sniper rifle. Each rifle was fitted with an optical sight, and was fired from a wrist-rest. The targets were analysed on the principles expounded by John Walter in *The Pistol Book* (Arms & Armour Press, 1983). **5.56mm Gewehr 41 Zf**: mean radius 10.3mm (0.406in) at 100m. The farthest shot lay 30.3mm (1.19in) from the centre. Thus, all thirty shots would have been contained in a 61mm circle.

The most curious looking of all the modern guns is the Austrian AUG.77 ('Armee-Universal-Gewehr'), developed and manufactured by Steyr-Daimler-Puch. Its futuristic lines, facilitated by extensive use of synthetic material, hide a gas-operated turning-bolt action efficient enough to have convinced the Australians, Irish, Malaysians, New Zealanders and others to adopt it at the expense of the British SA-80/L85A1. The AUG has also been seen in the hands of the SAS, in addition to Austrian counter-terrorist units operating at Vienna airport. Though the standard rifle chambers the 5.56mm SS109 cartridge, it is instantly convertible to a light support weapon merely by changing the barrel. Alternatively, a 9mm conversion unit transforms the AUG into an efficient submachine-gun.

140▲

7.62mm Gewehr 3 Zf: mean radius 13.2mm (0.520in) at 100m. The farthest shot lay 28.8mm (1.13in) from the centre. All thirty shots would have lain inside a 57mm circle, though fewer struck near the centre than in the G41 trial.
7.62mm Präzisions Scharfschützen-Gewehr 1 (PSG/1): mean radius 6.9mm (0.271in) at 100m. The farthest shot lay 15.4mm from the centre, and all thirty would have struck within a circle measuring 31mm – a very impressive performance indeed.

Although the chances of hitting a static target may seem reasonable enough, particularly when the rifle is fitted with optical sights, movement introduces another dimension. Appendix 3 indicates that the 7.62×51mm NATO SS77 bullet takes 0.77 seconds to cover 500 metres; at this range, a man walking at 5km/hr will have moved 1.08 metres (a little over forty inches); a man running will move more than twice this distance, and a decision must be taken as to how far to lead the target with the sights. And, if the man is also zigzagging, the chances of a hit are reduced still further.

Consequently, having approached as near to the target as they dare, snipers wait until they have a static shot; the special CTW forces, by and large, attempt to get to close quarters, where the first shots can be made to count by minimizing the firer/target distance.

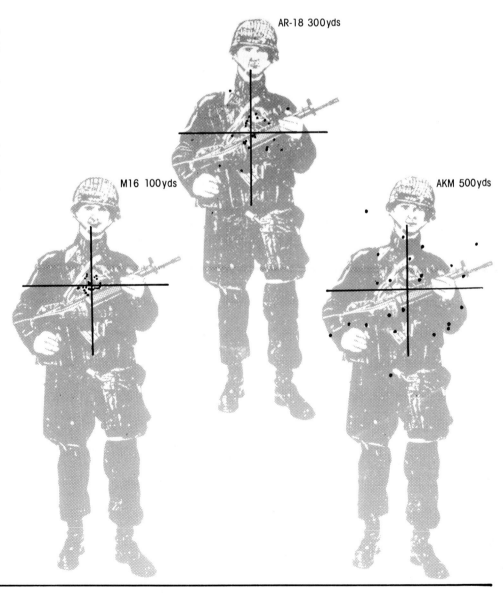

▲141   ▼142

Sniper rifles

GUNS AND THE SNIPER

The sniper continues to be an integral part of most armies, police and virtually all special forces. His brief remains the elimination of key opposing personnel (particularly officers or terrorist leaders) and counter-sniper activity. He is both well trained and specifically equipped, taking great pride in his marksmanship and – equally importantly – his ability to hide.

The widespread service introduction of intermediate cartridges, with their comparatively limited effective range, has failed to displace the traditional full-power cartridge/sniper-rifle combination necessary to engage targets successfully at 800 metres or more. At ranges below 500 metres, this chance must become a virtual certainty and few of the current crop of 5.56mm cartridges – particularly those fired from 1-in-12 pitch rifling – perform well enough to merit consideration. Thus, the old faithfuls have been retained: Britain, the USA and most of the NATO-aligned powers use the 7.62×51mm NATO round, though the French persisted with 7.5×54mm for many years and the Soviet bloc still clings to the venerable 7.62×54mm rimmed cartridge dating back to 1891.

The rifles, however, are subject to appreciably greater variation. This is partly due to the marked divergence of military and target-shooters' views of acceptable construction, and also to the varied theatres in which the sniper is expected to ply his trade. The target marksman, firing in relatively inconsequential circumstances, simply seeks the perfect strike on his target with total reliability; but the military must also consider the logistic implications, durability, and performance of man and equipment under the stress of shooting to kill. The delicate sights, triggers and accessories of many of the best target rifles are quite out of place on a battlefield, while the performance of standard military rifles rarely allows a certain 'kill' at 500 metres.

Sniper rifles and their sights, therefore, almost always represent a compromise. In addition, the counter-terrorist sniper often holds a watching brief and the provision of bipods on most of the new designs reflects the necessity to spend hours motionless, without losing concentration, yet remain sufficiently alert to make the first shot count.

Countries that still maintain something of a global presence – the USA, Britain, the Soviet Union and France – have relied on well-tried military-style rifles, accepting proven reliability and robustness at the expense of performance.

THE US ARMY AND USMC GUNS

When the US Army became officially embroiled in Vietnam, the North Vietnamese snipers soon wreaked considerable havoc. The Communists initially had little appreciation of the subtleties of sniping, and one-shot kills at ranges greater than 50 yards were rare. American counter-sniping was extremely effective at such short ranges and many of their opponents were soon killed. Ironically, this provided a form of natural selection; only the best North Vietnamese survived, becoming well-respected adversaries effective at ten times the early 50-yard maximum. Most of the sniper rifles recovered from the Communist Vietnamese have been Hungarian-made 48M Mosin-Nagant rifles, interspersed with a few Russian 1891/30 and Czech vz/54 examples.

The US Army, having used the earlier M1C and M1D (Garand) sniper rifles, with M81, M82 and M84 telescope sights, adopted the 7.62mm Rifle M14 National Match (now known as the M21) and 3>9× Leatherwood Adjustable Ranging Telescope sight in 1975. The USMC, disapproving of semi-automatic sniper rifles but in dire need of effectual alternatives, had standardized the M40 as early as April 1966. This militarized Remington Model 700 commercial bolt-action rifle was originally issued with a 3>9× Redfield optical sight, but will now be encountered with a fixed-magnification 10× Unertl pattern. The M40 has a standard barrel and a wooden stock; the improved M40A1, which shares the same action, has a stainless steel barrel and a fibreglass stock.

Severe problems were soon encountered in the hot and humid Vietnamese climate and unannounced inspections sometimes showed that as much as 60 per cent of the equipment was unserviceable. Though the rifles were reasonably durable apart from their wood stocks, which warped and mouldered, the optical sights proved to be the Achilles' heel. Detail complaints included the unnecessary zoom mechanism, poor focus at maximum magnification, ingress of moisture, poorly marked control drums, and failure of the mechanical range-finding systems. All these faults were to be expected when commercial telescopes attempted to withstand rigours of military service, but were a nuisance in the field.

Bolt-action rifles offer two considerable advantages: their shooting is generally better, owing to the lack of moving parts, and the mechanical noise generated by an autoloader is absent. With this in mind, Research Armament Prototypes of Rogers, Arkansas, has delivered a few Model 300

CLLRs (Convertible Long Range Rifles) to as yet unidentified US special forces. The bolt-action M300, which feeds from a box magazine, may be supplied in 7.62mm NATO and a new 8.58×71mm cartridge based on the 0.416in Rigby sporting rifle cartridge. Only the barrel, bolt-head and magazine need be substituted to change calibres. RAP's reasoning is that excellent long-range performance is indispensable to a sniper, and that this is better achieved by *increasing* cartridge power than by attempting to extract the maximum performance

possible from the existing 7.62mm NATO cartridge. There is even a bolt-action Model 500, in .50 Browning, which offers frighteningly potent performance in a gun weighing only a little over 30lb.

Most US SWAT and police teams use the M21 or, increasingly more widespread, the heavy-barrelled commercial version of the M16A1. The FBI Hostage Rescue Team uses the M40A1, while, in Canada, the Royal Canadian Mounted Police issues an optically-sighted commercial Winchester Model 70 bolt-action rifle.

THE BRITISH ARMY AND POLICE

The British sniper has been used to a bolt-action rifle, a 7.62mm NATO conversion of the Rifle No. 4 Mk 1(T) or 1*(T) known as the L42A1 or – for the police Blue Berets –

a variant called the Enfield Enforcer. Though optical sights have appeared on the L1A1, including the modern SUIT and SUSAT patterns, the autoloader has not proved entirely suitable for long-range work. The L42A1 has, however, been used with great success by the SAS, Marines and Paratroopers in Aden, Northern Ireland and the Falklands, with a 4× fixed-power L1A1 telescope sight adapted from the Sight, Optical, No. 32 Mk 3 of the Second World War era. The Enforcer, an adaptation of the Envoy target rifle, is usually encountered with a 4>10× Pecar telescope sight. It is more delicate than the L42A1, its variable-power sight and rather better trigger befitting less demanding police services.

During the early 1980s, experiments to replace the L42A1 have resulted in the introduction of a new rifle developed by the Olympic gold medallist Malcolm Cooper and Accuracy International. It is believed

Fig. 22. General arrangement drawings of the M85 sniper rifle. Courtesy of Parker-Hale Ltd.

143, 144. The standard British sniper equipment is currently the 7.62mm Rifle L42A1 (**144**), a descendant of the Rifle No. 4 Mk 1(T) and the venerable SMLE. The guns have served efficiently from Aden and Malaya to the Falklands and Northern Ireland (**143**). The police élite marksmen of Scotland Yard's D11 'Blue Berets' use a civilian variant of the L42A1 known as the Enfield Enforcer. Courtesy of Ian Hogg.

◄143   ▼144

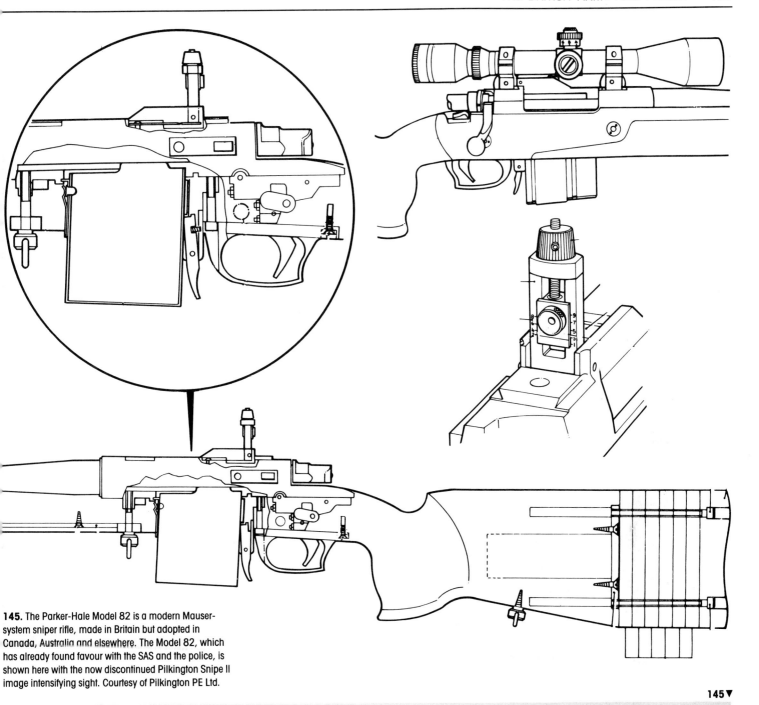

145. The Parker-Hale Model 82 is a modern Mauser-system sniper rifle, made in Britain but adopted in Canada, Australia and elsewhere. The Model 82, which has already found favour with the SAS and the police, is shown here with the now discontinued Pilkington Snipe II image intensifying sight. Courtesy of Pilkington PE Ltd.

145▼

HOW TO FIRE THE PARKER-HALE M85 SNIPER RIFLE

Starting with the gun empty, the safety catch **A** at OFF (forward) and the loaded magazine in the hand,

> close the bolt **B** and turn the bolt-handle down as far as it will go;

> insert the magazine **C** in the magazine aperture ahead of the trigger guard, press it home with the heel of the palm until the magazine-release catch **D** locks it in place;

> raise the bolt handle and pull the bolt **B** back as far as it will go, then push it forward to chamber a round and turn the bolt handle down again;

> if necessary, pull the safety catch **A** backward to ON. Do not apply the safety catch if the gun is not cocked, or if the bolt is open.

To fire:

> push the safety catch forward to OFF;

> take aim and squeeze the trigger **E**.

The process can be repeated until the magazine is empty, the action closing on an empty magazine:

> remove the empty magazine **C** by pressing the magazine-release catch **D** and simultaneously pulling the magazine box downward;

> insert a new magazine;

> open and retract the bolt when required, loading the chamber on the forward stroke.

To clear the gun:

> remove the magazine;

> set the safety catch to OFF (forward);

> open the bolt **B**, pull it slowly back and position the free hand to catch the chambered round as it is ejected;

> ensure that the breech is clear;

> close the bolt and squeeze the trigger.

The magazine can then be emptied and replaced.

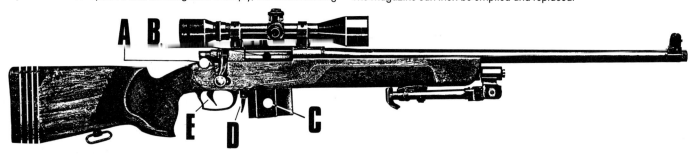

▲146   ▼147

that the PM rifle (or L96) is already replacing the Finnish-made Tikka guns previously favoured by the SAS. The Parker-Hale M85 ran the Cooper/AI design a close second in the trials, being recommended as 'fit for service', but a notable feature of the British trials was the poor performance of some of the most expensive European submissions.

The previous Parker-Hale sniper rifle (Model 82), using a Mauser action, is a strong, somewhat plain gun offering the excellent performance expected from the company with generations of experience of target shooting. It has been adopted by Australia, Canada and New Zealand, and has been used in small numbers by British special forces. Some guns are fitted with Pecar 4>10× optical sights, but the Australian and Canadian guns, at least, have

fixed-power 6×42 Kahles Helios ZF69 sights. The Model 82 has now been supplemented by the M85, offered to the British Army, and the M87 (currently interesting the Metropolitan Police). The M87 is essentially similar to the M85, but is shorter, lighter and lacks a bipod.

THE WARSAW PACT RIFLES

The standard Kalashnikov rifles, in 7.62×39mm M43, have much too looping a trajectory – and insufficient long-range accuracy – to be suitable snipers' equipment. For much of the post-war period, the Soviet Army and its satellites relied on the bolt-action Mosin-Nagant M91/30 sniper rifle, fitted with the 3.5× fixed-power PU

telescope sight. Though rather clumsy, and offering poor optical performance by Western standards, this combination proved in Vietnam that it was to be feared out to 500 metres or more.

The semi-automatic SVD (Dragunov) appeared in 1963, firing the full-power 7.62×54mm rimmed round and based on the Kalashnikov action. In Soviet service, the SVD is accompanied by the PSO-1, a 4× fixed-power optical sight that doubles as a passive infra-red detector. By the best Western standards, the SVD is somewhat crude, and its sight falls short of comparable German systems; however, like virtually all Russian-made weapons, the SVD and PSO-1 are robust and effective. The PSO-1 and image-intensifier night sights, the NSP-3 and PGN-1, are considered separately.

146, 147. Recently, trials undertaken in Britain to find a replacement for the venerable Rifle L42A1 have been resolved in favour of the Accuracy International PM (**146**), officially labelled the L96. This gun narrowly beat the Parker-Hale Model 85 (**147**). Courtesy of Parker-Hale Ltd.

148. A variant of the Parker-Hale rifle, the Model 87, has been developed for police marksmen – particularly Scotland Yard's élite D11, the 'Blue Berets'. Courtesy of Parker-Hale Ltd.

149, 150. The standard Soviet bloc sniper rifle is the SVD, or Dragunov, introduced in 1963 to replace the venerable bolt-action Mosin-Nagant. The SVD is a very light gun for its purpose, chambering the ancient 7.62×54mm rimmed round, but apparently performs well enough and has survived in service for twenty years without modification. Courtesy of Ian Hogg.

THE FRENCH GUNS

Owing to the adoption of the 5.56mm FAMAS rifle for general issue, the French army issues bolt-action rifles to snipers and special forces. The efficient Fusil à Répétition Modèle F1, Tireur d'Elite (FR-F1), with a fixed-power 4× Modèle 53bis optical sight, was used to good effect by GIGN personnel at Djibouti in 1976 (see page 48) and in the hands of French paratroops at Kolwezi, Zaïre, in March 1978, when European hostages were successfully released from the clutches of Communist guerrillas. The FR-F1 bolt system is a simple adaptation of the pre-war MAS-36, but the basic rifle has recently been transformed into the 7.62×51mm FR-F2 by adding a thermal jacket around the barrel, substituting synthetic furniture for wood, and relocating the bipod.

OTHER EUROPEAN GUNS

Few remaining NATO-aligned powers are required to protect interests as diverse as the Falklands and the Far East, or Alaska and Vietnam. They can be far more discerning where sniper equipment is concerned, but unanimity is still curiously absent. One of the most impressive of the bolt-action designs is the Austrian Scharfschützengewehr 69 (SSG.69), made by Steyr-Daimler-Puch AG on the popular Mannlicher-Schönauer bolt system. This beautifully made rifle is extremely accurate; indeed, its manufacturer claims that, with RWS Match ammunition, 10-shot groups of less than 10cm diameter can be achieved at 800 metres. At 400 metres, dispersion is a mere 13cm (5.1in) and a hit can be all but guaranteed. The SSG.69 has a wood or rotproof synthetic stock and a fixed-power 6×

42 Kahles Helios ZF69 telescope sight. It has been adopted by the Austrian army, and is used by military and paramilitary units worldwide, notably the West German counter-terrorist unit, GSG-9.

Not convinced by the claims of the proponents of bolt-action sniper rifles, Heckler & Koch has developed several special

151. The French use the FR F-1, a bolt-action gun derived from the prewar MAS-36. The FR F-1 chambers the otherwise little seen 7.5mm French service cartridge or, more recently, 7.62mm NATO. A modified rifle known as the FR F-2 is now entering service. Courtesy of Ian Hogg.

152. One of the most impressive of contemporary sniper rifles is the Steyr-Mannlicher, adopted by the Austrian armed forces and CTW units as the Scharfschützengewehr 69 (SSG.69). Military and commercial sales have been made to nearly fifty countries, and the SSG.69 is commonly encountered in the hands of the West German CTW group, GSG-9. It has also occasionally been used by the SAS and the Royal Marines in preference to the L42A1. Courtesy of Steyr-Daimler-Puch.

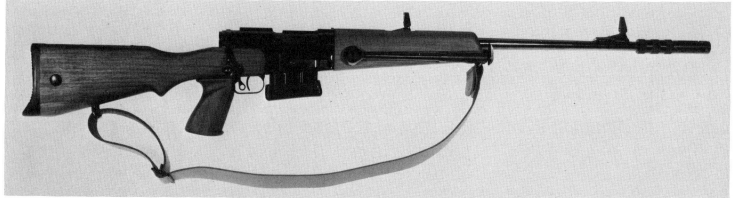

▲151 ▼152

153. Effectual camouflage is as vital to the sniper of the 1990s as it has always been. The rifle is a bolt-action pattern; guns of this type are still widely favoured, as they are comparatively simple, sturdy and much quieter in use than an auto-loader. Courtesy of Ian Hogg.

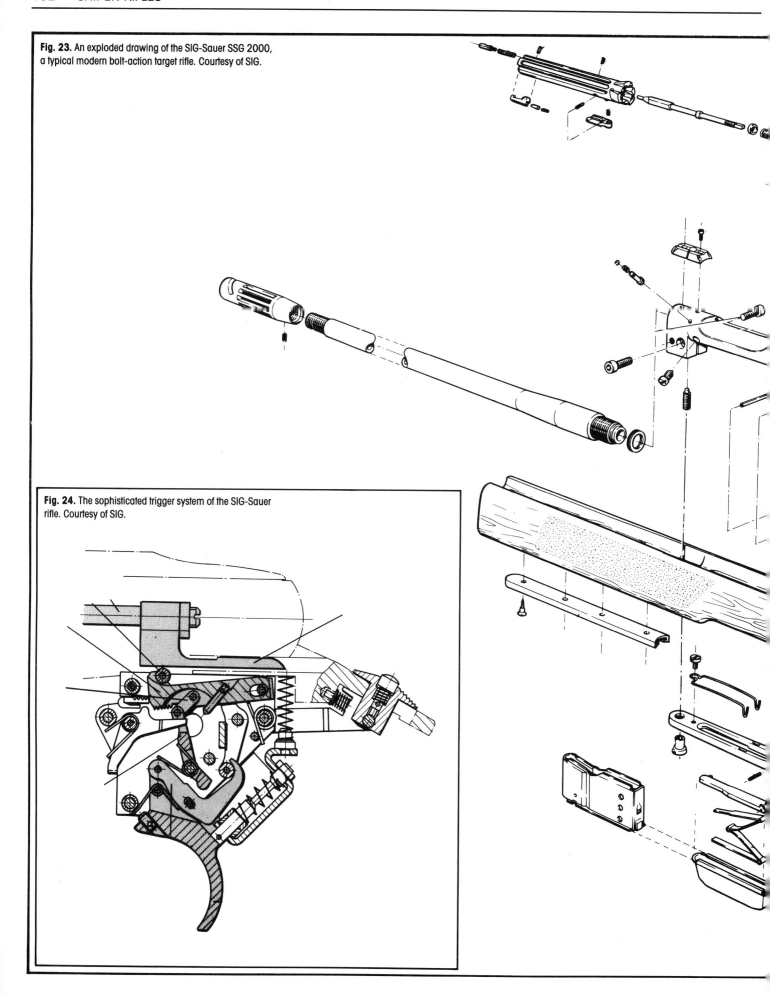

Fig. 23. An exploded drawing of the SIG-Sauer SSG 2000, a typical modern bolt-action target rifle. Courtesy of SIG.

Fig. 24. The sophisticated trigger system of the SIG-Sauer rifle. Courtesy of SIG.

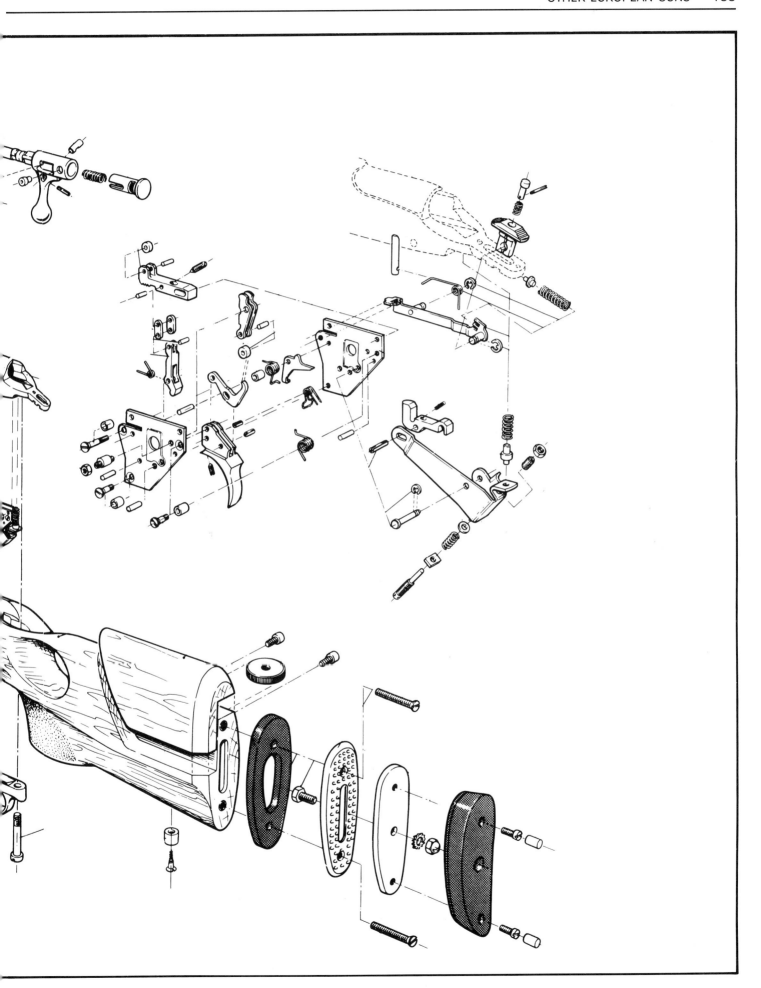

154-6

157

158

159

157–9. Other European sniper rifles worthy of note include the Mauser SG66 (**157**), with its unique ultra-short bolt system; the FN-Mauser (**158**); and the Tikka M55 Super Sporter (**159**). Small quantities of the Mauser and FN rifles have been acquired by police and CTW agencies in Belgium, Germany, Spain and elsewhere in Europe in recent years. The Tikka has been favoured by the SAS in .22-250, .243 and .308 Winchester, the calibre being selected to suit the application.

160. Another Finnish rifle which has occasionally been ▶ pressed into a sniping role is the commercial variant of the Valmet-made Kalashnikov copy, marketed in .243 and .308 as the 'Petra'. Courtesy of Sako-Valmet Oy.

154–6. Heckler & Koch has made a number of sniper rifles incorporating the proven roller-locked breech of the G3. These include specially selected, but otherwise standard G3A3 Zf, the improved G3 SG/1 used by the Bundeswehr and US special forces (**154**), and the perfected PSG-1 (**155**, **156** cased). Courtesy of Heckler & Koch GmbH, Oberndorf.

variants of the G3/HK33/G41 series. The original G3A3 Zf—simply a selected standard rifle, specially finished and fitted with an optical sight—was too much of an expedient, and was replaced by the G3 SG/1. These were based on unusually efficient, accurate G3 actions, identified at proof stage and fitted with a special set-trigger. Zeiss Diavari 1.5>6×42 optical sights are standard. Many G3 SG/1 have been purchased by the West German state police forces, though Heckler & Koch subsequently progressed to the Präzisions-Scharfschützen-Gewehr 1 (PSG-1). This much modified G3 has a heavy barrel, a greatly improved single

trigger, a competition-style adjustable palm-rest pistol grip and an adjustable butt. A 6×42 Kahles Helios ZF69 optical sight is standard, and performance is very good indeed. Mauser has offered an SG66 variant of its standard 'System 66' bolt-action rifle—with one of the shortest of all actions—and the highly sophisticated 2.5>10×56 Schmidt & Bender telescope sight. The Mauser has been seen in the hands of many German state police Special-Einsatz-Kommando, the Spanish Grupo Especiale de Operaciónes (GEO) and Israeli border guards.

Sauer and SIG have collaborated on the highly sophisticated SSG 2000.

Distinguished by an unusually effectual trigger system, this was built around the Sauer Model 90 bolt system with triple rear-locking lugs. The rifle has been offered in four chamberings—7.62×51mm NATO, 5.56mm, 7.5mm Swiss M11 and 0.300 Winchester Magnum—but has never sold in large numbers. The Swiss army has recently decided simply to purchase a special heavy-barrelled version of the standard 5.56mm Stg.90 (SIG), which will be issued as the SSG.90.

For such a sparsely populated country, Finland has a sizeable firearms industry. Commercial Tikka and Sako rifles have been purchased by many agencies,

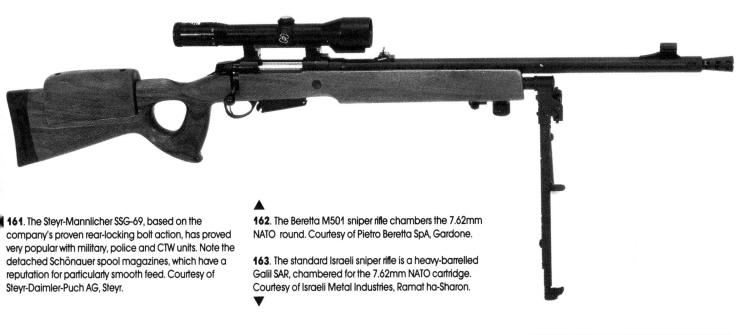

161. The Steyr-Mannlicher SSG-69, based on the company's proven rear-locking bolt action, has proved very popular with military, police and CTW units. Note the detached Schönauer spool magazines, which have a reputation for particularly smooth feed. Courtesy of Steyr-Daimler-Puch AG, Steyr.

162. The Beretta M501 sniper rifle chambers the 7.62mm NATO round. Courtesy of Pietro Beretta SpA, Gardone.

163. The standard Israeli sniper rifle is a heavy-barrelled Galil SAR, chambered for the 7.62mm NATO cartridge. Courtesy of Israeli Metal Industries, Ramat ha-Sharon.

including the SAS and the Pakistani special security services, and Valmet (now Sako–Valmet) has made a semi-sporting variant of the standard Kalashnikov-type assault rifle under the brandname 'Petra'.

The purpose-built bolt-action Valmet M86 sniper rifle has been purchased in small numbers by the Finnish armed forces. This impressive gun, though long and heavy (1,210mm, 5.7kg without sights), appears to derive more from traditional army-type sniper rifles than the target shooter's dream; and, despite the bipod and adjustable cheek piece, presents an unusually conventional appearance. It was designed expressly to guarantee hitting a 150mm-diameter target at 500m, with specially selected ammunition, and is claimed to group its shots inside 65mm at 300m. The Sako TRG-21 has also sold in small numbers, though the Finnish army, probably for reasons of economy, has now produced its own adaption of the tried and tested Mosin-Nagant bolt action.

SUPER-CALIBRE RIFLES

When the first edition of this book was published, attempts to interest the military in large-calibre sniping rifles had been comparatively unsuccessful. Though small quantities of AMAC LRRS (0.338/416 or 0.50) and Barrett Light Fifty guns were sold, often for the Special Forces, their public profile remained low. Much of the initial lack of enthusiasm stemmed from the fact that 0.50 machine-gun ammunition was designed not for extreme accuracy, but instead to give effectual scatter when fired continuously.

Once improvements in the cartridges began to be made, the value of hitting helicopters, vehicles and similar valuable equipment at long range could be clearly appreciated. The lesson was not really new; throughout the Second World War, the Red Army had retained its 14.5mm anti-tank rifles for use against vehicles long after their value against tanks had declined.

Typical of the current offerings in this field is the Barrett M82A1 Light Fifty. The manufacturer's literature draws attention to the fact that:

'Armored personnel carriers, radar dishes, communications vehicles, aircraft and area denial submunitions are all vulnerable to the quick strike capability of the Barrett 82A1 ... With decisive force, and without the need for manpower and expense of mortar or rocket crews, your forces can engage the opposition at distances far beyond the range of small arms fire ...'

The Light Fifty is a recoil-operated semi-automatic measuring about 61in (1550mm) overall, and weighs about 32.5lb (14.7kg). It feeds from a detachable box magazine containing eleven rounds, will usually be encountered with 10× optical sights, and fires 0.50 M33 Ball ammunition with a muzzle velocity of 2800fps. Recoil is claimed to be not unlike that of a 12-Bore shotgun, and the gun can actually be fired from the hip if the firer can lift it.

The success of Barrett, McMillan and guns of this general type in their intended role, and the usefulness of large-calibre machine-guns to down small helicopters—including one destroyed in Northern Ireland by the IRA—has inspired work to begin elsewhere.

The Hungarian M1 Gepard is an interesting single-shot rifle, chambered for the 12.7 × 108mm Soviet machine-gun cartridge. The bolt and the pistol grip are combined in one unit, which is withdrawn from the gun to allow a single round to be inserted, whilst a combination of an effectual muzzle brake and a buffer are used to keep the recoil sensation within reasonable bounds. The Gepard, about 1340mm long and weighing 15.5kg, is designed for use at ranges up to 1200 metres. However, the demise of the Soviet bloc has left it temporarily without a role; attempts are apparently being made to re-chamber it for the 0.50 Browning cartridge, but have yet to be satisfactorily concluded.

Designer Istvan Fellegi has also developed a semi-automatic Elefant rifle, chambering the 14.5 × 114mm cartridge developed for the original Soviet anti-tank rifles. This is a particularly potent round—much more powerful than the 0.50 Browning—and could ultimately find an important niche for special purposes.

164. The Barrett M82A1 'Light Fifty' long-range sniping rifle chambers the .50 Browning heavy machine-gun round in a successful attempt to increase destructive capability at long range. Courtesy of Ian Hogg.

Sniper sights

The most popular military sights remain 'open' types, which are usually very durable and easy to use. The rotary sight on the Heckler & Koch G3 and SIG SG540/550 series, or the new drum sight adopted for the US Rifle M16A2 are good examples of the current state of the art. In the 1950s, however, the British were prepared to adopt a non-magnifying optical sight with the abortive EM-2 rifle, in the hope that sighting would be facilitated and performance greatly improved. Though the rifle was abandoned, the principle of general-issue optical sights has persisted in British service, with the widespread issue of the Sight, Unit, Infantry, Trilux (SUIT, now known as SUSAT) for the L1A1 and its recent adoption for the Rifle L85.

However, optical sights suffer certain inherent problems. Not only are they complicated – and often too delicate to withstand the rigours of military service – but magnification of the target means that the firer's eyes see different images if both eyes remain open during shooting. Thus, though the sights improve deliberate shooting, they can hinder target location and (particularly) engagement of moving targets. The Austrian army, seemingly aware of this problem, has accepted an optical sight magnifying only 1.5 times with the AUG (Stg.77). Owing to the accommodating properties of the human eye, this sight can be used with both eyes open and permits a wider field of view than the British 4× SUSAT. It also allows the firer to spot potential threats that may lie outside the limited view through the sight.

INFRA-RED SIGHTS

Prior to the Second World War, the sniper was forced to rely solely on optical sights, reducing his effectiveness in twilight – despite the light-gathering properties of the better sights – and rendering him completely ineffectual in darkness. Though luminous 'night sights' had been developed for infantry rifles as early as the First World War, these simply consisted of bars and dots to facilitate alignment of standard open sights and still depended on the firer's capability to select the basic target.

By the 1940s, however, the value of infrared detection had been realized and several attempts were made to fit active detectors in rifle sights. These worked by emitting beams in the infra-red wavelength (longer than visible light, and hence undetectable by

165. The SniperScope was an early US attempt to provide an active infra-red sight. It is seen here on a T3 (M3) Carbine, which emphasises its bulk. Primitive it may have been, but the SniperScope undoubtedly improved marksmanship in poor conditions. Courtesy of Ian Hogg.

the human eye) to 'illuminate' the target zone, providing a picture at which the marksman could shoot once the reflections had been focused onto a converter unit containing a primitive photocathode. Photons, provided by the energy of the reflected illuminator beam, cause the photocathode to emit electrons. These electrons are focused onto a phosphorescent target screen, from which new photons are emitted to present the viewer with a reconstructed image. The faithfulness of reproduction depends on the gain in the system (i.e., the number of electrons released by each original photon). In the early sights this amplification was comparatively feeble; the reconstructed images, poor and lacking in detail. But they were appreciably better than not being able to see at all.

Early in the Second World War, the Germans adapted a vehicle-control system known as the Fahrzeug-Gerät 1229 to serve as a night-sight for the Karabiner 98k. The key component was a converter designed by the Forschungsanstalt der Deutschen

▲166   ▼167   168▶

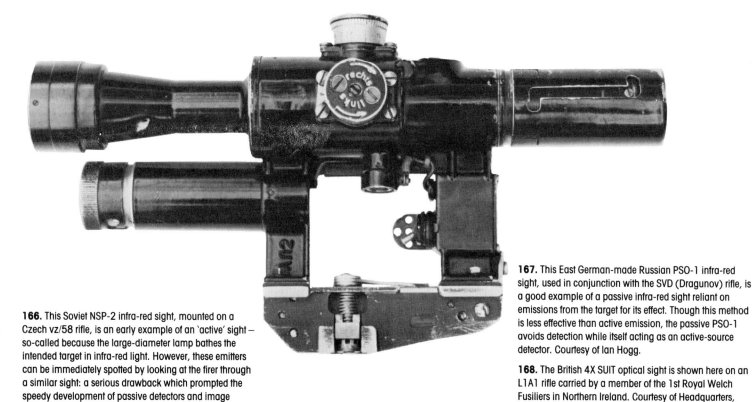

166. This Soviet NSP-2 infra-red sight, mounted on a Czech vz/58 rifle, is an early example of an 'active' sight — so-called because the large-diameter lamp bathes the intended target in infra-red light. However, these emitters can be immediately spotted by looking at the firer through a similar sight: a serious drawback which prompted the speedy development of passive detectors and image intensifiers. Courtesy of Ian Hogg.

167. This East German-made Russian PSO-1 infra-red sight, used in conjunction with the SVD (Dragunov) rifle, is a good example of a passive infra-red sight reliant on emissions from the target for its effect. Though this method is less effective than active emission, the passive PSO-1 avoids detection while itself acting as an active-source detector. Courtesy of Ian Hogg.

168. The British 4X SUIT optical sight is shown here on an L1A1 rifle carried by a member of the 1st Royal Welch Fusiliers in Northern Ireland. Courtesy of Headquarters, British Army Northern Ireland.

▲169

▼170

169. The US Varo AN-PVS4 second-generation image intensifier, detached from the gun. Courtesy of Ian Hogg.

170. This Eltro-Zeiss image-intensifying sight, mounted on a G3, is typical of the bulky first-generation designs. It weighs more than 5lb, but was much favoured by GSG-9 before being replaced by more compact second-generation patterns. Courtesy of Heckler & Koch.

Reichspost, Berlin, and perfected by Leitz of Wetzlar. The ZG 1229 Vampir consisted of a 13cm-diameter transmitter lamp, the converter tube, a magnifying objective lens and a power supply. The transmitter/receiver, which weighed 2.25kg, clamped onto the optical sight bracket of the Kar.98k, the Gew.43 or MP.43. Though their effectiveness was limited, the sights undoubtedly improved the performance of the sniper in marginal conditions. On the debit side, the power pack weighed nearly 15kg.

By the end of the war, the US Army had issued the SniperScope, which worked on much the same principle as the Vampir. It is shown here mounted on a variant of the M1 Carbine known as the T3 (or M3); excessive weight and limited sighting range made the SniperScope/Garand pairing too

heavy for combat duty. Yet these first-generation sights inspired a wide range of post-war experiments to improve the performance of infra-red detectors or 'collect' ambient light to intensify the true image. The discovery of lasers in 1960 presaged other possibilities.

The first infra-red sights, such as the ZG 1229 and – indeed – many later developments, suffer a serious problem: active emission of infra-red can be easily detected by the intended target, provided suitable equipment is available. Thus, counter-snipers can make use of a passive detector (i.e., one that does not emit infra-red) to locate the source of the illuminating beam. Passive infra-red location can also be used as a sight in its own right, but lacks range and definition capabilities. However, because the detector is usually infinitely

smaller than the transmitter, passive capability can be built into an optical sight such as the Soviet PSO-1 issued with the SVD rifle.

The PSO-1 is an ungainly, but effective fixed-power 4× telescope sight, with powered reticle illumination and excellent Carl Zeiss Jena lenses. In the bottom left-hand corner of a the image-field is a range-finding system based on a man 5ft 7in tall. Ranges up to 1,000 metres can then be set on the adjusting drum atop the sight, the uppermost chevron aligned on the target and the gun fired; three lower chevrons permit shooting at 1,100, 1,200 and 1,300 metres. The presence of infra-red emitters can be detected by setting the range-drum to 400 metres, pivoting the detector-plate into the field of view (the control lies on the left side of the sight ahead of the range

drum) and scanning the area. These emitters show as reddish-orange spots in the viewfinder. The uppermost chevron is simply aligned with the marks, and firing can commence. Unlike many of the more advanced sights, the PSO-1 is light, the SVD/PSO-1 combination weighing only about 9.6lb (cf., Walther WA 2000, 16.8lb).

The latest passive infra-red or 'thermal imaging' (TI) sights are appreciably better than their predecessors, but the sensor requires constant cooling and prevents TI sights entering widespread service. The most common coolant is liquid nitrogen, a tiny gas bottle being incorporated in the sight or its mount. For some years, the Italian Officine Galileo company offered a dual thermal imaging/image intensification sight which had the additional capability of superimposing both images.

IMAGE-INTENSIFYING SIGHTS

The principal alternative to the infra-red systems, with their detection and cooling problems, is image intensification (II). This is intended to give 'daylight' vision in twilight or semi-darkness, relying on the wavelengths of visible light rather than infra-red, and can do so surprisingly well. However, the sights are not as efficient as most fictional works would have us believe; for example, they are practically useless in woodland on moonless, overcast nights and – without filters – will black out under even street lighting. The accompanying chart illustrates the range of performance more graphically.

The image intensifiers rely on the image of an imperceptibly-lit target to excite electrons on a photo-sensitive plate. The ambient light is focused onto the front element of the converter unit by a system of lenses not unlike that of a conventional optical sight, with similar reticle adjustability for elevation and lateral deflection. In much the same manner as the infra-red sights, the converter relies on photocathodes to emit electrons when irradiated by photons supplied by the light from the target-image. The number of electrons emitted for each photon constitutes the sensitivity of the photocathode, but more than one stage can be built into the sight. The maximum practicable amplification is currently a triple-stage $40 \times 40 \times 40$ (64,000

171. The Pilkington Kite on a Canadian C7 rifle. Courtesy of Pilkington PE Ltd.

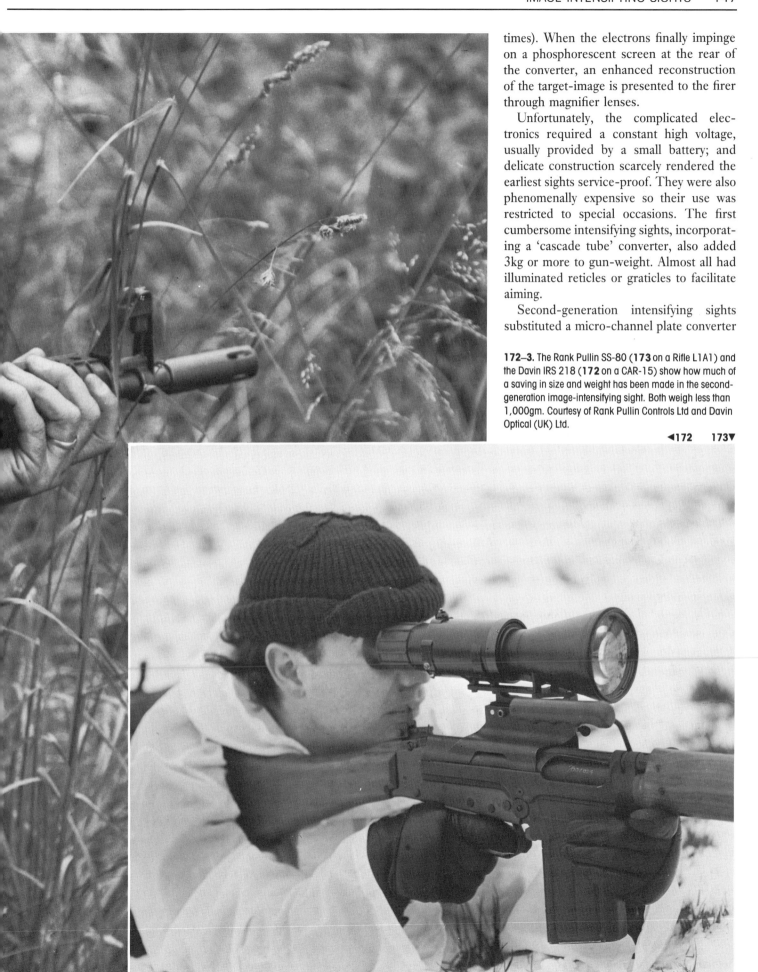

times). When the electrons finally impinge on a phosphorescent screen at the rear of the converter, an enhanced reconstruction of the target-image is presented to the firer through magnifier lenses.

Unfortunately, the complicated electronics required a constant high voltage, usually provided by a small battery; and delicate construction scarcely rendered the earliest sights service-proof. They were also phenomenally expensive so their use was restricted to special occasions. The first cumbersome intensifying sights, incorporating a 'cascade tube' converter, also added 3kg or more to gun-weight. Almost all had illuminated reticles or graticles to facilitate aiming.

Second-generation intensifying sights substituted a micro-channel plate converter

172–3. The Rank Pullin SS-80 (**173** on a Rifle L1A1) and the Davin IRS 218 (**172** on a CAR-15) show how much of a saving in size and weight has been made in the second-generation image-intensifying sight. Both weigh less than 1,000gm. Courtesy of Rank Pullin Controls Ltd and Davin Optical (UK) Ltd.

◄**172**   **173**▼

174–6. Illustrations from the Heckler & Koch catalogue show the difference an image intensifying sight can make under dusk or night conditions. The image shown here, which can only be taken as a guide, is obtained with Philips Elektro-Spezial BM8028 image-intensifying goggles, as part of the Laser-assisted Heckler & Koch INCAS system approved by the Bundeswehr and used by, among other agencies, GSG-9 and the Federal German police. The goggles weigh 1kg (2.2lb) and have a field of view of 48°. Virtually all image intensifiers washout colours, though this is usually of little importance to the firer. Picture **176** shows the laser unit built in to the rifle fore-end. Courtesy of Heckler & Koch GmbH.

▲174   ▼175

176▲

for the earlier cascade-tube converter. The bundle of fibre-optics through which the electrons are accelerated gives a shorter path and saves weight. For example, the British Pilkington KITE 4× Individual Weapon Sight (selected for the L85 rifle) is only 255mm overall, 73mm in diameter and weighs about 1,000gm. Requiring only two 1.5V batteries – 2.7V in the L85 system – it gives daylight vision under starlight conditions out to 600 metres. The image gain is controlled by the plate voltage. The comparable Rank Pullin SS80 Lightweight Night Sight is 285mm overall, has a maximum diameter of 90mm and weighs 940gm excluding the mounting bracket; its performance includes a magnification of 3.8× and a range of 400 metres under starlight conditions. The Rank Pullin SS82 Night Pocketscope is somewhat smaller – 230mm long, 70mm diameter and weighing 700gm – but achieves this by limiting performance to a range of only 210 metres with a 2× magnification.

LASER SIGHTS

The problems of infra-red sighting have led to laser-assisted illuminating systems such as the INCAS unit fitted integrally with some Heckler & Koch G3 and G41 rifles. This makes use of Philips Elektro-Spezial BM 8208 goggles-type image intensifiers worn by the firer, and a powerful infra-red laser unit adding only some 220gm to the basic rifle weight (4.3kg unladen for the G3, 4.1kg for the G41). The goggles offer the firer daylight firing under starlight conditions, at the expense of some inconvenience and restriction of peripheral vision. Target location is facilitated by the improved vision, whereupon the gun is roughly aimed at the target; the laser marker can then be activated to project an invisible beam in the vicinity of the target. This shows in the goggles as a dot of white light which is laid accurately on the target and the gun is fired. This system is simple, effective, and permits target illumination for only a second or two, hindering detection appreciably.

The NATO-aligned countries have a virtual monopoly of second-generation image-intensifying sights, many excellent designs being offered by Pilkington and Rank Pullin in Britain; Varo and Litton Industries in the USA; Philips and Oldelft in The Netherlands, and several companies in Germany. The Warsaw Pact is at an appreciable disadvantage, as the standard NSP-3 and PGN-1 sights are very crude by comparison with Western examples.

OTHER SIGHTS

Unfortunately, the infra-red, image-intensification/laser marker and similar systems are too expensive for general issue. Consequently, several attempts have been made to develop collimator sights – exemplified by the late, lamented Singlepoint – that appear to project an aiming dot on the target provided the firer's eyes are compatible with the principle of the system. This is an optical illusion, but an effective one; it undoubtedly promotes accurate snap-shooting for comparatively little investment, the Swedish Aimpoint sight costing hundreds rather than thousands of pounds. The South African Armson OES (Occluded Eye Sight) is also encountered.

Unfortunately, collimator sights are less useful in twilight and of almost no use in darkness (despite the illuminated reticle) if the target cannot be identified; firing from dark-to-bright conditions can also be problematical. They have taken several forms, some depending on firer having adequate binocular vision and others adapted for one eye. But despite their attractive features, none has yet been adopted for general use.

Machine-guns

By 1939, only the Germans had seriously challenged the traditional machine-gun concept, clandestinely developing the first true 'general purpose machine-gun' at Solothurn in Switzerland in 1929–30 and then producing the MG.34 – the first design to combine the advantages of a heavy design with the mobility of a light gun. The MG.34 could be mounted on the MG-Lafette 34, a heavy buffered-cradle mount for sustained fire, or transformed into a light belt-fed gun (weighing 27lb) with a small bipod.

177. These two members of 40 Commando, Royal marines, are pictured prior to the landings at San Carlos during the British campaign to retrieve the Falkland Islands. The man on the right carries a GPMG, while his companion has an L42A1 sniper rifle *and* an L2A3 Sterling submachine-gun. Both have a plentiful supply of ammunition for the machine-gun. Courtesy of the Royal Marines Museum, Eastney.

178, 179. The German MG.42, which succeeded the MG.34, was appreciably easier to make. The characteristic rattle of its 1,200 rpm cyclic rate was to be heard on many wartime battlefields. Allegedly based on a prototype captured when the Wehrmacht invaded Poland, the roller-locked MG.42 (**178** in the hands of an élite German Gebirgsjäger unit) inspired the current Heckler & Koch series. The West German MG3, made by Rheinmetall, is little more than a minor variant of the MG.42, sharing the remarkable exchangeable-barrel system. Courtesy of Ian Hogg.

THE SECOND WORLD WAR

This period was the proving ground for all the new machine-guns. Among the great successes were the Bren Gun (still in limited front-line service in 1986) and the Browning; disasters included many Italian and most Japanese designs. The MG.34, though excellent in some respects, merely paved the way for the roller-locked MG.42, and the crude, but otherwise efficient Russian Degtyarev was not perpetuated after 1945.

Several promising designs failed because resources were diverted to support existing production weapons, or where development was curtailed. For instance, the US Marine Raiders, Rangers, the First Marine Parachute Battalion and other élite US airborne forces used small numbers of Johnson light machine-guns, the perfected version of which, the Model 1944, weighed only 14.7lb with its monopod. The Johnson had some excellent features, including its un-

◄177
178▲ 179▼

usually low weight and quick-change barrel. Its advertising literature made much of these, claiming that 'official reports . . . tell of its efficiency under battle conditions and, above all, its flexibility. It has been used for single-shot sniping at ranges up to a thousand yards and has been fired full automatic from the hip at advancing groups of Japanese at ranges of a few feet.'

The Johnson was denied the opportunity of wider recognition by the understandable reluctance of the US authorities to concentrate production resources on anything other than the handful of existing well-tried designs – the Garand, the Browning, the M1 Carbine and the BAR. As a result, the 1941-pattern Johnson light machine-gun was more prone to jamming than some rivals, and somewhat less robust. But if the German FG.42 is seen as a milestone in smallarms history, a genuinely controllable rifle-size full-automatic, then at least a thought should be spared for the Johnson . . . doomed in the manner of the later Stoner Mk 23 Mod 0 light-machine gun in Vietnam.

POST-WAR ANALYSIS

As the majority of the operating principles had been established by 1945, most current guns are merely adaptations of pre-war designs. The Brownings, particularly, had been perfected prior to 1939. But if this is a reasonable assumption, contemporary assessments of the machine-gun's tactical role do not reflect former opinions. This is partly due to the adoption of comparatively low-powered intermediate ammunition with poor long-range performance, and also to the blurring of the distinction between infantry rifles and light machine-guns by the assault rifle.

The light support weapon (LSW) category contains a proliferation of belt- and box-fed guns, and a few, such as the Czech vz/52, which are convertible. Though belt-fed guns offer a higher rate of fire, they are useless if replacement belts are unavailable. Box-fed guns, conversely, may be reloaded from loose cartridges taken from the rifle-men – provided, of course, that the guns share common cartridges. The acknowledged poor long-range capabilities of the US M193 5.56mm ball have led to some armies retaining 7.62mm NATO support weapons such as the US M60 series or the FN MAG. However, the recent relaxation

▲180 ▼181

of the US Army requirement to pierce a standard US steel helmet at '800 metres or more' to *up to* 800 metres, has permitted adoption of the 5.56mm belt-fed FN Minimi.

180. The standard full-power machine-gun of the US armed forces is the M60 and its perfected adaptation, the M60E1. Unfortunately, the original gun had several bad features – such as the barrel-mounted bipod visible in this official US Army photograph of troops 'somewhere in America' in 1962. Courtesy of the Department of the Army, Washington DC.

181. Carrying the M60 by its bipod, as shown in this US Army photograph from Vietnam, placed unnecessary strain on the barrel. In addition, changing a hot barrel was needlessly complicated. The modified M60E1 went some way to rectify matters by improving the bipod, feed mechanism and sights. Courtesy of the Department of the Army, Washington DC.

182. The M60 and M60E1 are light enough to be fired from the hip if the firer is strong enough, but rather inconvenient to hold. Consequently, the Saco Defense Division of the Maremont Corporation has developed the M60E3 – with its lightweight bipod and auxiliary front pistol-grip – which weighs a mere 18.5lb. Courtesy of Saco Defense Systems.

THE US M60 GPMG

The standard US light machine-gun is the 7.62mm M60 series, the initial model of which appeared shortly before American embroilment in Vietnam began. Made by the Saco Defense Systems Division of the Maremont Corporation, the M60 was originally a highly unsatisfactory design for the world's most advanced industrial power. Not only had the feed system (culled from the German FG.42 and MG.42) been revised to its detriment, but the bipod was attached to the quick-change barrel – making the barrel change particularly awkward – and the sights were surprisingly poor. As a result of battle experience, however, the greatly improved M60E1 made its début. The bipod was moved to the gas cylinder assembly, facilitating barrel changing, the carrying handle was improved, the sights refined and a number of changes made to the feed mechanism and gas-system assem-

blies. As a result, the M60E1 has been improved to such a point that it is on a par with the MAG. Recently, the US Army has taken the Minimi after trials with a selection of indigenous and European guns, though certain sections of the US armed forces apparently still favour the Singapore-made CIS Ultimax (see below). The lightened Maremont-designed M60A3 was adopted by the USMC in 1983 and has also been procured in small numbers for special-purpose use.

THE STONER MACHINE-GUN

During the Vietnam war, abortive trials were undertaken with many machine rifles and light machine-guns, including the Colt-backed CMG-2 and the Stoner M63 series promoted by the Cadillac Gage Company. Colt, in fact, still offers a detachable heavy-barrel variant of the M16A1 which is greatly favoured by US Special Forces, SWAT Teams and other paramilitary groups. Dur-

182▼

▲183

ing the 1960s, the US Navy equipped many of its SEAL teams with the Stoner Mk 23 Mod. 0 light machine-gun for covert operations in Vietnam, arguing that the superior firepower of the comparatively light Mk 23 (which weighed only 11.68lb) and its capacity for sustained fire outweighed its suspect reliability and the occasional tendency to 'go auto' while in the single-shot mode. As the SEALs paid great attention to maintenance and could be relied upon to clean the guns almost daily, few operational troubles were encountered. It is interesting to speculate that the Mk 23 and its companion rifle, the XM22, could have been developed to a fully satisfactory service status had the project been granted the necessary resources.

THE BRITISH L4 AND L7 MACHINE-GUNS

Since 1957, the British army has been satisfied with the 7.62mm Gun, Machine, L7A1 and L7A2 – the British-made variant of the FN MAG that has performed well enough in Aden, the Falklands and elsewhere without ever entirely displacing the supposedly obsolete L4A4, a Bren Mk 3 converted to 7.62mm NATO. With its top-feed box magazine, the L4, which weighs 21lb, is

undoubtedly more accurate (and handier) than the belt-fed L7 series. Its principal drawbacks are limited magazine capacity and a comparatively light barrel which heats up rapidly. The Bren Gun is to be replaced in the late 1980s by the 5.56mm L86. However, it remains to be seen whether the mid- and long-range performance of the 5.56mm SS109 bullet will be deemed acceptable.

THE PRINCIPAL EUROPEAN GUNS

Apart from France and Germany, most NATO armies are satisfied with the MAG. The French have clung to the curious semi-delayed-blowback Arme Automatique Transformable (AAT) Mle 52 after the adoption of the 5.56mm FAMAS rifle, but suffer accordingly. The AAT 52 operates on the very margins of safety and trials have shown that it is particularly prone to jamming. As barrel changing is also problematical, it is hard to see the AAT in the vanguard of technology.

The German army machine-gun, the MG3 (and its various predecessors), derives directly from the wartime MG42. The roller-locking system is simple, effective

183. Among the comparatively unsuccessful 5.56mm light machine-guns tested by the US armed forces have been the Stoner 63A1 used by US Navy SEAL tests in Vietnam as the 5.56mm Machine-gun Mk 23. The gun was well liked, weighing less than 13lb, but was unreliable unless kept clean and had an unfortunate tendency to 'go auto' unbidden. Courtesy of Ian Hogg.

and reasonably reliable (in some tests, the MG3 has not performed as well as the MAG or the PK), barrel change is simplicity itself, and the feed is particularly smooth and effective.

Heckler & Koch makes a variety of 7.62mm-calibre machine-guns, though, as yet, they have still to displace the MG3 as the standard weapon of the Bundeswehr. However, they are popular among special forces because of their variety, flexibility and light weight. All share the standard roller-locking system, associated with the G3 rifle. Users of the H&K guns include GSG-9, whose G6 features an integral 4× optical sight and a special linkless feed

184, 185. The belt-feed FN MAG has proved an outstanding success, being adopted by many armies worldwide – including the British Army, as the L7A1 and L7A2 GPMG, or 'Jimpy'. Picture **184** shows a standard FN-made gun. The L7 is light enough to be fired from the hip, picture **185** showing two members of the 3rd Light Infantry fresh from range practice in Omagh, Northern Ireland, in June 1986. Note that the soldier on the right carries a magazineless L4A4 Bren Gun. Courtesy of Fabrique Nationale and Headquarters, British Forces Northern Ireland.

▼184

185▲

186, 187. FN also promotes the 5.56mm Minimi, an interesting light machine-gun capable of belt (**186**) or box-magazine feed (**187**). The Minimi is made in a number of varieties, including a 'Para' model with a rectactable stock and a short barrel. Courtesy of Fabrique Nationale Herstal SA.

186▲

187▲

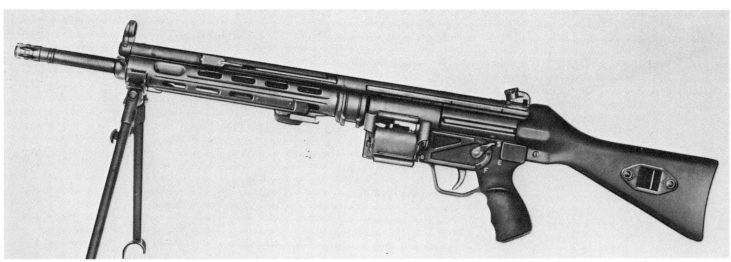

▲188

189▲   190▼

188–90. Heckler & Koch has made a variety of machine-guns built on the proven roller-lock. The full-power guns include the HK21A1 (**188**) in 7.62×51mm, while the HK13E (**189**) chambers 5.56×45mm. The HK12 handles the 7.62×39mm Russian M43 cartridge, while the HK21E (**190**) may chamber any of the three. Courtesy of Heckler & Koch GmbH.

system which can be loaded with clips or loose rounds, and replenished at any time. The ill-fated US Delta Force mission to rescue the hostages in Iran apparently selected the 7.62mm HK21A1 (an unsuccessful contender in the US JSSAP Squad Automatic Weapon competition) in the absence of a suitable full-calibre indigenous light machine-gun.

The Austrians, the Italians, the Portuguese and the Spanish have all used variants of the MG42, MG42/59 or MG3 at one time or another, though the Austrians are now issuing the heavy-barrelled LSW variant of the Steyr AUG and the Italians are experimenting with a number of LSWs submitted by Beretta, Franchi and others. The Swiss MG51 is essentially similar to the G3, but has a flap-lock rather than rollers.

THE 5.56mm DESIGNS

Many European arms-makers – including Beretta and Steyr-Daimler-Puch – offer 'machine rifle' derivatives of their basic assault rifles, although, despite the provision of heavy quick-change barrels, it is difficult to see these fulfilling the traditional light machine-gun role. This class shows the deficiencies of the all-purpose 5.56mm round most clearly, and it is hard to avoid the conclusion that the British 0.280in EM-2 or 6.25mm cartridges would have provided better overall performance in assault and sniper rifles, as well as light and even medium machine-guns.

The leading contender for widespread adoption appears to be the FN-made Minimi, which has caught the attention of the US Army (though a minority of its experts apparently favour the CIS Ultimax described below). The Minimi has been standardized as the US 5.56mm Squad Automatic Weapon M249 since 1982. It is an interesting design, feeding from box or belts at will, and will probably be adopted by the Belgian army in due course.

Heckler & Koch also makes a variety of 5.56mm machine-guns embodying the well-known roller locking system and externally all but indistinguishable from the 7.62mm (NATO and Soviet M43) patterns, though usually smaller and somewhat lighter.

191-4. Other contenders in the European 5.56mm LSW stakes include the British SA-80 LSW (191-2), the Italian Beretta AS 70/90 (193) and the Austrian Steyr AUG HB (194). As yet, none has seen sufficient service to be properly established and their future is by no means certain. Box-magazine feed is by no means ideal in a support weapon, particularly in a bullpup design which limits the cartridge capacity and makes alternative belt-feed (cf., Minimi) all but impossible. Courtesy of Heckler & Koch GmbH, Royal Ordnance Small Arms Ltd, Pietro Beretta SpA and Steyr-Daimler-Puch AG.

191▼

192▲

193▲   194▼

▲195

195. The most commonly encountered Soviet machine-gun design is the RPK and its small-calibre RPK-74 derivative, LSW variants of the standard Kalashnikov rifles. Generally encountered with 30- or 40-round box magazines (the protrusion of which hinders shooting when prone), they lack exchangeable barrels and are, consequently, incapable of sustaining fire for long periods. This photograph of Soviet army winter exercises shows two RPKs (centre and left), an AKM (right), and a holstered Makarov pistol worn by the squad leader. Courtesy of Ian Hogg.

196. The standard Soviet GPMG is the PK, another Kalashnikov design, handling the ancient rimmed 7.62× 54mm cartridge. Though the PK has an unnecessarily complicated feed system — owing to the design of the cartridge case and the closed-pocket belts — it is, none the less, a solid and reliable performer. Weighing a little under 19lb, the perfected PKM is comparable with the recent M60E3 US light machine-gun. Courtesy of Ian Hogg.

197. This photograph of joint manoeuvres undertaken by the armed forces of Russia, the German Democratic Republic and Czechoslovakia in September 1966 shows the ease with which a modern light machine-gun can be handled. Note the Czech paratrooper sitting atop the armoured personnel carrier, firing a vz/59 from the shoulder during Exercise 'Moldau' (Voltava). Courtesy of TASS.

THE WARSAW PACT GUNS: RPD, RPK AND PK

The Soviet bloc has approached machine-gun requirements in a different way, largely due to the early adoption of the 7.62× 39mm M43 intermediate cartridge. Soon after the appearance of the Kalashnikov assault rifle, development of a suitable 'squad automatic' or light support weapon commenced. The RPD appeared in 1952–3 and has remained in service for thirty years, requiring purely minor modification. Obsolescence in the Warsaw Pact countries has permitted countless thousands to be dispatched to terrorists, guerrillas and 'freedom fighters' throughout the Third World.

The RPD is gas-operated, weighing only about 15.7lb unladen, with a 100-round disintegrating-link belt carried in a detachable drum. Though reasonably reliable, belt-lifting capabilities in unfavourable conditions are marginal and newer versions with non-reciprocating cocking handles can jam solid if an attempt to cock them is made with the safety catch applied. In addition, the RPD lacks a detachable barrel and is incapable of sustained fire; this, and the comparatively poor long-range performance of its cartridge, compromises its effectiveness appreciably.

The RPD was replaced in Soviet service in the 1960s by the RPK, a 'machine rifle' derivative of the standard Kalashnikov. Like the RPD, the RPK lacks a detachable barrel and is similarly incapable of sustained fire. Its principal advantages are its light weight – 12.9lb with a loaded 30-round box magazine, 15.7lb with the 75-round drum – and a bipod that enhances accurate shooting.

However, the excessive protrusion of the 40-round box magazine below the receiver must often make covert shooting very difficult. Though top-mounted magazines such as the Bren type undeniably cause a blind spot to the front right of the firer, they do facilitate firing from cover.

The poor long-range performance of the 7.62mm intermediate cartridge has forced the Warsaw Pact forces to retain the rimmed 7.62×54mm cartridge for sustained-fire weapons. The needs were satisfied by two comparatively old designs – the SGM and the RP-46 – until the early 1960s, when the first examples of the PK entered service. This machine-gun takes features from many of its predecessors: the rotating bolt lock comes from the Kalashnikov rifle, parts of the feed system from the SGM and the Czech vz/52 light machine-gun, and the trigger from the RPD. The PK fires the rimmed ammunition from closed-pocket belts, inevitably complicating the feed system though the gun has a reputation for reliability unmatched by all but the MAG and the perfected M60E1. It is immediately recognizable by its unusually massive receiver – needed to house the feed – and the angular, skeletal butt. The original gun weighed a fraction under twenty pounds, but judicious modification after service reports led to the lightened PKM (18.5lb) and a number of specialized variants for tank and vehicle use.

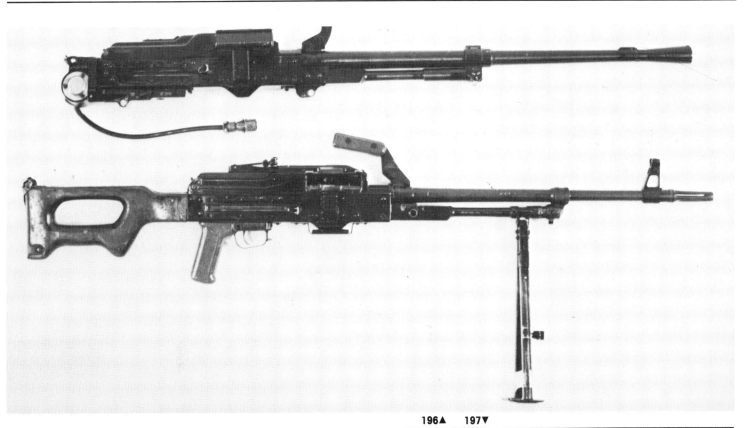

196▲   197▼

THE CZECH GUNS: vz/52 AND vz/59

The success of the PK series has rather overshadowed other achievements in the Soviet bloc. The Czech firearms industry, for example, has been allowed a measure of autonomy, resulting in several distinctive machine-gun designs. The interesting vz/52 light machine-gun offered convertible belt/box feed, with the trigger doubling as fire-selector, but was too complicated for its own good. Performance in dust and mud, particularly, was very poor: rather surprising, considering the achievements of the Holek brothers and their collaborators prior to 1939, when they had designed the precursors of the Bren Gun. The vz/59 machine-gun is a simplification of the vz/52, offering better performance but rarely encountered except in the hands of some guerrilla forces.

THE ULTIMAX

Developments in the Far East have been few and far between, though the Japanese have developed an efficient (if somewhat complicated) belt-fed general-purpose machine-gun known as the Type 62. The most impressive design has been the CIS

Ultimax, made in Singapore, which has already attracted special forces' interest. The Ultimax 100 Mk 2 and Mk 3 (the latter with quick-detachable barrel) are remarkable developments, particularly as they originate in the Far East rather than from one of the better-known manufacturers in Europe or the USA. The guns are the lightest in their class, weighing, with a loaded 100-round drum magazine, a mere 14.3lb. Unladen, the guns weigh 10.4lb with the bipod. The gentle recoil characteristics of the Ultimax permit single-hand firing in the manner of a large pistol, provided the firer's arm is strong enough. Most indepen-

dent trials have shown that the Ultimax jams very rarely, though early semi-disposable nylon-reinforced plastic 100-round spring-feed magazines were troublesome. Should the FN Minimi fail to impress the US Army during its probationary period, the Ultimax waits in the wings.

SUSTAINED-FIRE WEAPONS

The classic sustained-fire guns have been the Maxim, Vickers and Browning designs, few of which have much relevance in the modern army. However, the Australian and other armies have successfully converted some 0.30in Brownings to 7.62mm NATO and, as the gun is strong and reliable, there may still be life in the design: the principal goal of all armies, after all, is efficiency and this can sometimes still be fulfilled by supposedly obsolescent guns. This is particularly true of the heavy support machine-

guns, discarded by most theorists in the 1960s but subsequently found to be indispensable in Vietnam, the Arab-Israeli Wars and the South Atlantic. The 0.50in Browning machine-gun is still being made by Fabrique Nationale, the Saco Defense Systems Division of the Maremont Corporation and Ramo, Inc.

The powerful cartridge and sustained-fire capability of the Browning M2 HB having proved indispensable, further development in this class will surely occur. Saco has produced what it calls the 'Fifty/.50', a simplified lightweight variant of the M2 offering all-welded receiver, a better charging system, an adjustable fire-rate and a greatly improved barrel-change system. FN is currently developing a 15mm-calibre derivative of the Browning, but few details are available and it is believed that trials are still continuing. There is an enlargement of the Kalashnikov-designed PK, the NSV, chambering 12.7×108mm ammunition.

199. The classic heavy sustained-fire machine-gun is the .50 M2 Browning, an old but effectual design dating back to the 1930s. Despite efforts to phase the large Browning out, it made a glorious comeback in Vietnam and the Falklands, and, thus far, none of its rivals has proved as efficient. The gun illustrated is Saco Defense's 'Fifty/.50', a modernised lightweight version of the basic design weighing just 56lb. Courtesy of Saco Defense Systems.
▼199

Support weapons

SHOTGUNS AND GRENADE-LAUNCHERS

The use of the shotgun in war has a long pedigree, dating back to the 'trench guns' of the First World War when similar guns, loaded with buckshot, were carried by men guarding prisoners of war. During the Second World War, 'lethal ball' rounds were loaded for the Home Guard, whose shotguns often represented the sole local deterrent to German invasion.

The renaissance of the fighting shotgun occurred during the Malayan Emergency, when FN-Browning autoloaders were issued to the British-backed police forces and, subsequently, to the SAS. They were then used in Borneo, during the period of Indonesian insurgency, and by the US

Forces in Vietnam. The Delta reconnaissance teams of the Special Operations Group (SOG) favoured the Ithaca M37, while the USAF Combat Security Police used a selection: the Remington M870, the Ithaca M37 or the venerable Winchester Model 12.

The rapid rise of urban terrorism, and Counter-Terrorist Warfare (CTW) operations, has led to a resurgence in interest in the combat shotgun. Its advantages include awesome close-range firepower – the 450-grain 12-bore slug will blow a small rock into powder at close range – and the ability to handle not only a wide variety of loads, but also, with suitable adaptors, a selection of grenades. The shotgun is indispensable in close-range urban warfare even though its use is a political minefield.

The fighting in Vietnam, together with the extensive urban experience of SWAT

teams, persuaded the US authorities to investigate short-range weapons. The Special Purpose Infantry Weapon (SPIW) programme was adjudged a failure, as attempts to fire flechettes – small-calibre dart-like projectiles, enthusiastically promoted by Irwin Barr of Aircraft Armaments Inc. – as well as 40mm grenades from a single 'infantry weapon' failed to challenge the established M16 rifle/M203 grenade-launcher combination. The AAI-designed XM19 was finally rejected in 1973. The latest US Army Close Assault Weapons System project (CAWS), promoted under JSSAP, is investigating the perfection of a combat shotgun. The goal is a versatile

200. One attractive feature of the shotgun is its ability to handle a variety of cartridge-loads. These include several types of slug, buckshot of varying sizes, rubber ball and rubber shot, and plastic baton rounds. Courtesy of Pietro Beretta Spa.

200▼

201. The Beretta RS202 M1 12-bore pump-action shotgun. Courtesy of Pietro Beretta SpA, Gardone.

202. Beretta's M3P 12-bore shotgun, with a detachable box magazine and a folding butt, provides the Franchi SPAS 12 with effectual competition. Courtesy of Pietro Beretta SpA, Gardone.

206. The Franchi PA-3 pump-action 12-bore shotgun saw police use prior to the emergence of the SPAS 12. Courtesy of Colin Greenwood and *Guns Review*.

203. A Mossberg M500 Persuader 12-bore pump-action shotgun, widely favoured by US police units. Courtesy of O.F. Mossberg & Sons, Inc., North Haven.

204. Another of the many US-made pump-action shotguns favoured for police SWAT and CTW use is the 12-bore Savage Model 69-N, with a corrosion-resistant nickel finish and a seven-round tube magazine. Courtesy of the Savage Arms Company, Westfield.

207. Franchi's SPAS 12 shotgun has gained much attention for its militaristic lines and widespread SWAT/CTW use. Courtesy of Luigi Franchi SpA, Fornaci.

205. Winchester's Model 1300 Stainless Marine Defender, a 12-bore pump-action weapon with a five-round tube magazine beneath the barrel, is a popular 'security shotgun'. Courtesy of the US Repeating Arms Company, New Haven.

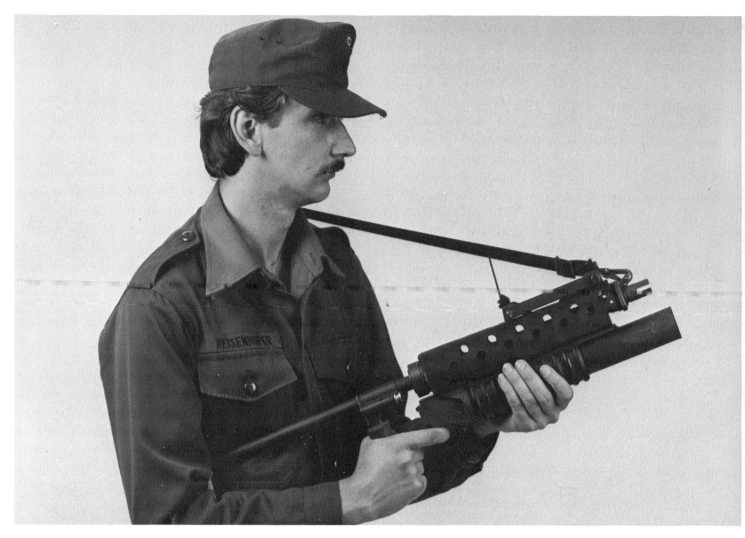

weapon that can be used on raids, in close combat, in ambushes, on search-and-destroy missions and in poor visibility, as well as for guard duties, policing and survival. Among the more arcane developments, such as Heckler & Koch's extraordinary combat shotgun, have been a series of more conventional European submissions, typified by Franchi.

Very few European manufacturers make combat shotguns, preferring the more traditional sporting and target-shooting markets. The American manufacturers, however, offer a variety of guns. The pump-action is greatly favoured, its mechanical action being regarded as more reliable than the gas-operated automatics. Ithaca Gun Co. offers a selection of guns, including the M37, the Deerslayer, Handgrip and Stakeout – the last, a particularly compact design – in addition to the semi-automatic Roadblocker. Mossberg offers the Model 500 Milsgun, the P6 and P8, all pump-action; Smith & Wesson, prior to quitting the shotgun business in 1985, had the Model 3000 and the experimental AS; Remington has

made the Models 870 and 1100 Sidewinder; and Winchester has a selection of pump-action guns, including the Defender.

European interest is comparatively more recent, though both FN and Beretta have made pump-action patterns. Among the most interesting of all the combat shotguns are those made by Luigi Franchi SpA of Fornaci/Brescia. The PA-8 is a relatively conventional pump-action design, but the SPAS-12 (and its prototype, the SPAS-11) is a gas-operated semi-automatic (SPAS = Special Purpose Automatic Shotgun). Manipulating a function selector under the black high-impact polymer fore-end allows the SPAS-12 to revert to pump action if desired. The shotgun has a pistol grip and a folding stock; and the under-barrel magazine tube is loaded, with the breechblock closed, by depressing a catch on the left side of the receiver. The magazine will hold eight 2.5in or 2.75in cartridges, or nine 2in. They can be intermixed without affecting the autoloading action. The muzzle of the 20.3in barrel is threaded for chokes, grenade-launchers or Franchi's shot

diverter, which changes the shot-pattern from circular to a flattened oval – useful in close-quarter firing when the problem of bystanders does not arise.

The SPAS-12 has encountered considerable commercial, police and paramilitary interest, but has been joined by the SPAS-15 and SPAS-16 developed for the US Army CAWS trials. Though the basic convertible manual/automatic action has been retained, the latest Franchi designs feature detachable box magazines. Though these are bulky, protruding some way beneath the receiver, they greatly facilitate loading and, by no means unintentionally, the selection of specific cartridges for particular tasks. This is hindered by a conventional tube magazine, in which the state of loading can be difficult to determine.

The Beretta designs include the RS202 and RS202P, now known as the M1 and M2, together with the M3P – a convertible manual/automatic shotgun, with a detachable box magazine, developed for the CAWS competition and not unlike the Franchi SPAS-15.

208. The US M203 grenade launcher, generally encountered on the M16A1 rifle, can be adapted to suit other systems. Here, an Austrian soldier demonstrates the M203 attached to the Steyr AUG barrel.

209. Though a little large for CTW operations, the US Mk 19 Mod. 3 automatic grenade thrower provides efficient saturation coverage at surprisingly long ranges. Developed by the US Navy for riverine operations in the Mekong Delta in South Vietnam, the Mk 19 has been used extensively by SEALs and other specialists. Courtesy of Saco Defense Systems.

Guns such as the Beretta M3P and the Franchi SPAS-12 will fire with equal facility a wide variety of ammunition including conventional heavyweight lead slugs, lead shot of varying size (to suit varying operations), rubber slugs or balls, plastic baton rounds and tear-gas cartridges, as well as lachrymatory and smoke grenades. This versatility has weakened the case for specialized grenade-launchers such as the obsolescent US M79. US special forces now rely more on the M203 40mm launcher, developed by AAI and adopted in August 1969. The single-shot M203 is comparatively light, adding about 1.36kg to the basic weight of the M16 rifle, though the latter's fore-end is discarded. The M203 unit comprises a breech-loaded barrel assembly (revealed by sliding the barrel forward), together with its trigger system, a quadrant sight and a new M16A1 handguard, squarer than normal and pierced with holes. To load the M203, the catch on the left side of the barrel must be depressed, whereupon the unit can be slid forward and a fixed 40mm round inserted. The barrel is then replaced. the safety catch in the front of the trigger guard pushed to its forward position, and the launcher trigger squeezed.

The M203 has a quadrant sight attached to the left side of the M16A1 carrying handle, and a ladder-type sight on the hand-guard which can be used for rapid firing in conjunction with the standard rifle front sight. This facility can be used when precise shooting is not required. The maximum effective range of the combination is about 350 metres, minimum effective safe firing range being about 80 metres for the high-explosive grenades.

The US armed forces also make use of an automatic 40mm grenade-launcher, developed by the US Naval Ordnance Station in Louisville, Kentucky and introduced for riverine patrols in Vietnam in January 1968. For land service, the Mk 19 Model 3 – made by Saco Defense, Inc. of Saco, Maine – can be mounted on the M3 Tripod, the M31C or M4 pedestals, the Mk 16 Stand or ring mounts. Belts of 20 or 50 40mm rounds are fired automatically, using advanced-primer actuation to restrict recoil. The Mk 19 weighs 72.5lb (33kg) without its mount, but can fire a selection of high-explosive, dual-purpose anti-tank/anti-personnel grenades with a maximum effective range of 1,650yd (1,500m).

The Soviet Union also uses an automatic launcher, the 30mm AGS-17, which belt-feeds 29 rounds using blowback principles. The 'Plamya' (Flame) is said to have a maximum effective range of 2,750 metres.

Elsewhere in Europe, Franchi makes a 'Lanciatore Terrestre Multiplo', an interesting lightweight spigot-pattern launcher which fires French Luchaire AP/AV700

grenades. The ultra lightweight LTM, which weighs only 11kg (24lb) with its field mounting, makes it a popular, portable means of delivering effective support fire.

British police and special forces make limited use of the Grenade Discharger L1A1 – recognizable by its FAL-like pistol grip – which is electrically fired and can project grenades to 100 metres, though the special forces prefer the M16A1/M203 combination. As a safety feature, the safety button protruding beneath the action immediately behind the L1A1 discharger cup must be depressed with one hand while the other squeezes the trigger. The 1.5in

210. The Franchi SPAS 12 combat shotgun is shown with an array of cartridges, chokes, the diverter (which produces a special flattened shot pattern), a grenade-launching cup and a smoke grenade. Courtesy of Precision Arms Ltd.

211. Heckler & Koch's solutions to grenade launching include this 40mm Gr.P. Courtesy of Heckler & Koch GmbH, Oberndorf. ▼

Webley-Schermuly and the 37mm ARWEN are also used to propel smoke, CS gas and baton rounds for anti-riot purposes.

Heckler & Koch, with typical inventiveness, offers a number of grenade-launching systems, including the 40mm Granatpistole and a special barrel insert/discharger cup conversion for the P2A1 signal pistol. The Granatpistole and the similar MZP-1 (with a smaller 100m sight) are special single-shot launchers firing standard US 40mm ammunition. The Gr.P is operated by pressing down on the locking-latch on the left side of the standing breech, and tilting the barrel downward to allow insertion of a cartridge. The breech is then pushed shut until the locking catch engages its grooves; the hammer is thumb-cocked; the radial-lever safety catch is rotated downward to 'F'; and the Granatpistole can be fired. A large-leaf ladder sight atop the breech is graduated from 150 to 350 metres in 50-metre increments, being used in conjunction with

the muzzle sight. There is also an auxiliary backsight, shared with the MZP-1, with a standing block for 50m and a small pivoting leaf for 100m. The Granatpistole is 28.9in overall, with the sliding tubular stock extended, and weighs 5.8lb with its sling.

The West German equivalent of the M16A1/M203 combination is the TGS system (G3 or G41 fitted with the HK79 launcher), used in small numbers by the Bundeswehr and GSG-9. The grenade-launcher consists of a pivoting barrel unit, combined with a new fore-end. To load, the latch under the breech is released and the rear end of the barrel drops down under gravity. A 40mm grenade round is inserted and the barrel closed until it is caught by the latch. The bolt-type firing pin protruding from the HK79 ahead of the rifle magazine is pulled back, and, provided the crossbolt safety catch displays red, the trigger on the mid-point on the left side of the fore-end (immediately below the cocking handle)

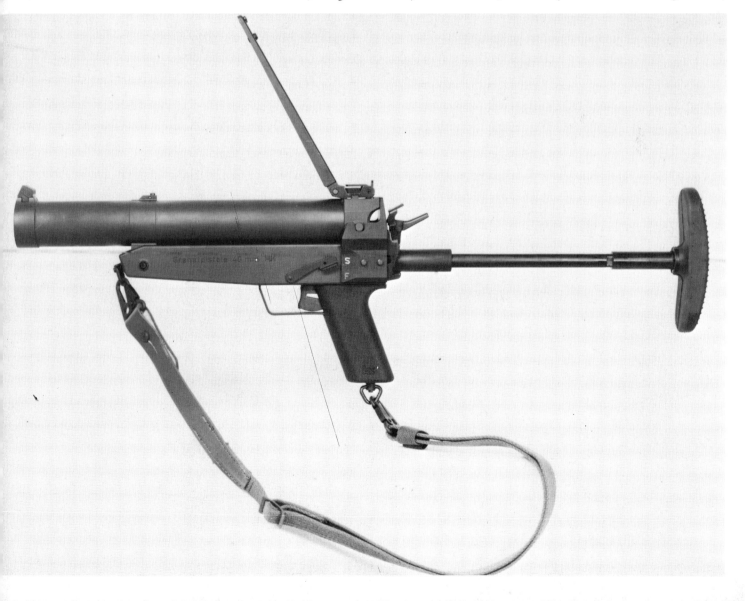

fires the gun. An additional ladder sight, graduated 50–200 metres in 50m increments, lies on the receiver immediately ahead of the standard rifle backsight. The HK79 adds about 1.5kg to the standard rifle, the G3-TGS weighing about 5.5kg and the G41-TGS 5.35kg.

The simplest way of firing grenades from military rifles is with the aid of an auxiliary muzzle fitting. Though this type of grenade has been used for many years, its special blank ammunition complicates logistics – and courts the potentially disastrous use of ball cartridges by mistake. In the 1960s, however, the Belgian Mecar company developed and patented a 'universal bullet trap' allowing conventional ball ammunition

▼212

to be used in safety. The Mecar-BTU device traps the bullet in the grenade-tail, using the energy of the ball-cartridge propellant to project the grenades. The system will handle virtually any modern military round (including 7.62×39mm M43 Russian, 7.62×51mm NATO and 5.56×45mm M193 or SS109) provided the rifle has an external flash-suppressor diameter of 22mm. As this is already more-or-less standardized on NATO guns, largely by agreement among the manufacturers themselves, the utility of the Mecar-BTU ammunition is immediately apparent. (The muzzle of the M16 series, however, tends to be nearer 21mm and the grenades do not fit sufficiently tightly for optimal **performance.**

This problem is cured by fitting a specia clip between the suppressor and the rifl barrel.)

212. The ability to fire conventional rifle grenades, from guns such as the FN FNC, is most useful. Among the most popular are the Belgian Mecar 'Bullet Trap' pattern, which can be fired in conjunction with standard ball cartridges rather than requiring special blanks. Courtesy of Fabrique Nationale Herstal SA.

213. The Heckler & Koch G41-TGS. Courtesy of Heckler & Koch GmbH.

214. The Greener Light Harpoon Gun, now made in the USA, is a handy line-throwing system based on the Peabody-Martini block-action breech. Courtesy of Navy Arms Company.

213▲

214▲

Ammunition

The efficiency of small-arms ammunition has been the subject of many reports, opinions and claims. It is probably true to say that it has excited greater controversy than practically any other single facet of small-arms technology, and also that few of the basic rules have yet been cut in stone.

The principal problem is that few authorities, owing largely to use of differing criteria, have been able to agree basic parameters. Even within the confines of NATO, national preference and national prejudice have often played their parts to the full. Thus the British initially refused to accept the 7.62 × 51mm and 5.56 × 45mm rounds, both of which were designed in the USA.* Some commentators have even seen in this the root of the problems with the current service rifle, the L85A1, which was originally designed for a short-lived 4.85mm round.

The search for the optimum military cartridge has been under way since the invention of smokeless powder more than a century ago. Many authorities in the early 1900s championed 6.5mm or 7mm (the 7 × 57mm Mauser being a particular favourite), but decisions taken by those who were concerned only with long-range striking power ensured that rifle cartridges issued in the armies of the Big Four—the USA, Britain, France and Germany—did not drop under 0.300-calibre until recent times. The lessons of the First World War, and many subsequent studies suggesting that effectual combat range did not exceed 400 metres, were simply ignored by high-rankers with the power to ensure that they had no effect on tactical doctrines.

This the Germans changed in the Second World War, with the introduction of the short 7.9mm assault-rifle cartridge. The Soviet Union followed almost immediately, but the US Army stoutly refused to compromise when the British produced their 0.280 round in the 1940s. Ironically, the ballistic properties of the 0.280 were not dissimilar to those of the 7 × 57mm Mauser.

It was a surprise, therefore, particularly after forcing the 0.30 T65E3 cartridge on NATO, when the US Army suddenly championed the 0.223 (5.56mm) round and the lightweight AR-15.

The earliest rifles, soon reclassified as XM-16, were tested extensively in Vietnam in the early 1960s. There, the slow 1-in-14 rifling twist promoted horrible wounds that shocked even the firers.

Though still satisfying the Geneva Convention, which accepted nothing less than a fully metal-jacketed projectile, the bullet from the 5.56mm cartridge operated on the limits of stability and was found to cartwheel when it struck the target, inflicting an inordinate amount of tissue damage.

Once the rifles were tested in arctic conditions, however, accuracy deteriorated to unacceptable levels. This forced a change to 1-in-12 rifling and, ultimately, the acceptance of a Belgian-designed cartridge. This was undoubtedly a better compromise, but the extraordinary wounding capacity of the original US cartridge was lost. A more recent alteration to 1-in-7 rifling has now restored much of the hitting efficiency, apparently by increasing the rotational velocity of the bullet to a point where it begins to fly apart on striking the target.

This simply highlights that cartridge design is inevitably a compromise, and that no single cartridge can possibly satisfy all the roles in which it is used. The needs of each class of weapon are different—e.g., a handgun, which is used only at very short range, must drop an assailant as rapidly as possible whilst a rifle bullet must retain sufficient striking power at long range.

Theoretically, military ammunition must conform with the Geneva Convention; in practice, terrorists and fanatics cannot (and, indeed, do not) subscribe to such restrictions. Most soldiers know the value of soft- or hollow-point bullets, which create far greater wound cavities and give much greater kinetic shock than standard

jacketed patterns, which often simply pass through tissue to continue on their journey with energy only slightly diminished.

There is little doubt that commercial hollow-point ammunition is being used in Yugoslavia, as many wounds bear silent witness. There is also no doubt that men of the Special Forces—faced with the need to make rapid kills with the least possible commotion—will also use non-standard bullets if necessary.

A favourite method used in the past has been to load revolver cartridges with wadcutter projectiles, or simply to reverse conventional bullets in their cases. Though these expedients greatly reduce effective range, the projectiles have a tremendous stopping effect in relation to comparatively low penetration.

Many studies have shown that, to give effectual levels of hydrostatic or kinetic shock,† a projectile has to be travelling at 2,000fps or more. This is regularly achieved in the modern assault-rifle cartridges, but eludes virtually all standard pistols. Attempts have been made to rectify this deficiency with special designs such as the Glaser Safety Slug, whose bullet contains metal shot set in a polymer matrix. The projectile case supposedly ruptures on striking the target, allowing the shot to scatter. Alternatively, cartridges such as the French Très Haute Velocité (THV), which are loaded with lightweight projectiles moving at very high speed, are designed to

---

* The root of this controversy is sometimes seen in the US rejection of the British 0.280 round in the late 1940s, at a time when the US Army was unwilling to accept any cartridge that offered substantially less power than the 0.30 M1906.

† Hydrostatic shock is based on the theory that a vessel containing liquid will rupture at the weakest point when an attempt to compress the liquid is made. As the human body is largely liquid, so the argument goes, damage arising from hydrostatic shock may occur when it is struck by a high-velocity bullet. Kinetic or sonic shock occurs when a rapidly moving bullet imparts energy to tissue, causing it to expand momentarily to many times the volume of the final wound channel and create a temporary vacuum into which air flows rapidly. Though the effects are very short lived, the pressure is so great that organs may rupture some distance away from the point of strike.

enetrate the body armour from which a Glaser Slug may simply bounce.

Attention has regularly been drawn to the unsuitability of many conventional tests conducted on ballistic gelatine, chosen because of its supposed similarity to flesh. Assessments of permanent and temporary wound cavities mean very little if, as can often happen, a slow-moving handgun bullet is prevented from expanding by a layer or two of clothing plugging its nose cavity.

The arguments will doubtless continue to rage; some US Army experts argued for many years that the 0.45 pistol cartridge was too powerful to train inexperienced recruits, whilst others averred that 0.45 was the minimum calibre permissible in a military handgun. Now that the 9mm Parabellum cartridge has been substituted, the FBI and others are realising that the declining efficiency of full metal-jacket projectiles arises in direct relation to reduction in calibre, and that excessive penetration is no substitute for stopping power. The most important contributor to the latter is bullet design—not calibre, nor even velocity. The theoretically feeble lead-bulleted 0.22 rimfire is a much more effectual hitter than the 0.25 ACP loaded with a jacketed bullet, whereas a jacketed 0.45 ACP is far inferior to a 9mm Parabellum hollow-point.

CARTRIDGE DIMENSIONS

Round	Case length mm	Diameters head mm	rim mm	bullet mm	Total length mm	weight gm	Bullet weight gm	Velocity mps
0.577in Mk 9	50.0	16.9	19.1	14.7	62.2	46.3	31.1	387
0.450in Ball Mk 3	59.0	16.8	19.1	11.7	81.0	49.1	31.1	401
0.303in Ball Mk 2	56.1	11.6	13.5	7.9	77.5	26.9	13.9	609
0.303in Ball Mk 7	56.1	11.6	13.5	7.9	77.2	24.9	11.3	744
0.30 Ball M2	63.2	11.8	11.9	7.8	84.5	25.7	9.7	835
0.30 Carbine M1	32.6	9.0	9.1	7.8	42.3	12.5	7.3	580
7.9mm sS ball	56.8	11.9	11.9	8.2	80.5	26.4	12.8	810
7.9mm Pist.Patr.43	32.8	11.8	11.9	8.2	47.4	16.2	8.2	700
7.62mm M43 Type PS	38.6	11.2	11.3	7.9	55.6	16.4	8.0	710
7.62mm NATO	51.1	11.8	11.9	7.8	70.7	24.3	9.3	823
5.56mm Ball M193	44.5	9.5	9.5	5.7	57.3	11.8	3.6	970
5.45mm M74	39.5	10.0	10.0	5.6	56.5	11.5?	3.5	>900
7.62mm Type L	53.3	12.3	14.4	7.9	76.5	22.6	9.6	863
9mm Pist.Patr.08	19.0	9.9	9.9	9.0	29.6	12.3	8.0	335
0.45in ACP	22.7	12.0	12.0	11.5	32.3	21.2	14.9	250
0.50in Ball M2	99.0	20.3	20.3	13.0	138.0	116.6	45.9	853
0.280in Ball Mk 1Z	43.3	12.0	11.9	7.2	64.4	20.7	9.1	772
6.25×43mm	43.3	11.9	11.9	6.3	63.0	15.4	6.2	817
4.85×49mm (in IW)	49.1	9.5	9.5	5.0	62.3	11.6	3.6	950

RANGE/EFFECTIVENESS

All figures in yds

	Effective range average	expert	Maximum sight range	Maximum wound range	Approx maximum range
Matchlock musket	75	125	§§	300	1000
New Land Pattern musket	75	125	§§	300	1000
Baker Rifle	150	250	200*	500	1200
Brunswick Rifle	175	300	300	500	1350
P/51 Rifle-musket	250	400	900	1800	2750
P/53 Rifle-musket	300	500	1000	1750	2900
Snider	300	500	1000	1750	2900
Martini-Henry	300	550	1450	2200	3350
Long Lee-Metford	300	600	1900**	2300	3740†
SMLE Mark 3	300	600	2000**	2250	3585††
Garand	300	600	2000	2200	3500
FG.42	300	600	1200§	2800	4700†††
MP.43 series	250	400	800§	1600	3175
AK47	250	.400	800§***	1440	3000
L1A1 (FN FAL)	300	600	600	2150	4000
M16 series	250	400	500	950	2880
SA-80 (L85A1)	400	500	‡	1100	2985

*Not all fitted with adjustable sights.
**Plus extreme-range sights on the left side of the stock, graduated from 1,600 to 2,900 (later 2,800) yards.
***The AKM is graduated to 1,000m, except for the 800m-sight on the Hungarian pattern.
†With Mark 2 Ball ammunition.
††With Mark 4 Ball ammunition.
†††With sS (heavy ball) ammunition.
‡Fitted with a SUSAT optical sight as standard.
§Figures in metres.
§§Only suitable for firing at point-blank range, owing to the absence of proper sights.

Boat-tailed, or streamlined bullets offer considerably better performance at long range (cf., flat-base 0.30 M2 bullet in the Garand and the boat-tail sS pattern in the FG.42). The heavier boat-tailed US 0.30 M1 bullet will carry up to two thousand yards farther than the M2. In the 1920s, British trials showed that the maximum range of the Swiss M11 cartridge – with a boat-tail bullet weighing 174 grains – was 4,457yd at an elevation of 34° 42'.

Other maximum ranges include 1,600yd for the 9mm Parabellum and 1,640yd for the 0.45 ACP (when fired in short-barrel pistols), 2,200yd for the US 0.30 M1 Carbine cartridge, and 7,275yd for the 0.50 AP M2 in the Browning machine-gun.

The effectiveness figures are much less generous than those often given elsewhere, but assume the firer is engaging a single target (i.e., the muskets are not being used for volley fire against massed ranks). It is practically impossible to engage a man-size target at 1,000yd and guarantee a hit, even with the best sniper rifle/optical sight.

PERFORMANCE OF 5.56×45mm BALL SS109D (WEIGHT: 4gm, 62gn)

Gun: FN FNC-80 or Minimi. Source: information supplied by Fabrique Nationale, Herstal, Belgium.

Details	0m	100m	200m	500m	1000m	1500m	2000m
velocity (mps)	946	831	734	480	259	170	110
energy (mkg)	196.9	152.0	118.6	50.7	14.8	6.4	2.7
Max. trajectory height (m)	na	0.02	0.07	0.68	6.88	30.53	100.03
Range to max. traj. ht. (m)	na	51	104	278	618	919	1274
flight-time (s)	na	0.11	0.24	0.75	2.28	4.67	8.50
elevation	na	2'5″	4'32″	15'15″	59'58″	2°43'22″	6°17'29″
descent angle	na	2'15″	5'21″	23'46″	2°21'40″	7°9'	19°51'8″

Maximum range: about 2,900m.

PERFORMANCE OF 7.62×51mm NATO BALL SS77, BOAT-TAIL (WEIGHT: 9.33gm, 144gn)

Gun: FN FAL, or MAG. Source: information supplied by Fabrique Nationale, Herstal, Belgium.

Details	0m	100m	200m	500m	1000m	1500m	2000m
velocity (mps)	840	770	700	515	310	239	188
energy (mkg)	335	281	232	126	45	27	17
Max. trajectory height (m)	na	0.02	0.08	0.77	5.46	20.84	54.33
Range to max. traj. ht. (m)	na	51	103	272	583	891	1175
flight-time (s)	na	0.12	0.26	0.77	2.09	3.93	6.36
elevation	na	2'38″	5'22″	16'42″	52'9″	2°3'11″	3°55'20″
descent angle	na	2'42″	6'7″	23'7″	1°40'45″	4°23'19″	8°23'57″

Maximum range: about 4,000m.

The Table shows key data for selected ranges. The diagram below indicates the salient details. If the performance of the 7.62mm bullet at 1,000m is taken as an example, it is seen that the muzzle velocity of 840mps has dropped to only 310mps when the striking point is reached. To hit the target requires that the gun barrel be elevated to a little under one degree; however, as the maximum height of the trajectory is no less than 5.46m above the line of sight, there is a considerable 'safe distance' in which a man will not be struck – permitting covering or 'overhead' fire when required. Owing to the effects of air resistance, the trajectory is asymmetrical and the bullet drops at an appreciably sharper angle (1°40') than it rises. As a result the vertex of the trajectory lies at 583m rather than the midway point. The difficulties of hitting moving targets at long range is obvious in the flight-time, as a little over two seconds elapse before the bullet strikes the target. If the range is doubled, to 2,000m, the flight-time is almost 6½ seconds. For the smaller 5.56mm bullet, the time to 1,000m is comparable with that of the 7.62mm pattern; at 2,000m, however, the former takes two seconds longer than the latter to reach the target.

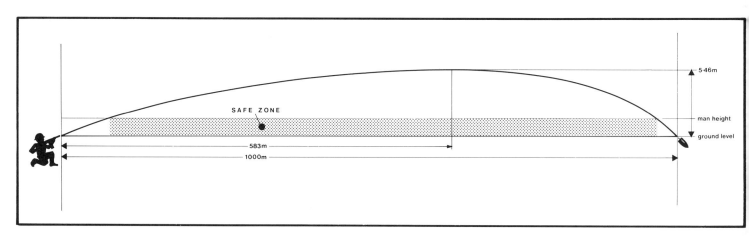

AMMOCHART: WEIGHT AND QUANTITY

Cartridge	weight gm	number of rounds in 10lb	per kg	per lb	Cartridge	weight gm	number of rounds in 10lb	per kg	per lb
0.577in Mk 9	46.3	98	22	10	5.45mm M74	11.5*	394*	87*	39*
0.450in Ball Mk 3	49.1	92	20	9	7.62mm Type L	22.6	201	44	20
0.303in Ball Mk 2	26.9	169	37	17	9mm Pist.Patr.08	12.3	369	81	37
0.303in Ball Mk 7	24.9	182	40	18	0.45 ACP	21.2	214	47	21
0.30 Ball M2	25.7	176	39	18	0.50 Ball M2	116.6	39	9	4
0.30 Carbine M1	12.5	363	80	36	0.280in Ball Mk 1Z	20.7	219	48	21
7.9mm sS Ball	26.4	172	38	17	6.25×43mm	15.4	294	65	29
7.9mm Pist.Patr.43	16.2	280	62	28	4.85×49mm	11.6	391	86	39
7.62mm M43 Type PS	16.4	277	61	28					
7.62mm NATO	24.3	187	41	19					
5.56mm Ball M193	11.8	384	85	38					

Note. Quantities are given to the nearest whole numbers, and are calculated without including packaging, clips, chargers or magazines. *Approximate figures: no cartridge for weighing.

Index